Reviews of *Chance*

5 stars - The Real Thing, by Marian Coombs (an [illegible]m Reviewer)

Dr. Staple's memoir is effortlessly dramatic. Born Irmgard Johanna Lorch in the Rhineland, she underwent a "metamorphosis from a little girl in Hitler's Germany to a biologist in post-war London." Indeed, of all the identities Dr. Staple seems to have worn in her long life, that of Scientist is the most innate, pronounced and enduring. The discussions of her creative scientific work are humorous and clearly written.

4 stars - Courage, Determination, and Creativity, by Shirley Rosenthal (an Amazon.com Reviewer)

This is a fascinating account of what it meant to have had the author's life interrupted by Hitler's Germany. The determination, creativity and courage displayed by the author and her family make a compelling story. Reading about the early scientific finds was amazing. I found the book very interesting, written in a straightforward manner in keeping with the emotions expressed and the experiences outlined. I would recommend this book for anyone interested in learning about the period of life so dependent on the political upheaval in the wartime and post-wartime era.

4 stars - A Real Life "Atonement," by Anne Mcenany (an Amazon.com Reviewer)

I read "Chance and Choice" at the same time that I read "Atonement" by Ian McEwan and I was struck by the similarities in circumstance and description of war-torn England. Joan Lorch Staple's tale of her first 30 years highlighted the struggles of families throughout Europe, the hardship of continuing one's education during wartime, as well as the simple pleasures of girlhood.

I was struck by this young feminist as she stood side-by-side with her male peers in the lab, unafraid and confident in her knowledge and skill. This book would be a good read for any young woman thinking about a career in science.

About the Author

Joan Lorch Staple, Ph.D. is Professor Emerita of Biology at Canisius College in Buffalo, NY. She lives with her husband, Dr. Peter Staple, in Williamsville, NY. The first volume of her memoirs, *Chance and Choice: My First Thirty Years*, was published in 2007 and is available at Amazon.com.

COVER PHOTOS

Front

Center: The Staple family. Eastbourne, England.
March 1959.

Bottom left: Alan and Gregory Staple on Dartmoor,
Devonshire, England. Summer 1962.

Bottom right: Joan Lorch Staple with Leo and Foxy.
Birmingham, AL 1962.

Back

Top: Dr Joan Lorch in her lab. Buffalo, NY. 1970.

Bottom: Portrait of the author by Molly Jarboe

CHANGE AND CHALLENGE

MY LIFE AFTER THIRTY

Joan Lorch Staple

Author of *Chance and Choice: My First Thirty Years*, 2007

Copyright © Joan Staple 2009
Joan Lorch Staple has asserted her right under the Copyright, Designs and Patents Act, 1988, to be identified as the author of this work.
All rights reserved.
This book may not be reproduced in whole or in part, by mimeograph, photocopy, or any other means, electronic or physical, without express written permission of the author.
ISBN 978-0-557-08292-6

Jan. 2011

To Marge
with love from
Joan

- I dedicate this book to my family and friends – both old and new – whose valuable comments I internalized before following one of my favorite author's advice:

"Don't try to figure out what other people want to hear from you: figure out what you have to say. It's the one and only thing you have to offer." Barbara Kingsolver

CONTENTS

INTRODUCTION

"If you cannot - in the long run - tell everyone what you have been doing, your doing has been worthless." Erwin Schrödinger, 1933 Nobel Prize winner in Physics

My life story begins with *Chance and Choice: My First Thirty Years*, where I describe my childhood in Hitler's Germany, my family's emigration to England, and how I became a biologist in war-torn Britain. That story ends with my 1952 marriage to Peter Staple, a doctoral student at King's College, London. My sons, Greg and Alan, commented somewhat wistfully, "What a pity your book ends just before we were born, surely *the* most important event of your life." Touché!

This sequel, which you can enjoy without having read *Chance and Choice,* not only relates the joys and tribulations of raising a family, first in rural England and later in the United States, but also continues the story of my scientific research with the one-celled creatures called amoebas. You will get reacquainted with these amazing animals as well as the equally engaging species of humans, who also make the laboratory their home.

While these memoirs focus largely on my family and work, I also tried to convey the flavor of places and times long gone: a London psychiatric ward in the era of Freudian analysis, the racially segregated society of Alabama, the counterculture of the Sixties, and lastly the atmosphere of a Jesuit liberal arts college challenged by the concept of sexual equality.

Throughout this story change is evident, both in my personal life as well as in the world around me, and every change brings a new challenge. Writing itself is a challenge, but in Nadine Gordimer's words, "writing makes sense of life."

Joan Lorch Staple
Williamsville, New York
May 2009

1. The Disciples of Freud

"When making a decision of minor importance I have always found it advantageous to consider all the pros and cons. In vital matters, however, such as the choice of a mate or a profession, the decision should come from the unconscious." Sigmund Freud

A Miracle Drug from New York

The Ward Sister ushered in a handsome, smiling man.

"Wow," I thought, "a film star for sure."

"Mrs. Staple, dear, this is Dr. Kohn, our consultant psychiatrist to see you."

"How do you do?" Sister withdrew and the gorgeous chap sat down by my bed.

It was May 1952 and I was a Nuffield post-doctoral fellow in the Zoology Department of King's College, London, studying the relationship between a cell's nucleus and its cytoplasm. Until recently I considered myself a healthy twenty nine year old woman, newly married to a colleague and Ph.D. student, Peter Staple. So why did I find myself in the "rheumatic diseases ward" of London's Hammersmith Hospital, surrounded by elderly arthritic women? It is a sad story.

All my life I had suffered from eczema, which had lately flared up and covered most of my body. My dermatologist, Dr. Gold, told me about a "wonder drug", Cortisone, which had recently been synthesized, and was said to *cure* arthritis and possibly other inflammatory diseases, including eczema. Cortisone, a steroid, was available as an experimental drug in the USA and, to a very limited extent, in England. Through my American relatives, I was able to obtain a small quantity of this drug, and Dr. Gold, desperate to find *something* to help me, was happy to administer the pills. He had no idea what dose might be suitable. But the miracle happened: within a few days my sore, crusty, weeping skin had been replaced with a new smooth pink epidermis. I continued taking the pills until none were left. I felt exhilarated, jubilant, euphoric – drunk! Peter and I had been married for two months and had planned a honeymoon trip to the French Riviera – postponed because of my skin condition. Maybe we could go after all! Then came the crash: not long after the last pill, the eczema came back with a vengeance, my hair started falling out by the handful, I was covered with festering sores, my mood plummeted, I cried non-stop, had hot flashes, alternating with bouts of violent shivering and was in such bad shape that Dr. Gold had me admitted to a hospital ward, where clinical trials of Cortisone were in progress.

My friendly nurse had warned me:

"If you keep on crying, luv, they'll send you to the Maudsley."

"What's that?" I sobbed.

"The Looney Bin, dear, yes, that's where you'll be, so you better cheer up, here's a clean hankie for you."

Looking at Dr. Kohn through my tears, I recalled her words. So *that's* why he was here: to take me to the Looney Bin! Well, I hated this arthritis ward with its long rows of beds and sad crippled old ladies. I was confined to bed, which made me hot and itchy, but there was nowhere else to go. Across the street I could see Holloway Prison for Women with its barred windows, and I felt I was worse off than the inmates. At least they were allowed to walk in the yard. Meanwhile Dr. Kohn chatted with me and I thought if all the doctors at this Maudsley Hospital were like him, it might be quite a nice place!

"Would I be allowed to get out of bed?" I asked "Our patients are only in bed at night; we have large common rooms and a garden to walk in."

"Are the inmates really crazy, Dr. Kohn?"

"No more so than you are, Mrs. Staple, I believe you'd fit in very well. So think about it and tell Sister what you have decided."

He left and I was hooked. As soon as a bed was available, I said good-bye to my fellow patients and was transferred to Maudsley Hospital on Denmark Hill.

Ward Six [1]

Maudsley Hospital, named for an eminent psychiatrist, opened in 1923 as a teaching and research facility for the University of London's Institute of Psychiatry. Unlike its sister-hospital, the venerable Bethlam (Bedlam), which dates back to the twelfth century, the Maudsley accepted only voluntary patients. Admissions were quite selective, since the hospital had to provide a variety of conditions for the psychiatric residents who came from all over the world to study there.

Ward Six, my home for the next few months was called the "convalescent ward", perhaps because some of the patients were recovering from leucotomies (lobotomies), a brutal surgery, performed on persons with intractable symptoms of various psychoses, usually schizophrenia. One has to keep in mind that this was in the 1950s, a few years before psychoactive drugs became available. There were neither tranquilizers nor anti-depressants. The post- leucotomy patients were quiet and docile; they wore colorful bandanas because their heads had been shaved. I was often mistaken for one of them; having lost most of my hair, I resorted to various scarves. My scalp was too sore for a wig.

Gradually I got to know the women on Ward Six and some of them became my good friends. They suffered from a variety of conditions, none of which would be considered for long-term inpatient treatment nowadays: post-natal depression, eating disorders, asthma, attempted suicide, obsessive-compulsive disorder and panic attacks. I was the only eczema case and my fellow patients actually *envied* me because I looked so terrible!

"It's obvious you are sick, Joan, nobody would accuse *you* of being a hypochondriac."

"My husband thinks I'm faking, I should be taking care of our home."

"My boss is going to stop sick pay, he says I look just fine."

"Mum won't look after the baby much longer, she says I'm just damned lazy."

These were remarks I heard every day from my healthy

---

1 Fortunately this Ward bore no resemblance to the one described by Anton Chekhov in his famous short story also entitled *Ward Six*.

looking ward-mates, who spent a lot of their time curling and coloring their hair, applying makeup and fussing over their clothes. Conversely I envied *them* because I was bald and could only wear loose-fitting soft cotton gowns.

The "queen bee" of our little community was Sister Tauber, who was in charge of Ward Six. A vivacious Austrian refugee, she was a niece of Richard Tauber, best known for his tenor role in Léhar's operetta *The Land of Smiles*. She had a good voice herself and went about her duties singing and smiling. This petite curly headed lady knew everything about everybody and, in spite of her cheerful demeanor, kept strict discipline in her realm of disturbed women. Most of us were on edge; so minor disputes easily mushroomed into noisy quarrels. When Sister was off duty (always a different day of the week) chaos was apt to break out and I felt very insecure. The nurse who usually took over was a recent German immigrant who spoke little English, so the patients were quick to take advantage of her. It was rumored that mental patients were apt to "act out" during the full moon. I don't know if there is any truth in this but noticed extra nurses on duty on moonlit nights.

One of the things we bickered about was music. The ward had a record player and a variety of records for us to play. In the age of the Walkman and MP3 it seems strange that the whole ward inevitably shared the music, which not surprisingly, led to some disagreements! The one record everybody loved was *The Blue Tango* by American composer Leroy Anderson. It was the hit single of 1952, both in England and the U.S. We sang it, hummed it, danced to it and wore out several records. Over fifty years later, I can still hum it and am instantly transported to Ward Six when I (rarely) hear it on the radio.

Almost everybody on the Ward smoked. Patients provided their own cigarettes but were not allowed to own matches or lighters. Nurses passed these around as needed, along with small scissors, used for needlework or to cut our nails. I found the smoky atmosphere very irritating, but Sister Tauber suggested that if I smoked myself, I'd feel a lot better about it. Smoking was soothing and highly recommended. Sister even bought me a pack of cigarettes but I never opened it. All this seems ironic now in view of the fact that Richard Tauber died of lung cancer just a few years ago.

The Doctors

What about the doctors on Ward Six? What did they do and – most important – where was the charismatic Dr. Kohn who had lured me here? To answer the last question first: I never laid eyes on Dr. Kohn again. He had admitted most of my fellow patients, and we sadly came to the conclusion that acting as bait was his sole function.

But yes, there were doctors who visited Ward Six. Two kinds of doctors in fact. We called them the "physical" and the "mental" doctors. Like every patient, I was periodically examined by an internist (the "physical doctor") who kept track of my general health. Then there was my "mental doctor", a psychiatric resident, whose task it was to treat the condition for which I had been admitted. She was Dr. Ada McQuaide from Montreal. The attending in charge of Ward Six, Dr. Kraupl-Taylor, was, like Sister Tauber, a refugee from Vienna, and a disciple of Freud. Unlike her, he kept a low profile. I saw him only twice: on admission and on the day before my discharge. His policy was to leave the treatment of patients entirely to the residents, but I gathered that he held weekly conferences at which each case was discussed in detail. I never received a definite diagnosis. Dr. McQuaide thought my condition was due to the sudden withdrawal of the very high dose of Cortisone with which I had been treated. Nowadays much more is known about corticosteroids and, while still extensively used in moderate doses, they are tapered off very gradually, *never* stopped abruptly. I was indeed lucky that no permanent damage resulted from my hit-or-miss steroid therapy.

So what did McQuaide actually *do* to treat my condition? After spending the first six weeks or so taking a detailed history, she began classical Freudian psychoanalysis. We patients called it "the talking treatment". Twice a week McQuaide called me into one of the little offices on Ward Six where I made myself comfortable on an old couch, which sagged under the weight of the confessions it had heard. McQuaide sat at a desk behind me and listened to anything I wanted to say. Sometimes she took notes (I heard her pencil scrape). She hardly ever spoke. It was weird. I tried to provoke her into talking to me by asking questions – or by remaining stubbornly silent throughout the session. No effect.

Sometimes I cried, occasionally I fell asleep. Nothing disturbed McQuaide's composure. After a few weeks I got used to this routine and gave up expecting any feedback. Actually just lying there quietly and being listened to made me feel better; the hot flashes subsided temporarily, and my skin felt a little less itchy. Looking back on this type of therapy, I think it was pretty useless and a waste of time. Freudian psychoanalysis is rarely used nowadays, being too expensive and time consuming. Informal talk sessions among us patients were much more useful. I guess they were precursors of what is now called group therapy. We chatted away while knitting or working on our occupational therapy projects.

One day it was announced that a doctor specializing in sex and marriage counseling was on the ward and we were encouraged to set up an appointment with him. Most of us were young married women and felt this might be interesting. I signed up and was promptly seen by Dr. Bloom, a restless young man with greasy hair, who paced up and down the small consulting room. He asked a few perfunctory questions but did not appear to listen to my answers. Every few minutes he looked at his watch. I felt *he* needed help and was glad when our time was over.

The next morning there was great excitement round the breakfast table. Tabloid newspapers were being passed around and guess who was on the cover? Our nervous sexologist, Dr. Bloom! He had kidnapped his two young children from the house of his estranged wife and taken them out of the country. Police were searching for the three Blooms. Now I understood! No wonder he was agitated with all that on his mind. So much for marriage counseling.

Just when I got used to McQuaide and her silent ways, she announced that her rotation on Ward Six was over and she would be moving to the Pediatric Ward. I was stunned. I guess I actually liked her! Dr. Tong took her place. I don't remember much about him except that I felt that I had to start all over again and was too weary to bother. My condition had deteriorated over the weeks, and even the ministrations of a consultant dermatologist were of no help.

Social Life

Mealtimes were social occasions on Ward Six and the food was actually quite good. We patients took turns setting the table, working in pairs. First we were issued 20 sets of silverware, counted in our presence. The meals were served family style and anorexics were gently encouraged to try "just a bite". Nobody was allowed to leave the table until the silverware was collected *and counted.* If even one teaspoon was missing we waited patiently until it was found – usually on the floor. Then the tables were wiped down and we went our separate ways. I'm not sure why there was all this fuss about the cutlery, but think these items were considered potential hazards, along with penknives, nail files and belts – all confiscated on admission.

An important part of our social life on Ward Six was occupational therapy (OT). There were facilities for finger painting, basketry, pottery and other crafts. I was not allowed to get clay or paint on my sore fingers, but painting with big brushes was OK. You were supposed to express your feelings in paint. Some of the results were striking – blood red paint dripping from black storm clouds, daggers piercing hearts and exploding brains in brilliant hues. The sewing teacher helped me make a cotton skirt, but I really hated sewing *and* the skirt. On the other hand, I constructed a beautiful waste paper basket of which I was very proud. When handling the reeds and twine became too painful, I switched to making tablemats, wrapping brightly colored raffia round a core of rope. I got inspiration from the Folk Arts Museum nearby. We used those mats for over thirty years! One of the attractions of OT, at least for some patients, was the fact that you met *men* there. Male patients had their own dormitory and dining room, but many activities were co-ed. We even had dances. I don't remember meeting any interesting men, but had several friends among the women.

Marion was one of them. Like me, she was a newlywed, and

sad to live apart from her husband, who was in the diplomatic corps and traveled a lot. Marion was unable to accompany him because she got panic attacks on trains and ships. Nor could she stay home alone – for the same reason. She firmly believed these attacks would kill her, and lived in constant terror of them. She loved children and hoped to have a baby. But she was also convinced that giving birth would kill her! Marion was given the "talking treatment" but also some injections (I don't know what) which actually *caused* small panic attacks. Rather brutal treatment I thought. Since Marion spoke fluent French, we often conversed in that language for fun – and to discuss our fellow patients. We befriended a new patient, a very pretty young French woman, recovering from a suicide attempt. Jeanette, who spoke only French, had met her husband, an English businessman, in Paris. They were married and, after a short honeymoon, she accompanied him to London. There he abandoned her (he had another wife).

It took me a while to understand why Sheila was in Ward Six, there seemed to be nothing wrong with her. She told us that she was *terrified* of horses; if she should happen to *see* a horse, she would die. Well, horses were not common in London, but they did exist. One might see some fine steeds on Rotton Row in Hyde Park, where the gentry rode around in circles. Or perhaps a brewery wagon might come by, drawn by a pair of huge Percheron horses. So Sheila was unable to leave her home, for fear a horse might appear. I'm not sure what her treatment was.

Both Judy and Melanie were new mothers, unable to care for their babies. They cried all day because they *missed* their babies, yet they felt they could not touch, let alone nurse, the newborns. They had been in the Maudsley for many weeks, while their mothers looked after the little boys. Both were skinny, haggard and in despair. We would now call their condition post-natal depression. Or maybe they had Post Traumatic Shock Syndrome, since both mothers had very traumatic deliveries, which they insisted on recounting in great detail. Judy and Melanie were eventually treated with ECT (electro convulsive therapy) and made full recoveries.

Mrs. Morrison was in her sixties, a pleasant woman who loved to help with cleaning the ward (we all had assigned chores), in fact she was only really happy when mopping tables or floors. She seemed to spend the rest of her day washing her hands, which were chapped and raw. "Everything here is dirty," she said, "it's even worse than my flat." She ran off: "Excuse me, I must wash my hands."

Then there was Betty, an administrative assistant and private secretary to a business tycoon, who lost her job because she was suddenly unable to type. Why? Well, her hands shook so much that she couldn't hit the keys. I found this hard to believe because she did fine embroidery and played the piano, all without a tremor. Only typing caused her to shake. Her treatment involved hypnosis and she eventually got her job back. All the others recovered too and went back home. But I was still there! It seemed like forever.

Exorcising the Demons

As a physiologist, I found it interesting to watch the various treatments given to my fellow patients. I already mentioned leucotomy (called lobotomy in the U.S.) for which the Maudsley was famous in the forties and fifties. A Portuguese neurologist, Egas Moniz, invented this controversial brain surgery, which was very crude by modern standards. He was awarded the Nobel Prize in 1949. Another rather brutal and dangerous treatment was known to us as "Insulin Shock", later called Insulin Coma Therapy (ICT). Since this treatment was administered right in our dormitory, I was able to watch the procedure, which was always done very early in the morning, before breakfast. The patients were injected with insulin to bring down their blood sugar and induce insulin coma. After a while, they were "revived" with a glucose injection. According to the patients, it was a horrible experience and felt "like dying". They woke up soaked in sweat and ravenously hungry. Even emaciated anorexics, who normally refused food, ate every morsel of the big post treatment breakfast served in bed. After a bath they slept the rest of the morning. This treatment, although successful for many disturbed patients, was eventually given up because of the high risk of death, and was replaced by Electro Convulsive Therapy (ECT).

I did not actually see ECT administered, but observed its

effects. Again this was done before breakfast, on Tuesdays and Thursdays. The patients were given a sedative, taken to the treatment room, and were soon back on the ward. They remembered nothing of the procedure. In fact they had memory problems for weeks after their course of treatment, but they did seem much less depressed.

I witnessed one "miracle cure": a tiny old lady was admitted one evening, screaming and protesting loudly. She spoke a language nobody could understand and was terrified of Sister Tauber, who tried her best to soothe her. Sister tried a few German words, but that made the old lady even more hysterical! Early next morning she was taken for her first ECT treatment from which she emerged a little calmer, although still frightened and unable to communicate. After the second treatment she was a different person: she introduced herself, smiled and conversed in heavily accented English. She explained that she was a Polish Jew (used to speaking Yiddish at home), had survived a concentration camp, and was really happy to be in England. Her son, who visited her, told us that her condition emerged after her rescue from the camp, and this was not her first stay at the Maudsley. The ECT "cure", although impressive, was not permanent.

Weekends

Weekends were quiet on Ward Six since many patients went home "on pass". If your doctor considered you well enough to try a home visit s/he would sign your pass, and a responsible relative had to sign you out. Many patients were too scared to even apply for a pass; they felt secure and sheltered in the hospital and afraid their condition would get worse at home. Others couldn't wait to get out – and those were considered almost ready for discharge. All that summer Peter picked me up on Fridays after work and we spent weekends in our flat in Kentish Town. He shopped, cooked and did all the housework, as I was not able to do much. Sometimes close friends visited us, but I never went out because I was too embarrassed to be seen. This was not the way we had envisaged our first year of married life. However, we still hoped to start our family soon and, after getting the OK from my doctors, ceremoniously threw away my diaphragm and any other contraceptives lurking in the flat.

Sunday afternoons were terrible, since I had to get ready to return to the hospital. The separation was painful, yet we both realized that I was not well enough to stay home alone on weekdays. So, at about 5 pm, after our "teatime", I started the long return trip, which involved a walk to the Underground Station and two different buses. On the final lap I usually met other returning patients, and we were glad to see each other and chat about our weekend experiences. The bus ended its journey at Denmark Hill and our helpful conductor would shout: "Maudsley Looney Bin – All Change!" It was the last straw. Sunday supper always included a bright red jellied fruit salad. That, and the *Blue Tango* playing in the background, cheered me up sufficiently to face another week on Ward Six.

As autumn approached and the weather got colder, I was no longer able to make the journey home and Peter came to visit me instead. Sister Tauber, who, as I mentioned, knew everything about every patient, was the first to notice that I was pregnant. She allotted me one of the two tiny private rooms available on Ward Six, for which I was truly grateful. It enabled me to escape from the smoke, listen to my own little radio and – most important – have some privacy. The rest of Ward Six soon realized what was going on when extra glasses of milk appeared at my place setting, and I was served an egg *every* morning. What luxury! Although World War II had ended seven years ago, some food rationing remained in place until 1954. Once pregnancy was confirmed, a woman was immediately issued a new ration book, and soon an extra bottle of milk would appear on her doorstep for all the neighbors to see.

The Great London Smog

One weekend stands out clearly in my memory: that of the *Great London Smog of 1952*. Anybody who lived through those terrible days will never forget them. The fog started on Thursday, December 4th and at first seemed just like any other "normal" foggy day, so common in London at that time of year. But it soon became apparent that this was different: by Friday the grayish fog had turned into acrid yellow *smog*, a dense mixture of fog and carbon particles from smoking chimneys, commonly known as "pea soup". An unusually cold air mass and the absence of wind had trapped this toxic mixture over London. Visibility became close to zero, surface traffic came to a halt, and just breathing was a chore.

At the Maudsley all weekend passes were cancelled. Although we kept windows tightly closed and curtains drawn, the smog penetrated into the common room and our mood plummeted as we groped about in the dim light, wheezing and coughing, worried about our spouses at home, as well as about Mary, our asthma patient, who was making ominous rasping sounds. Visitors were welcome at weekends but, since surface transportation had virtually shut down, we had no hope of seeing anybody. Gloom and doom continued on Saturday. The BBC periodically announced the number of hospital admissions and deaths caused by smog inhalation. By Sunday, December 7th London hospitals had run out of beds and undertakers out of coffins.

The annual Smithfield Cattle Show, an important event, where cattle breeders from all over Great Britain display their most prized animals, was being held at Earls Court in London, and some of the first smog casualties reported were cattle, including a very valuable Aberdeen Angus bull. All the animals were young and in prime condition. The news media made much of this, and I think the animal -loving British public was more outraged by the reports from the Smithfield Show than by the fact that an estimated 4000 humans lost their lives in London that weekend. And the death rate remained above normal for weeks to come. The number of deaths attributable to the smog was similar to that caused by the flu epidemic of 1918!

Prime Minister Harold MacMillan's Conservative government tried to cover up the fact that pollution from burning raw coal, both in domestic fireplaces and factory furnaces, caused the problem. It took four years of political battles to get the Clean Air Act of 1956 passed. This act outlawed the burning of cheap "dirty" coal and established "smoke-free zones" where only smoke-free fuels could be used. As a result London became a much cleaner and healthier city for the next 25 years or so. In 2002, on the 50th anniversary of The Great Smog, newspapers ran articles pointing out that London air was again heavily polluted; not by chimney smoke,

A normal London smog, mild compared to the one on December 5 -9, 1952

Much has been written on the great smog of 1952, see for example The Guardian (UK) November 30, 2002 and Science December 13, 2002. Vol.298, page 2106

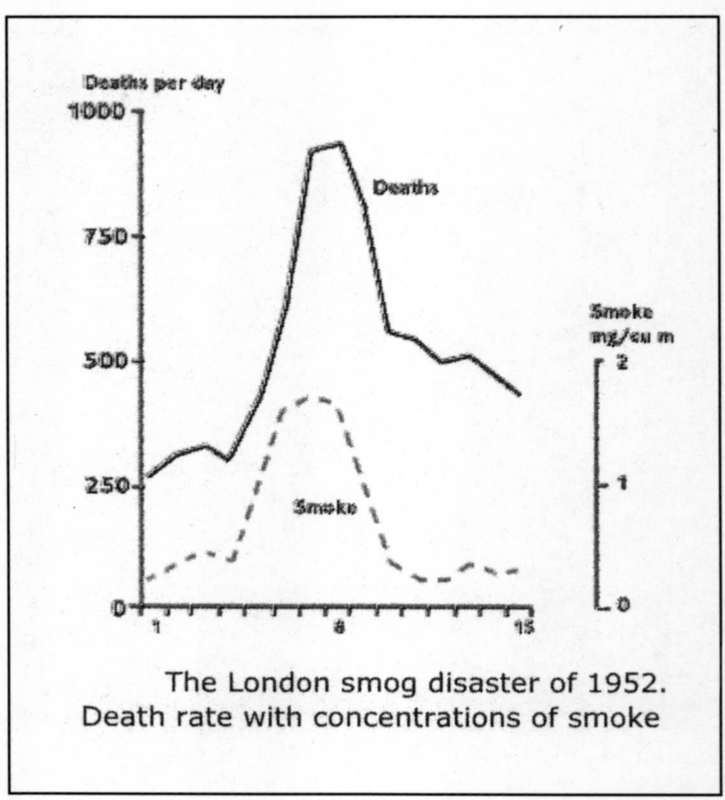

The London smog disaster of 1952.
Death rate with concentrations of smoke

but by automobile emissions, and deadly smogs could easily recur. Looking back on that week in December 1952 and its consequences, I am reminded of the current debate on climate change and global warming. Again big business interests are trying to cover up the fact that human activity contributes to the adverse effects of climate change. It is my opinion that, unless we are willing to change our lifestyle drastically, disaster is inevitable. Indeed it may already be too late to avert it.

Back to Ward Six and that smoggy Saturday. While patients and nurses were sitting around in the gloomy fumes, listening to the gloomy BBC, the door was suddenly flung open and guess who staggered in: my husband, Peter! He looked dazed and exhausted, having walked for miles ("I just followed the curb") from the nearest underground station. Immediately our mood lifted. Everybody scurried around to bring Peter food and, of course, cups of strong tea. How he managed to get there is a mystery; I guess love conquers all obstacles! Sister Tauber, usually a strict disciplinarian, chose not to notice that Peter was still with us on Sunday morning. That afternoon the smog thinned out a little and he was able to take the usual bus route back to Kentish Town. A weekend to remember!

Uncle Willy to the Rescue

In mid-December, a professional society of psychiatrists held their meeting at the Maudsley Hospital and there was great excitement to get the place spruced up and super tidy, in case the distinguished visitors should tour the facilities. Dr. McQuaide asked me whether I would consent to be presented as a "case" at one of the sessions. She no longer worked on Ward Six but told me she would really like to do this, since she was very interested in my condition, something I had never noticed during the months I was in therapy with her! I thought it would be interesting and might even lead to useful suggestions for treatment, so I agreed. During my career as a biologist, I had attended many professional meetings – but never as an "exhibit."

When the time came, McQuaide took me to the large tiered lecture theater of the adjacent Institute of Psychiatry and made me wait *outside* while she gave a brief introductory talk. Then she took me to the podium where I was confronted by hundreds of psychiatrists, mostly men, gazing at me curiously. They asked questions, which I answered to the best of my ability. Some of the questions, like "what does it feel like to lose all your hair?" were silly (I thought), so I gave silly answers. Was I allowed to ask questions in turn? Absolutely not! Did anything useful come of this case presentation? I don't think so.

One of the distinguished visiting psychiatrists was my "Uncle" Willy (Dr. Willy Mayer-Gross) whom readers of my first volume, *Chance and Choice,* may remember as the man who helped me find a wonderful flat in Chelsea. He was not my real uncle, but a second cousin and good friend of my father's. My parents, who lived in Birmingham, were understandably distressed about my long stay in the psychiatric hospital and had asked Willy to look into the situation. Since he had traveled from his home in Scotland to attend the conference, he took the opportunity to visit me on Ward Six. Sister Tauber and the rest of the staff were noticeably impressed; I guess he was a well known figure in the world of Freud's disciples. It was good to see Uncle Willy, and we had a long chat. He had talked to the attending in charge, Dr. Kraupl-Taylor, ("former student of mine, not a bad chap") and seemed familiar with my history.

"Do you think they are doing you any good here?" he asked. I admitted that I didn't think so.

"All right, I am arranging your transfer back to Hammersmith Hospital, where you will receive intensive therapy for your skin condition."

"What about the 'talking treatment', Uncle Willy?"

"You don't need it; the main thing is to get you well enough to go home before your baby is due."

He was as good as his word. After a few weeks (including Christmas) in a private room at Hammersmith Hospital, where I was given daily soothing baths, various ointments, as well as *very* low doses of cortisone, I was discharged home, not cured of course, but considerably better. I was determined to stay away from hospitals and, with Peter's encouragement, enjoy the last few months that the two of us would have on our own. It was January 1953 and our baby was due in May. My skirts felt tight and I was looking forward to shopping for clothes for the baby and for me. I had not been in a store for six months.

It was great to be home, and there was another happy event that month: Peter was awarded his Ph.D. from King's College, University of London. I was not well enough to attend the big ceremony and reception at Senate House but enjoyed hearing about the pomp and circumstance of the occasion and seeing him in his resplendent purple regalia with the yellow silk facings of the Faculty of Science. I had missed my own Ph.D. ceremony four years earlier, because wartime conditions made elaborate celebrations like this inappropriate, and clothing coupons did not include academic regalia!

Peter Staple, B.D.S.,Ph.D. in his academic regalia. London, January 1953

Looking back on my stay in the psychiatric ward, I am surprised how vivid these memories are. After all, over half a century has passed since that time, so I ask myself why these few months had so embedded themselves in my mind. What, if anything, happened to me during that time and did the psychoanalysis have anything to do with it? Does lying on a couch and babbling about oneself to nobody in particular really affect the brain? At the time I did think so. Being forced to stop *doing* things and to reflect on my life made me calmer. Maybe talking about one's life, *even without input from a listener* helps to clarify one's thoughts. However, the objective of my hospital stay was to cure, or at least alleviate, my eczema, as well as all the horrid steroid withdrawal symptoms. This was not achieved. The "physical" treatments were purely symptomatic: lotions and oatmeal baths to soothe the itching and phenobarbitone to help me sleep. Yes, I was kept on barbiturates even while pregnant, nowadays considered a big risk to the baby.

So, did I waste six months of my life? It certainly seemed so at the time. To add insult to injury, my condition was caused by inappropriate use of cortisone, i.e. it was an iatrogenic (doctor-caused) illness. However, in retrospect I feel that the Maudsley was the right place for me, whether my condition was psychosomatic, neurotic or autoimmune, it really makes no difference. It was also a learning experience. As a result of spending so much time thinking about myself, I understood myself a little better, and no doubt that's a good thing. Something else I learned: the medical profession knew virtually nothing about most of the conditions I saw on Ward Six, including mine. The treatments seemed to be empirical, even arbitrary. I would like to think that, with the development of psychoactive drugs, new techniques of psychotherapy, and a more enlightened attitude, some progress has been made in treating psychiatric patients.

It is harrowing enough to spend months in hospital without the additional worry of how to finance such a stay. I was spared this anguish: the National Health Service covered **all** medical expenses. This was true not only for episodes of sickness but also for all childbirth related expenses. Thank goodness we still lived in England!

Fever

Not long after getting home I developed a cold, which turned into pneumonia. I had a bad cough and high fever for what seemed like a long time. A nurse came to care for me, and our doctor looked in daily, so I avoided going to a hospital again. Slowly I got better, and one thing was obvious: my eczema had almost completely cleared up! I was reminded of Oma, my late grandmother, who had a German proverb for every occasion. While giving me bad-tasting medicine she always said: "Bös muss bös vertreiben," meaning, "evil must drive out evil." Well, it certainly worked in this case. Our family doctor was not too surprised by this "miracle cure". He told us that deliberately induced fevers had been used since antiquity to treat certain diseases, and until quite recently, "malaria therapy" was used to treat often fatal neurosyphilis. With the advent of penicillin, tertiary syphilis fortunately became a rarity. We kept all this in mind and, much later, when the eczema returned, I tried "fever therapy" with moderate success.

But for now I was feeling really well. My hair was coming back and resembled a newly seeded blond lawn. I was getting larger every day, and it became difficult to tie my shoes, but on the whole I enjoyed my pregnancy and marveled at the new life stirring inside me. More than "stirring": kickboxing would be a better term!

I started to think of the birth process and read a book popular at the time called *Childbirth Without Fear* by Grantley Dick-Read. In Dr. Dick-Read's view, a woman should not experience pain during normal childbirth. It is, after all, a natural process, which non-human mammals undergo without undue discomfort. In the 1920s, when Dick-Read practiced obstetrics, it was the custom to anesthetize women during labor and delivery, using drugs such as chloroform, which often had adverse effects on the baby. Dick-Read argued that these drugs were unnecessary if the birthing woman was adequately prepared for birth. He believed that the pain experienced by a woman in labor was due to *fear*, which in turn creates tension and pain. Eliminate this fear and labor will be pain free. Dick-Read was a pioneer in what is now known as the "natural childbirth", or better, "prepared childbirth" movement which advocates husband-coached breathing exercises and relaxation during labor. As far as I know prenatal classes and systems such as the Lamaze method were not available at the time. Although I read Dick-Read's book with interest, I did nothing to prepare for the event. Having heard the gruesome stories regarding labor and birth that circulated in Ward Six, I was a good candidate for the "fear-tension-pain" syndrome.

During my ninth month of pregnancy I went to the Middlesex Hospital to be examined by Mr. Winterton, the same OBGYN who had removed my ovarian cyst four years ago. He said the baby was lying in a breach position - feet down - but managed to turn it around by pummeling my abdomen. Then he pronounced everything in good order, said good-bye and "did not expect to see me again." It was not the custom for the attending obstetrician to be present at *normal* births; he would only be called if some form of intervention became necessary. So far so good.

2. Motherhood

"Though motherhood is the most important of all professions – requiring more knowledge than any other department in human affairs – there was no attention given to preparation for this office."
Elizabeth Cady Stanton

Childbirth without Fear?

May 1953 was an exciting month in London. Preparations for the coronation of Queen Elizabeth II, which was scheduled for June 2, were in full swing. Millions of people were expected to descend on London, including royalty and dignitaries from all over the world. Queen Elizabeth had in fact been reigning since February 1952 when her father, King George VI died of lung cancer. But it took well over a year to prepare for the official coronation ceremonies.

Among the people who came to London to see the coronation procession was a pretty blond young woman from Germany called Margaret. She planned to find a position as an "au pair girl" for a few months, which would enable her to be in London at this exciting time without incurring great expenses. At the back of her mind was the thought that she might even find an English husband and never return to Germany. We interviewed Margaret, liked her and hired her on the spot. Although my skin condition was much improved, I was still unable to do many household chores, such as washing and scrubbing. The household appliances we now take for granted either did not exist or were prohibitively expensive, and I anticipated a lot of washing once the baby was born. Disposable diapers (called nappies in England) were not around either, but "Nappy Laundries", which collected dirty nappies and delivered clean sterilized ones, were starting to appear in the big cities. They were costly and not always reliable, sometimes leaving the client's baby bare-bottomed ("sorry about that, our van broke down"). All in all an au pair seemed like a good idea.

Margaret moved into our top floor flat at 50 Gaisford Street in Kentish Town early in May. She did all the housework and was good company for me during those last few weeks of waiting. Her English improved daily and she loved to roam about London, watching the preparations for the big event. Of course she hoped that I would be in hospital during coronation week, so she could participate in all the celebrations. As it turned out I complied. Not only that, but I went into labor on Whitsunday, a holiday weekend in England, so Peter was home.

At the crack of dawn on May 23, I suddenly realized I was lying in a big puddle and understood that my amniotic sac had ruptured (the breaking of the waters), signaling the beginning of labor. Although I felt only a few contractions, Peter and I decided to take a taxi to the Middlesex Hospital because the tube did not run very frequently so early on a holiday. I was excited and imagined birth to be imminent! Well, I was admitted and Peter was sent home. There was actually no bed available, but I was offered a cot in a cubicle and told not to worry, surely a bed would become vacant by the time I needed it. After spending an uncomfortable and lonely morning on that hard cot, I was joined by a young medical student called Joe Miller.

"I'm supposed to attend several different births," he explained while patting my legs tentatively. "This is my first and I'm quite nervous."

I told him it was my first baby too and we were in this together. From time to time a nurse examined me, told me it would be "many hours yet" and gave me some pills. As the afternoon progressed, the contractions became more frequent, the pain got worse, and Joe and I got more anxious. So much for *Childbirth Without Fear* – where are you, Dr Grantley Dick-Read? It occurred to me that it would be comforting to have Peter there, but this was years before hospitals realized that the father-to-be might indeed have a role to play in the birth of his child. Peter told me later that he had spent the day sailing on Regents Park Lake, his last carefree weekend for years to come!

The midwife looked in and assured me that everything was perfectly normal; yes, the contractions would be "uncomfortable", the cervix was dilating, which is a slow process, especially in the absence of amniotic fluid. (So was it *my* fault that my waters had broken so early?) "You agree, Mr. Miller?" Joe nodded and tried to look professional. He sprawled on the only chair in my cubicle, so I had to put up with lying on the cot. Nobody suggested that I might be more relaxed walking – or waddling – around the ward.

Just as my contractions were coming really hard and fast, I was moved to the delivery room, where I had to climb on a flood-lit table, surrounded by a lot of people. My feet were stuck into stirrups, adding to my "discomfort" and I realized I was in second stage labor. Suddenly I heard bells ringing! No, not church bells - even in my stupor I recognized the obstetrics ward bell signal for "normal delivery". I had learned about the bell system from my sister-in-law Diana, now a physician, who was my roommate while she was in medical school. Every medical student had to observe several different kinds of birth, and the bell signal assured that students would not waste their time attending a normal birth when what they really needed to see was a forceps delivery. Diana had reminded me of the bells and sung the "signals" for me during her last visit.

The pain and pressure were now so bad that," normal delivery" bell notwithstanding, I was convinced that my demise was imminent.

"Am I dying, doctor?" I whispered. The young resident looked startled:

"NOT AT ALL, on the contrary, YOU ARE GIVING BIRTH!" he exclaimed.

Suddenly the searing pain stopped and, about the same time, I heard a new sound: the robust cry of a baby. Somebody held up the baby for me to see "Here is your son!" But he was quickly taken away while I delivered the placenta, and then the resident repaired a small tear. They actually administered an anesthetic for that – well, better late than never. I was exhausted, exhilarated – and ravenously hungry.

"I'll bring you a cup of tea, luv, and maybe a biscuit; dinner is over I'm afraid," the friendly nurse announced. Visiting hours were over too.

I learn to Be "Mummy"

Next morning I found myself in a real bed – one of twenty in the maternity ward. It would have been nice to see my son, to see Peter – *and* to get something to eat. All of that took a while, but I was offered another cup of tea, the English panacea for all that ails you. Then, at last, came the baby, neatly bundled up and fast asleep. He was beautiful, with lovely pink skin and a few wisps of soft blond hair. I knew that breast milk doesn't come in for a few days but it's important for baby to get the colostrum, so I tried my best to connect his sleepy baby mouth with my nipple. Wow, it worked! He sucked vigorously, making funny little snuffling noises. To my surprise it was both painful and pleasant at the same time. The pain was due to contractions of the uterus – a good thing actually because it helps to get the uterus back into shape. Soon the babies were returned to the nursery and – finally – we hungry mums got breakfast: bacon, eggs, tomatoes, baked beans, buttered toast, and of course, gallons of milky tea. While relaxing after breakfast, it occurred to me that I was really lucky to have survived this terrible experience and wondered what had happened during my labor to cause all that pain. Surely, I must have been close to death! Carefully I crawled to the foot of the bed and extracted my file from the rack attached to the bedrail. I opened it: there was only one page covered with scrawls in "doctor's handwriting". The time of admission was noted and a few other unremarkable data. The pills I had been given were Pethidine, the anesthetic was Trilene. Then one phrase caught my eye:

7:15pm normal delivery.

So this was all perfectly normal, just as the midwife had told me! OK, maybe somebody should have warned me. Or perhaps not. In my case prenatal ignorance was bliss – until the time of reckoning was upon me!

Later that day Peter appeared and we admired our baby together. After narrowly ruling out Derek and Colin, we decided to name the baby **Gregory Clive**. I'm really not sure how we chose the names; neither was in our families. But we did not want something as common as Mike or John, nor anything bizarre, so he'd have to spell it every time somebody asked his name. We thought Gregory sounded nice and we referred to our son's crying as "Gregorian chant". We *never* called him Greg – well, not until we became Americanized many years later. It is strange how Americans, who love long words such as elevator (lift), baby carriage (pram) and automobile (car), mutilate their first names, creating atrocities like Chuck, Hank and Bud.

On the maternity ward we mums were kept busy. The babies were brought in every four hours for nursing. Breastfeeding was the norm, and the nurses spent many hours, making sure we understood exactly what to do. We were taught how to change nappies and, a week later, after the umbilical cord stump had dropped off, how to bathe and dress a baby. There was physical therapy to get us back into shape, and still enough time to rest. The babies were kept in the nursery, and although I was assured that Gregory seldom cried, I worried about that. Visiting hours were strictly limited, as was the number of visitors per bed and there were no phones within hearing distance.

I mention all these details because I have noticed that nowadays, i.e. in the twenty-first century, new mothers are given virtually no chance to relax and enjoy their newborns. They are often discharged from hospital within twentyfour hours of giving birth, long before any stitches, let alone the baby's navel, have healed. Breast-feeding is not established yet - and may never be - nor do the young mothers learn anything about baby-care. A sign of progress? I don't think so. On the other hand, the management of labor and delivery has improved greatly and has become much more humane. Women are encouraged to have a significant other present and are given many more options regarding their birth experience.

Almost all of us on the ward were first time mums. Hospital beds were scarce after the war, and were not assigned to experienced mothers unless there was a medical problem. I did not even realize that until, about 2 years later, I was pregnant again, and *not* entitled to a hospital bed. Meanwhile I enjoyed my stay at the Middlesex. I was in a somewhat privileged position because it was here, at the Medical School that I had studied for my Ph.D. in the late nineteen-forties. Former colleagues came over to visit, and sometimes I had lunch with them in the staff dining room. This was a special treat for me because I well remembered that, six years ago, when I was a graduate student, women were not permitted in the Medical School dining facilities. *Definitely* a sign of progress!

The Coronation

The coronation of Queen Elizabeth II was scheduled for June 2, 1953, ten days after Gregory's birth, the very day on which we were due to be discharged from the hospital. The procession would actually pass close to the Middlesex and both staff and "mums" were looking forward to the spectacle, which would be visible from the roof. It was estimated that three million people would line the route of the procession, most of them sleeping in the streets the night before, including our au pair girl, Margaret. The streets would of course be closed to regular traffic. The hospital made a decision not to discharge anybody on that day. I don't think it occurred to me to leave earlier. Peter and I would celebrate the coronation with the other young families on the roof of the Middlesex. There was another treat in store: the hospital had rented several television sets, so that patients unable to get to the roof could still see the procession, and all the preparations prior to the great day. I had seen TV on a visit to New York a few years ago, but this was a first in England. The BBC did a magnificent job covering every aspect of the ceremony. I read that they were flying films to Canada and the U.S. several times that day to enable "the colonies" to witness the great event almost in real time.

Not surprisingly, most of the baby girls born that week were called Elizabeth. Babies born on Coronation Day were given a special silver commemorative plaque. There was another big event to celebrate that week: the first ascent of Mount Everest by the New Zealander Sir Edmund Hilary and Sherpa Tenzing Norgayg. They had actually reached the peak on May 29, but the official announcement was withheld until Coronation Day. Thus there was non-stop rejoicing and much pomp and circumstance on June 2, 1953.

The weather was overcast as the golden stagecoach, drawn by its magnificent team of horses, slowly passed by. Queen Elizabeth, sitting next to her handsome consort, Prince Phillip, looked radiant. I did not see their children, Prince Charles, 5, and Princess Anne, 3 years old, but they appeared later on TV, standing on the balcony of Buckingham Palace. As I write, the Queen is over 80 years old and as popular as she was during the first year of her reign. She has had a lot of sadness in her life, but I doubt she will ever resign in favor of her aging son, Prince Charles. That night the sky lit up with a huge fireworks display. There were colorful "tableaux" depicting the Queen, as well as the usual multicolored rockets. I was glad to be far enough away to dampen the noise, which made many of us nervous, being too reminiscent of the firebombs and rockets of WWII. Even now, over fifty years later, I am not too keen on fireworks.

Life with Baby

The Visiting Nurse stood on our doorstep when we got home to our top floor flat at 50 Gaisford Street in Kentish Town. Her mission: to make sure the new baby did not share the parents' bed where he might be smothered "Even a drawer would do" she said. I proudly showed her the carry cot (portable bassinet) and other baby equipment, most of it passed down from my brother Walter and sister-in-law Diana's children, now four and five years old. Although I pretended I had everything under control, it was reassuring to have Nurse there for a little while. Although Gregory weighed a robust 7 ½ pounds, he seemed tiny and fragile to me. I loved him to distraction and it was scary to be left in sole charge of him. Gregory seldom cried, and soon allowed us to sleep most of the night. And of course we had Margaret, a hard-working girl, who never tired of carrying Gregory up and down the stairs.

You may wonder why this baby couldn't just stay put in the flat. Where was he going? The answer is that English babies had to be out in the "fresh air", no matter what the weather, yes even in smoky, sooty NW London. Babies lived in their prams (baby carriages). Every four hours or so they were picked up to be nursed and changed, maybe played with for a few minutes, then put back outside. This custom originated in the 19th century when infant mortality was high – the major cause of death being tuberculosis to

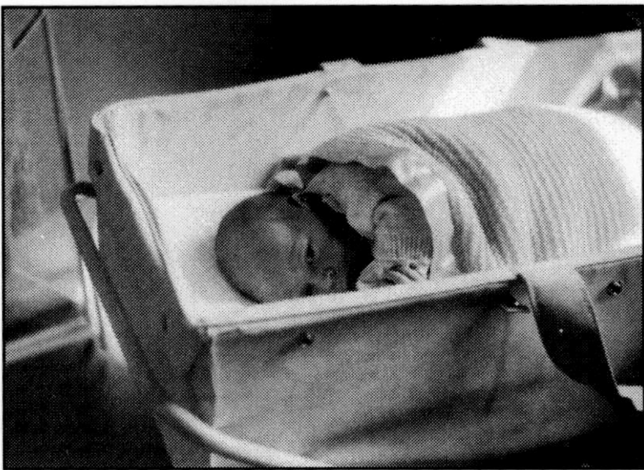

Gregory in his carrycot. London, June 1953

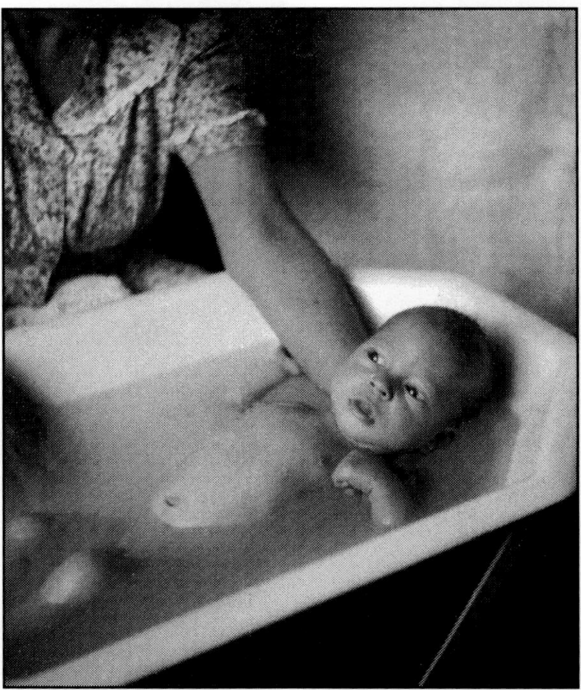

Gregory enjoying his bath, June 1953

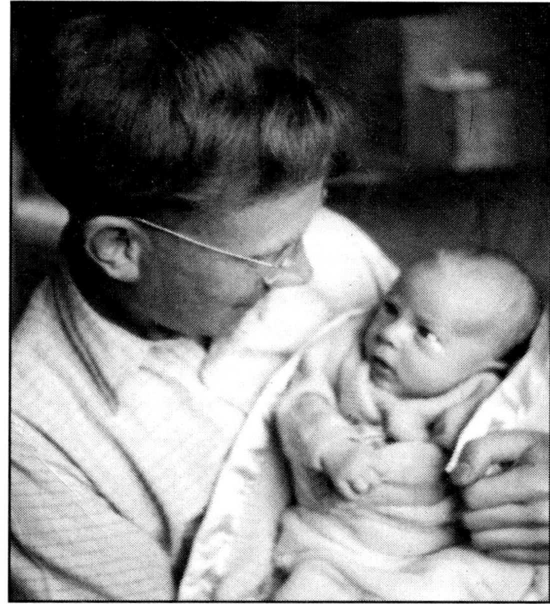

Proud father: Peter with two-week-old
Gregory Clive Staple

Nappies drying in our backyard in Kentish
Town Summer 1953

which newborns had virtually no resistance. The chance of acquiring TB was much higher in a crowded house than out in the yard – or street. Our flat was not crowded, nor did we have TB. No matter: babies belonged outdoors.

Just behind our house was a day nursery, run by London County Council for the benefit of single working mothers. Margaret and I often stood at the window, and watched the nurses as they tended the babies. We used binoculars, so as not to miss a thing. All the babies were out in the yard. When the nurses came to pick them up, we knew it was feeding time and Margaret rushed down to get Gregory. If we were uncertain about anything we consulted our friendly neighbors. Soon we got the hang of it and Gregory was thriving. The Visiting Nurse discontinued her visits, since I was now able to walk to the baby-clinic for periodic weighing and checkups. The clinic not only provided advice and immunizations, but also gave away National Dried Milk (baby formula), cod liver oil, Marmite (a brown gooey yeast paste rich in B vitamins) and something called National Orange Juice. The latter was so bitter that most babies spat it out instantly. Gregory was no exception, and we soon switched to Ribena (blackcurrant juice), equally rich in Vitamin C – but expensive. I did not require formula, since I was nursing, so I got free liquid milk instead. I mention these details to illustrate that, although taxes were high in England, the National Health Service, which took effect after World War II, assured that mothers and infants were well taken care of.

Another invaluable source of information and reassurance regarding babies was Dr. Spock's book *Baby and Child Care,* published in the U.S. in 1946 by Pocket Books for 25 cents. My New York relatives sent me a copy and I instantly related to Spock's attitude and style of writing. Although an expert in both pediatrics and psychoanalysis, his approach was non-authoritarian. He believed that each baby was an individual, and that mothers, not pediatricians, knew their own babies best. He advised us anxious mums to observe our babies and do what appeared best at the time, e.g. if the baby cries, pick it up. If it appears hungry, feed it. Of course this approach is intuitive and makes sense. But other authorities had told us to keep a rigid schedule for babies, e.g. feed exactly every 4 hours, don't spoil the baby by picking it up and other nonsense. I practically memorized *Baby and Child Care,* and the flimsy paperback fell apart before I became pregnant again. Fortunately an English edition became available by then. By 2007 the book has sold 50 million copies, second only to the bible!

It amuses me that young mothers in the twenty-first century feel they must exercise and/or diet to get rid of their "baby fat". That thought never occurred to me. Indeed the word "exercise" was not in our vocabulary and after years of rationing, we were glad to eat whatever was available. What is now called "exercise" was built into our lifestyle. With the new baby came a lot of washing – all done by hand, wrung out (strength training) and carried down from the third floor (Stairmaster) to the backyard to be hung on the line (stretching) in the hope it might dry. Since rain is not uncommon in England, you could never be sure of that.

Gregory was bathed and fed (his second "meal") at about 10 am, then I carried him and all his bedding down to the pram, which was stored under the stairs. His pretty white cover soon got spotted with soot particles blown in our direction from nearby coal-burning railways. The Clean Air Act, triggered by last year's Great Smog, was not implemented till the late 50s and London was really a dirty city. Dressed in his hand-knitted woollies and tucked firmly into his blankets, he was sound asleep when I wheeled the pram out the front door to be parked on the sidewalk right in front of our house. This was a good spot because we could watch him from the living-room window – again using binoculars, to make sure he had not kicked off the blankets. Actually, most passers-by would stop to tuck in a restless baby, pick up dropped toys, and rock a crying infant for a while. When my Aunt Franzel came to visit us from New York, she was absolutely horrified that this *beautiful* baby was put out in the street for most of the day. "He will be kidnapped," she moaned. As the Brits would say "Not bloody likely!" Everybody had more than enough kids in Kentish Town; there were prams lined up outside every building, evidence of the post-war baby boom.

If it started to rain, Margaret or I would race down our 48 steps to save the laundry ("cardio" exercise), but usually left Gregory securely under his pram hood unless there was a thunderstorm. We hung the laundry on the ceiling rack in the kitchen or draped it around the living-room fireplace. Soon it was time to run down again to pick up the baby for his "lunch" (2pm). Then I took him for a long walk up Highgate Hill (more "cardio"), while Margaret walked to the grocery shop, butcher and greengrocer. On a fine day we used the pram to take the bed linens and towels to the Laundromat. The laundry came out of the spin dryer not dripping, but definitely wet. It was piled on top of the baby, wheeled home and hung on the line (weight-lifting *and* stretching exercise).

After our walk it was teatime, then the six o'clock feeding, a little playtime and off to bed – yes indoors this time. Margaret rocked Gregory to sleep before she went off-duty, while I cooked dinner. Peter came home about seven, hungry and tired after a long day in the lab. He would wonder what I did all day and whether I was bored? Missed my work? A resounding NO to all of that.

Teatime with Aunt Diana. L to R: Janet Lorch, Peter with Gregory, Diana Lorch, Robbie Lorch. Summer 1953

A Horrible Birthday

While Gregory and I were in the Maternity Ward, the question of circumcision was raised. Both Peter and my parents felt that the little boy should be circumcised, not for religious, but for "hygienic" reasons. Newborn circumcision was not covered by the

National Health Service and therefore was not routinely performed in British hospitals. A commission set up to study this topic found that there was no medical rationale for removal of the foreskin of a healthy infant.[1]

The pediatrician who checked Gregory at birth saw no reason to perform this surgery and I agreed with him. However, after we got settled at home, the men in the family somehow persuaded me that circumcision was a good idea, and it was arranged for a *Mohel* (a Jewish doctor specially trained and certified to perform ritual circumcision) to come to the flat to do it. This was June 12, 1953, the day before my 30th birthday, and I was planning a little dinner party. Gregory was nearly 3 weeks old. The *Mohel* appeared early in the morning and asked if he should say prayers, which we declined. I kept well out of the way, while Peter held the baby, and soon the procedure was over and Gregory was comforted by his morning "meal". Peter went to work while I got busy preparing for the party.

Shortly before the guests were due to arrive, I decided to nurse and change Gregory, hoping he would then sleep through the dinner. He was awake but not crying, just lying there quietly, with an odd look on his little face. I felt something was wrong. When I picked him up, I was appalled to find that he was lying in a pool of blood! The next few hours are a blur in my memory: the first guest, my friend Dorothee, arrived at this very moment, and the two of us, with the bleeding baby in tow, took a taxi to the Middlesex Hospital, while Peter and Margaret stayed home to cope with the dinner. The admitting pediatrician was the very doctor who had checked Gregory three weeks ago, and had recommended against circumcision. He did not mention this fact. On the contrary, he was very reassuring, and did his best to stop the blood leakage by applying a dressing to the minute organ. I was told to nurse Gregory at hourly intervals to prevent dehydration and the doctor pointed out that, what appeared to be a "blood bath" was really bedding soaked in urine tinged with blood. At some point the *Mohel* appeared on the scene, very upset to find his patient in hospital. The problem was, of course, that the baby was much too old for a "ritual circumcision", which is

1 Recently there has been some evidence that circumcised men are less likely to acquire AIDS.

normally performed on the eighth day of life and does not involve sutures. We did not know this, but the *Mohel* should have warned us.

Meanwhile Peter and our guests celebrated my birthday – and Gregory's birth – without us. We were reunited the next day and all was well. But I made a silent vow not to get involved with any more circumcisions, no matter how many sons I might be blessed with in the future!

Baby on the Beach: A Holiday in Devon

When Gregory was just over three months old, we decided to be adventurous and take him on a seaside holiday in Devon. Peter's parents lived in Bovey Tracey, so we planned to introduce them to their first grandson on our way West to the beaches. Traveling about 200 miles with a baby would not be considered an adventure nowadays, but in 1953 England there were only two-lane roads, most of them quite narrow and winding, especially in Devon. Undeterred, we rented a car and borrowed a somewhat dilapidated baby carriage, small enough to be carried on top of the car's trunk. Our idea was to strap Gregory's carry-cot (car-bed) onto the old pram when going for walks. It looked weird, but worked out fine. We loaded the car with nappies and all the other stuff babies seem to need, not too bad since he was fully breast-fed and too young to require a highchair or playpen.

Bovey Tracey, a market town, considered the gateway to Dartmoor, is a pretty place with houses mainly built of gray Dartmoor granite. Our last visit there had been in 1951, when Peter introduced me to his parents as his fiancée. We stayed in the delightful small hotel owned and managed by Peter's "maiden aunts", Anne and Elizabeth Hebditch. After all the family had doted on Gregory, we were on our way to the nearby beaches of Torcross and Beesands. Peter enjoyed introducing me to a part of the country he knew very well, having spent all his childhood holidays here. He had attended boarding schools since the age of seven, so he was only with his parents and sister during vacations, mainly in summer. We spent our time exploring and lazing around the somewhat gravelly beaches,

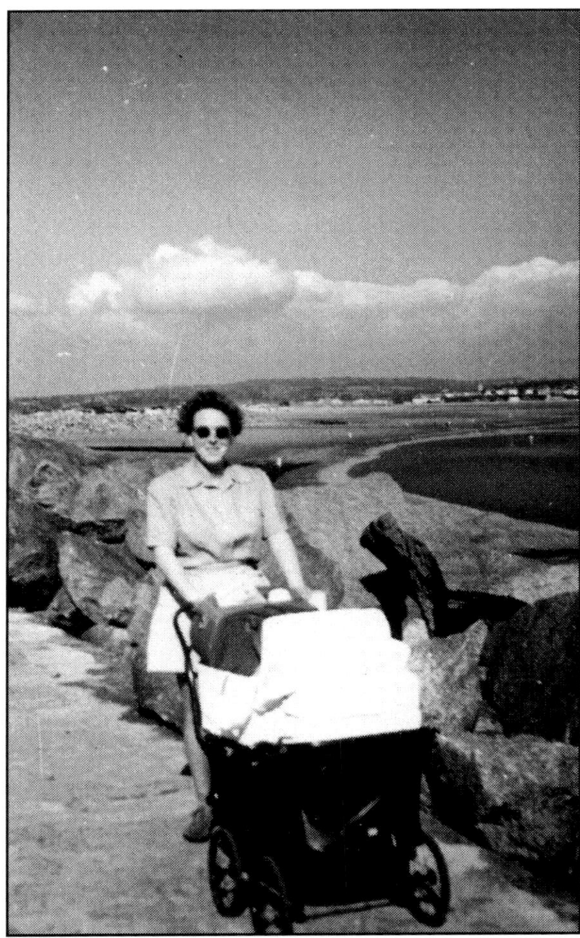

Our trip to Devonshire. Summer 1953

Our trip to Devonshire. Summer 1953

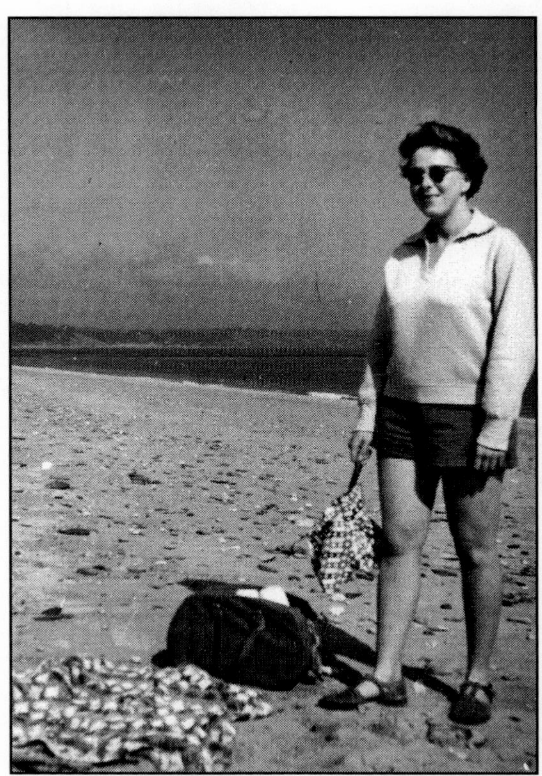

Our trip to Devonshire. Summer 1953

which were deserted in September, although it was still quite warm. We had found a small boarding house, where the owner allowed me to wash and hang out laundry, so all went well. Yes – until I noticed a painful swelling in my left breast. The doctor at the local "cottage hospital" diagnosed a breast abscess, prescribed hot compresses, and told me to stop nursing *immediately.* I was in shock: my poor baby would starve! It had never occurred to me that I might bottle-feed; my plan was to eventually wean Gregory to spoon food and a cup. But not yet!

With the help of the visiting nurse, who provided the necessary equipment and showed me how to prepare bottles, we survived. But not without a struggle! Gregory vigorously refused to suck on the rubber nipple for two days (it seemed much longer) and subsisted on milk I managed to spoon into his mouth. Meanwhile I was in much pain, and had to pump my breasts at intervals. So I was glad to be home again, by which time Gregory had adjusted to the bottle, and was also beginning to eat a little baby cereal and applesauce. Back in Kentish Town, my own doctor was appalled at the treatment I got in Torcross, and told me I should have continued nursing on the unaffected breast. He prescribed penicillin, which quickly cleared up the lingering abscess.

A House of Our Own

When Gregory was about three months old Margaret returned home to Germany (still single!) and I was pretty confident that I could cope by myself. However, the baby got heavier all the time and I was longing to move to a little house *without stairs* somewhere in the country, where the air was free from soot. Peter was now a Nuffield Post-Doctoral Fellow doing research on the effect of the anti-convulsive drug *Dilantin* on oral tissues. He enjoyed his work, but of course his income was minimal – certainly compared to that of a dentist in general practice, as his father never failed to point out.

My father-in-law had hoped that his son would join him in his dental practice in Tonbridge, Kent, after leaving the British Air Force where he served as a dental officer during World War II. But

Peter opted to study for a Ph.D. instead, which turned out to be a good idea, because that's how we met! All that is described in my previous book *Chance and Choice, The First thirty Years*.

Our bungalow at 13 Broadbridge Lane, Smallfield, Surrey

In spite of our limited income, and keeping in mind the inconvenience of a long commute to London, we decided to move out to Surrey. Our new home was a small brick bungalow in a village called Smallfield. Its floor plan was typical of English houses: an entrance hall into which opened the doors of the living room, dining room, kitchen, bathroom, lavatory (called the loo) and two bedrooms. All the rooms were small by American standards and did not interconnect, i.e. it was the opposite of a typical open plan ranch house in the U.S. Everything was painted a dull cream, and a coal-burning fireplace in the living room provided the only heating. Well, we soon made some changes, such as breaking down the wall between the small dining room and kitchen to create one unit, and installing an anthracite- burning stove, which not only heated the living room, but also supplied hot water to radiators in the hall and bedrooms. The radiators did not actually *heat* these rooms, rather they "took the chill off", so that on entering the hall one could feel that one was indoors. This was quite unusual in England at that time! In addition we put colorful wallpaper on selected walls. Gregory's room was painted a cheerful yellow and had "night sky" paper on the ceiling, so he could look up at the moon and stars as he lay in his crib.

Our nearest town was Horley, which was exactly halfway between London and Brighton, so train connection was excellent. We moved in soon after Gregory's first birthday and it was wonderful to have a big backyard where Peter soon planted fruit trees and established a vegetable garden. Instead of walking up steep Highgate Hill, I now pushed the pram through country lanes where Gregory was delighted to spot pigs and cows, as well as quacking ducks and hissing geese. His favorite walk was to visit "Big Pig", an enormous sow who wallowed in deep mud and made wonderful noises, which Gregory tried to imitate. We had a picture book showing this very sow (I thought) and I had to read the story of Big Pig every evening until the book fell apart.

Gregory neither crawled nor walked until he was about 18 months old. Since I did not know when babies are *supposed* to walk, it did not bother me. He liked to sit on his blanket (no playpen needed) and play with colored blocks, with which he built elaborate towers. I was convinced he would become a famous architect. Much later, his favorite toys were model soldiers, and I envisaged a future general.

We did not own a car but managed to get around quite well on our bicycles, once Gregory was able to sit on the baby seat. Peter left home very early in the morning to bicycle to Horley station from where he caught the train into London, followed by a ride on the tube to King's College Hospital on Denmark Hill, where he worked. There was a bus service between Smallfield and Horley but, unless it was raining heavily, we both preferred to ride our bikes. Occasionally I took Gregory into town by bus to do some shopping, but getting the pushchair (stroller), the baby and the shopping bags on the bus was much more trouble than using my bike, equipped with baby seat and basket. The grocery store in Horley delivered once a week, while the local butcher and greengrocer would come to our house every day if necessary, as did the milkman and bakery van. Nobody on our street owned a car or a refrigerator, so the daily food deliveries made sense.

Our street, called Broadbridge Lane was a short dirt road lined with bungalows on one side and separated from the real street by shrubbery. It was an ideal environment for young children, who

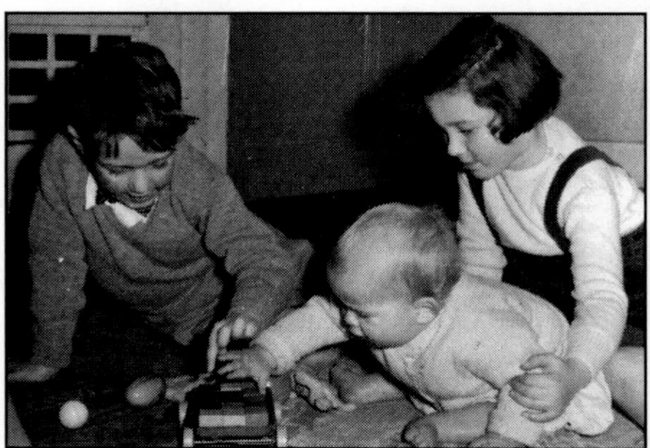

Gregory with cousins Robbie and Janet Lorch, 1954

Gregory in our backyard in Smallfield

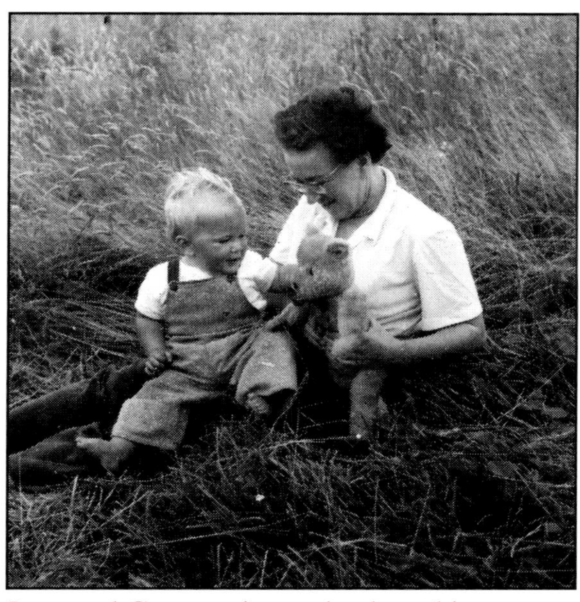

Joan and Gregory in our backyard in Smallfield

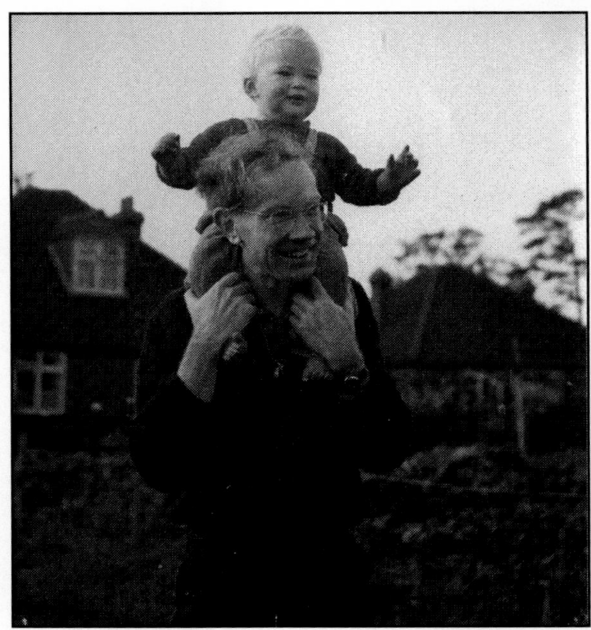

Peter and Gregory, Fall 1954

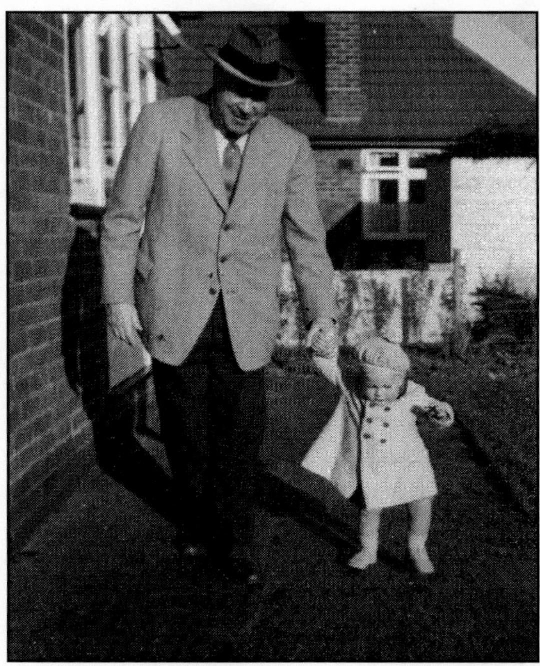

Gregory's first steps! With Papi (Sali Lorch), Smallfield, Fall 1954

could safely ride their tricycles and play in the lane, which also provided big puddles to jump over (or fall into). Peter and the other dads on the lane threw ashes from the fireplace into the potholes without lasting effect.

Fixing potholes in Broadbridge Lane, Spring 1955

I soon made friends with my neighbors, most of whom had young kids. I particularly remember the Thompsons with their six boys, all under eight, who ran wild, while their mother tried desperately to adjust to life without servants, having just moved to Smallfield from the Fiji Islands. Their bungalow had the luxury of electric under-floor heating, which the Thompsons, being used to a tropical climate, kept on year-round. The youngest Thompson boy, Will, was an adventurous toddler, apt to get into mischief. It was not unusual for his mum and/or older brothers to come running down the lane, searching for the missing tot. Once he was found asleep at the bottom of a large empty dustbin (trashcan) where one of his brothers had put him "to be safe" and then forgot all about it. Another time, when Will was still missing at bedtime, his distraught mother called the police, who told her that, indeed a little boy had been found. Will had wandered across the road to the large hospital where he joined a group of child patients in the playground. He was given dinner along with the other kids and only at bedtime did the nurses realize that they had an extra child!

Next-door to the Thompsons was the home of the Stone family, with three little blond girls, Margaret, Christine and baby Susan. They occupied the only two-story house on Broadbridge Lane, and all the toddlers acquired their stair climbing skills at the Stones'.

My parents, who still lived in Birmingham, did not visit us very often because my mother was in poor health, and found the train journey tiring. She suffered from anemia and digestive problems. After many tests she eventually underwent surgery for "stomach ulcers". At least that's what the surgeon told her. However, he informed Papi and me that Mutti actually had a malignant stomach tumor, and that he had performed a partial gastrectomy. Cancer was such a terrible condition that doctors usually withheld the diagnosis from the patient. Nobody ever mentioned the dreaded word; it was as taboo as sex. Neither chemotherapy nor radiation treatment existed in the 50s. The survival rate for stomach cancer patients was less than 50%. I traveled to Birmingham, with Gregory in tow, to help care for Mutti after her discharge from the hospital. During her slow convalescence she was entertained by watching her little grandson's antics. I spread the baby blanket on the floor in her bedroom; so she could watch Gregory, who would patiently arrange colored blocks in precarious piles, which eventually collapsed, causing him to burst into squeals of laughter.

My mother made a fairly good recovery. She complained that she had to eat frequent small meals and still had some discomfort, and she wondered whether her "ulcers" were recurring. Considering that she had virtually no stomach left, her ongoing symptoms were not surprising. It did not occur to us to tell her the truth, namely that she was a cancer survivor who had beaten the odds, and was indeed lucky to be alive! But her lack of a stomach had tragic consequences a few years later when an overdose of sleeping pills – instantly and irretrievably absorbed by the intestines - led to her untimely death.

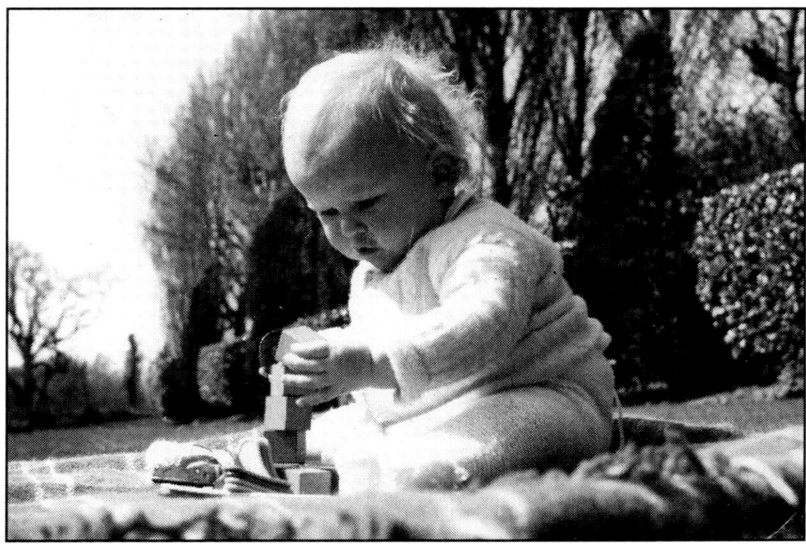

Gregory loves his blocks. Birmingham, 1954

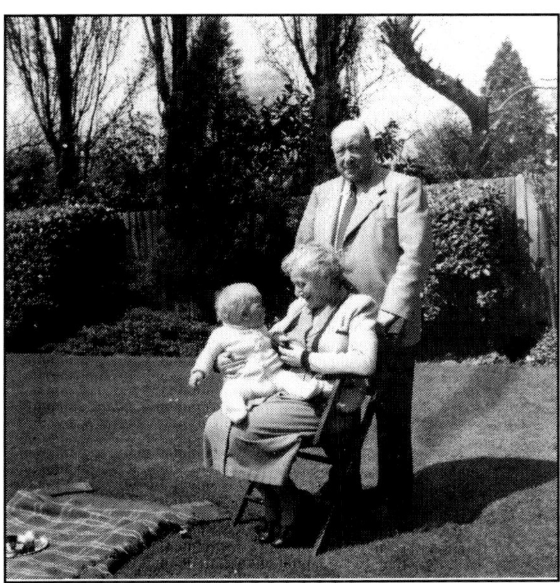

Gregory with his grandparents, Mutti and Papi, in Birmingham, England, 1954

My Baby Brother's Just Come Out

I have often been asked how I felt about giving up my research, which involved nuclear transplantation in amoebas, and had completely dominated my life for the last few years, and becoming what is now called a "stay-at-home-mom". It was certainly a big change, indeed a "paradigm-shift". I definitely missed my paychecks. Although I had subsisted frugally on "soft money", i.e. scholarships and grants, for the last ten years, I had never felt poor or deprived. I had my own flat and traveled to conferences or just for fun. Now, Peter's Nuffield Fellowship, very adequate for a single person, had to support three (and soon four) of us. So I noticed the difference in my financial status.

But, contrary to expectation, I hardly missed London or my lab. I became fully absorbed in running my small household and raising Gregory. It was fascinating to watch him and the neighborhood tots develop. I enjoyed being completely in charge of my domain, and not having any boss to report to. I also liked the company of the neighborhood women. Being used to the predominantly male world of science, this was something completely new for me. We helped each other with shopping ("I hear Mr. Collins[2] is getting some calves liver in tomorrow!") and childcare ("if you stick your safety pins into a bar of soap then they'll slide through the nappy more easily"). We rejoiced together in successes ("Susan went potty all by herself") and commiserated over our sorrows ("Trevor has measles"). We shared recipes and the produce of our gardens. We picked berries, and I experimented with different ways of preserving them. Peter expected me to cook his favorite dishes, which included grilled kippers or lambs' kidneys for breakfast, entrees such as jugged hare or shepherd's pie for dinner, and fruit pies or steamed puddings doused with custard, for dessert. He was a good cook himself, but usually too busy to teach me, so I was grateful for advice from my neighbors. Peter did show me how to iron his shirts, but somehow they never turned out right. Doing the laundry offered opportunities for innovation: I used the garden hose to soak sheets hanging on the clothesline; they then dried with hardly any wrinkles, eliminating

---

2 Our local butcher – more about him later!

the need for ironing, which I hated. Maybe I invented "drip-dry"!

On cold windy days the sheets froze solid but eventually the ice would sublime, leaving a nice smooth texture. We all did our big laundry on Mondays and agreed that on that day nobody would light a bonfire in their backyard. Much to our chagrin, our husbands *loved* burning rubbish, the smokier the better. It's a "guy thing" I guess. Other threats to the white sheets were the birds that devoured our raspberries and then showered the laundry with bright red droppings, interspersed with purple mulberry blobs.

Washing soiled nappies was no fun, but I entertained myself with recalling the names and metabolism of the bile pigments (bilirubin, biliverdin etc) so clearly displayed, and was grateful to be in my kitchen rather than taking a biochemistry exam. None of my fellow-housewives had a college education and I think we only talked about kids, food and laundry. This was our "shop-talk". The men's conversation across the garden fence covered such grave topics as gardening, football (meaning soccer) and even a little politics. My reading was limited to picture books and women's magazines, especially one called *Nursery World*, which, amazingly, is still flourishing. I even contributed an article entitled *Grousewives*, in which I tried to explain why housewives with degrees in the natural sciences adapted better to their new status than liberal arts graduates. Reading it now, about 50 years later, it all seems rather silly and certainly dated. It was quite a change from my previous publications in scientific periodicals such as *Nature*.

Peter and I decided we would be ready for another baby (hopefully a girl!) when Gregory was about three years old. Spring would be a good time – easy to dry the next set of nappies. Pregnancy sickness – which I had not experienced previously - dominated my life in the fall of 1955. Fortunately, Gregory was a pretty independent toddler and took the situation in stride. Instead of me running after him with the potty, *he* brought the potty to *me* when I threw up. Cooking smells made me nauseous, so Gregory, tired of sandwiches, usually went out to eat lunch with one of the neighbors. Of course my friends offered all sorts of good advice and, when nothing worked, concluded that I must be carrying a girl this time. Why are females always blamed for all problems? Our family doctor simply said it was a common affliction and would stop after the third month. And indeed it did! He also informed us that, because of the post-war shortage of hospital beds, I would probably not be eligible for a hospital birth. The decision was based on the mother's health as well as her social circumstances. My chances were slim, since this was my second pregnancy; I was in good health and, according to the Visiting Nurse, "lived in luxury". By this she meant that we had not only an indoor toilet and running water, but even *hot* running water.

The baby was due in early April, and Gregory, encouraged by neighborhood gossip, referred to it as "my baby sister". I was assigned a midwife, aptly named Sister Speed, who provided prenatal care during the winter months, gradually increasing the frequency of her visits towards spring. Sister Speed and her little black Ford were well known in Broadbridge Lane and she knew all the children by name, probably having delivered most of them herself. When her car was parked at our house (#13), the kids came running, begging her to let them "hear the baby". Sister was prepared. She handed out stethoscopes, always giving priority to "big brother Gregory", and soon she had as attentive an audience as any specialist on hospital grand rounds. I felt safe with Sister Speed and did not mind her following of urchins; indeed I preferred them to medical students.

We had bought a set of trundle beds for Gregory's bedroom and now allowed him to make the change from his crib to the lower bed. We thought by the time the new baby was ready for a bed, he'd be able to climb to the upper one. Eventually that happened but not without many intermediate problems. Sister Speed was delighted with the high bed and decided that would be the ideal "delivery table". It was firm and, most important, she would not have to bend down. So everything was set as we awaited the new arrival, tentatively named "Claire".

Peter and I had a bet regarding what would appear first: the daffodils or "Claire". Easter Sunday was on April Fool's Day that year and I was fooled by a few fake contractions. Easter Monday is a holiday in England, so Peter was home and he stayed an extra day since he had a bad cold. So he was still in bed when, early on Tuesday, April 3,1956, I started labor in earnest. This time I

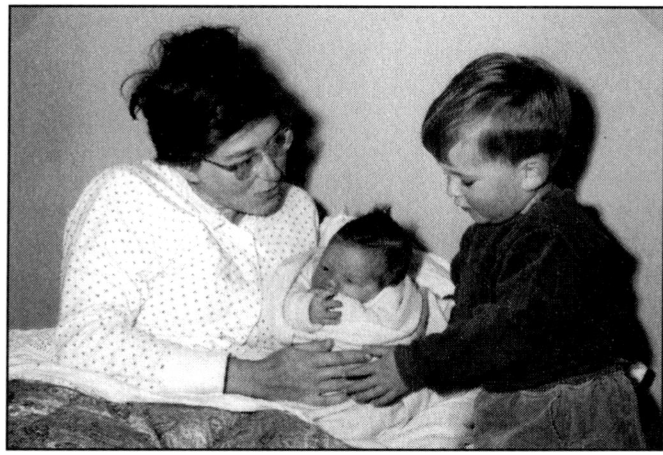

Hello, baby brother! Joan with Alan (one day old) and Gregory. Smallfield, April 4, 1956

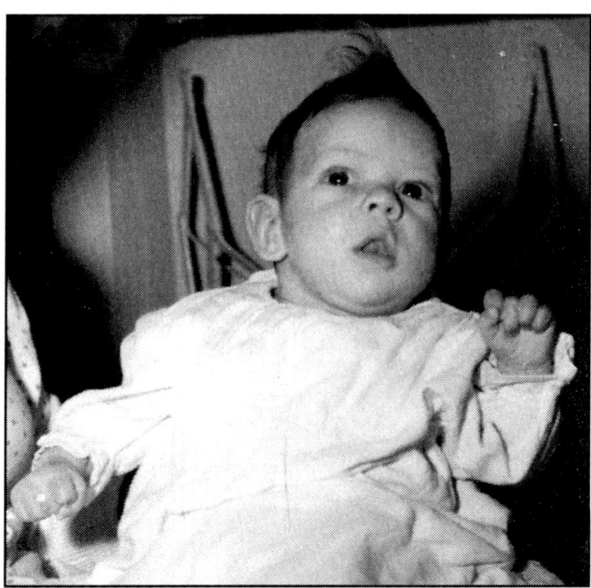

Alan Hugh Staple, May 1956

knew that it would be a slow process, so did not call Sister Speed immediately. I waddled around and inspected our spring flowers. Eventually Sister came by, leaving the Ford's engine running, while she quickly checked me and rushed off to another laboring mum. This process was repeated several times until, to my relief, she decided to send her colleague to the other mum ("it's her sixth, she'll be fast") and stay with me.

At this point my next-door neighbor and good friend, Mrs. Cant, came over to invite Gregory to lunch, which he happily accepted. Sister Speed asked Peter to boil a kettle and, nervous as I was, I asked if she would be "sterilizing instruments". She laughed heartily at the idea.

"No, luv, I have no instruments, but it's time for me cup o' tea".

So we all had tea and waited some more. Sister wore neither a mask nor gloves, but she made Peter don a mask because of his cold. As the pain got worse I was offered an anesthetic called "gas and air", actually a mixture of nitrous oxide ("laughing gas") and oxygen. This was self-administered, i.e. I held the mask to my face during a contraction. If I left it there too long I got drowsy and automatically dropped the mask, thus stopping the flow of gas. Peter, sniffling behind his surgical mask, supervised the procedure. Sister pointed out that, as a dentist, he should be familiar with nitrous oxide. I don't think he had a clue, but his presence was comforting, and overall this was a lot better than my previous experience at the Middlesex Hospital with its stirrups, glaring lights and hordes of spectators. When the head crowned, Peter administered Trilene, a more powerful anesthetic gas, while Sister gently eased the little body out. There were some anxious moments (of which I was not aware) until a few slaps on the bottom induced the baby to take his first breath. Yes, it was a BOY!

I was allowed to hold him immediately, while Sister waited patiently for the placenta. Then she washed me, wiped the baby clean, threw the disposable sheets as well as the afterbirth into our anthracite stove, and was on her way to check on her other patient. She had telephoned our doctor (who was on standby all day) and soon he appeared to examine the baby, repair my re- torn perineum, and, most important, have a glass of sherry with us to drink to the baby's health. To my relief he did not mention the word "circumcision". It was nearly 7pm when Mrs. Cant brought Gregory over. She had explained to him that he had a baby brother, and his comments were, "But it's got long hair like a girl." Then he ran off to spread the news along Broadbridge Lane shouting,

"My baby brother's just come out!"

I was too weary to check on the daffodils but yes, they were out too, and I could see them from the bedroom window early next morning. Thanks to Mrs. Cant, who invited Gregory to sleep over, the three of us had a peaceful night. But before we could sleep, we had one more decision to make: what would we call our new son? We decided to name him Alan Hugh, preserving the initials of Peter's father (Arthur Hubert), who had died two months before.

"Two Boys are easier than One…

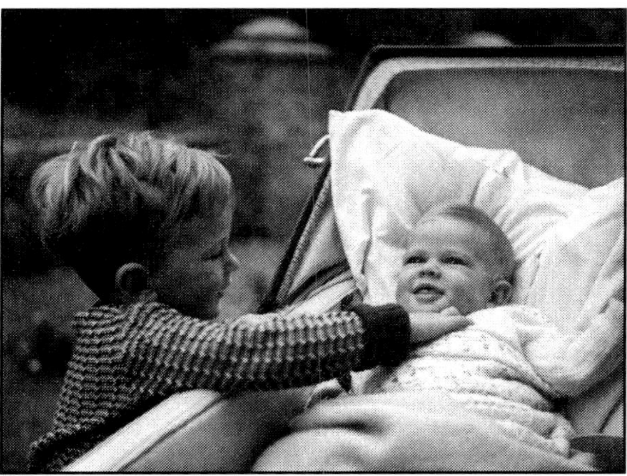

"Tickle, tickle…" Fall 1956

… they entertain each other." This is a myth, no doubt propagated by the baby-food industry. Gregory, so independent while I was pregnant, suddenly decided that he could not walk to the village for our daily shopping trips. He had asked why the baby had to be pushed in the pram (baby carriage) and, on being told that babies' legs were too weak to stand on, he collapsed on the floor, pronouncing that *his* legs were weak too. This condition was miraculously cured by the appearance of a beautiful red and yellow tricycle on his third birthday, about six weeks after Alan's birth. He was happy pedaling his little trike up and down bumpy Broadbridge Lane, going through as many puddles as possible.

Dr. Spock, the baby guru, suggests that, in order to avoid jealousy, the older sibling should be encouraged to help with the new baby's care, since it was *his* baby too. At first this approach worked: Gregory was delighted to squeeze bath water over Alan's head. "Shut eyes!" he warned. He would fetch a *clean* nappy, but wisely ran away from the soiled ones. He "helped" to feed Alan by sucking on the other breast. But one day he had obviously reached a decision. "Mummy", he said firmly, "that baby, it's *your* business, and I'm going out to play." Well, I was glad that he had regained his independence and his strong legs.

A few days after Alan's birth Peter had to attend an out-of-town dental meeting, so my sister-in-law, Diana, kindly came to stay with me, leaving Janet and Robbie with their nanny. She came in their 1938 Austin, named "William", a two-seater convertible with a "dickey"(rumble seat) in the back. Walter and Diana loved this car from the day they acquired it during their engagement at the end of World War II, and indeed it is still in driving condition 70 years later. All that week it rained steadily, a gentle spring rain, and I remember huddling in "William" with the raindrops drumming on the convertible roof, as Diana took me and the boys out for tea in Horley.

Sister Speed looked in most days to make sure everything was going all right. In addition, I had a "home help", supplied by the local government, to help me with chores the first two weeks. She pointed out that it was *not* her job to do the spring-cleaning, only to cook and to wash clothes for mother and baby. Even so, Diana and I seemed to be busy all the time. It soon became apparent that Alan was not as placid a baby as Gregory had been, although they were the same birth weight (7 ½ lb.) and were treated much the same way (I thought). Peter and I had attributed Gregory's behavior to our parenting skills, but perhaps it was just beginner's luck! Alan seemed to need very little sleep, certainly less than I did, and was colicky much of the time, spitting up milk all over

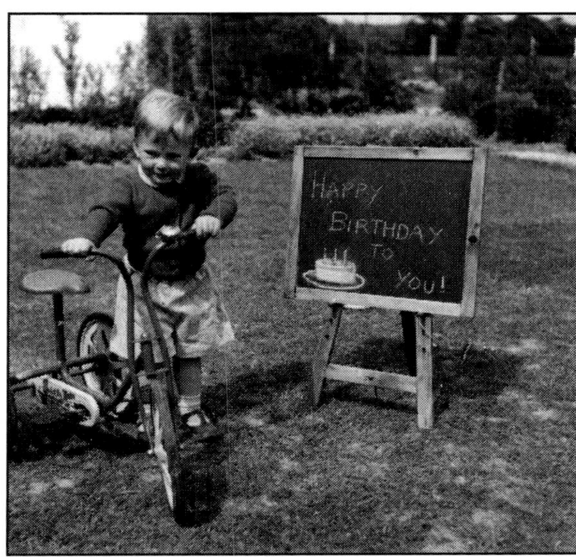

Gregory's third birthday, May 23, 1956

A friendly race on Broadbridge Lane, Smallfield. 1958

my shoulders. Unlike Gregory, whose growth curve resembled that in Dr. Spock's book, Alan gained very little weight. According to the baby clinic, there was nothing wrong with him; maybe he was "teething", they said. This was the standard explanation for crying babies, but I found it discouraging and tried various supplements with little success. Things slowly improved when Alan was able to eat solid food. My old lab-coats, which I wore around the house, were brightly decorated with pureed beetroot, carrots and spinach.

Gregory refused to share his bedroom with Alan ("he 'sturbs me"), so Peter and I kept his crib close to us. Of course he "sturbed" us too, so eventually we ended up sleeping in the living room, while our sons occupied *both* bedrooms, not exactly what we had planned. On Gregory's third birthday my brother and family drove over from Iver, Buckinghamshire, and Gregory enjoyed playing with his big cousins, Janet and Robbie. A gentle pony gave rides to all the neighborhood kids, so everybody had a great time.

In the summer of 1956, we decided to take a week's holiday by the seaside together with Peter's sister, Betty Buddle, and her family. We did not see much of the Buddles, who lived in Kent, since neither of us owned a car, and travel was difficult with small children. The eight of us settled into a spacious house, close to the beach at Shoreham[3] and we hoped that Gregory would get to know his cousins and have fun. Betty and her photographer husband, Jim, had two daughters: Anne, aged five, and Tricia, two years old. Anne was a serious girl and mature for her age. She took charge of her little sister as well as Gregory, and loved giving Alan his bottle. Since neither Betty nor I normally got away from our children for a whole day, we took turns going on daytrips with our husbands, leaving all four kids behind. Until then, I had harbored the vague notion that I would like to have a family of two boys and two girls. Just one day at Shoreham in charge of the four preschoolers did much towards changing my mind about that!

An important part of my daily routine was listening to the radio (called wireless in England). No, I'm not thinking of the nine o'clock news, which was so essential during the war, but something much more gentle: from 1.45 to 2pm the BBC Home Service aired

---

3 Shoreham is near Wothing, about 40 miles from Smallwood

Gregory with cousins Tricia and Anne Buddle.
Shoreham, Sussex, July 1956

Alan likes the seaside!

Listen with Mother, a wonderful program designed for pre-school children. Gregory seemed to know when it was time and came running when he heard the signature tune (Fauré's *Berceuse*). He was ready on his little chair close to the radio when the announcer opened with the familiar words

"Are you sitting comfortably?"

"Yes" Gregory replied solemnly.

"Then I'll begin", said the lady.

Both of us listened attentively to the stories, songs and nursery rhymes. Not having grown up in England, I was unfamiliar with the children's songs and stories that "everybody" knew, including Peter, who could recite whole passages from Winnie the Pooh. With the help of the Oxford Book of Nursery Rhymes and *Listen with Mother* I caught up with British early childhood literature. Gregory and I made the acquaintance of Peter Rabbit and Toad of Toad Hall, of Christopher Robin and friends, Alice in Wonderland and other beloved characters. Looking back on these daily fifteen minutes, two things strike me: unlike most contemporary TV children's programs, this one required the toddler to pay close attention since there were no visuals to supplement the spoken word. Secondly, it was not intended to be a baby-sitting service: mothers did not use this program to have a little time to themselves; it was definitely *Listen* ***with*** *Mother.* The narrator would ask questions, and both of us answered as best we could.

I have read that *Listen with Mother* had over a million listeners per session. It ran from 1950 to 1982, when it was replaced with *Watch with Mother*, which is still being televised in England at 1:45pm every weekday. After we said good-bye to the wireless lady, Gregory willingly snuggled down for his nap, humming the day's featured nursery rhyme.

Now it was my turn: *Woman's Hour* aired from 2-3pm. This show, designed for us home-bound mothers, was a mixture of news, music and fiction, which easily held my attention for an hour, the only time during the day that I was able to sit down for such an extended period. Nursing Alan at the same time did not interfere with my concentration, and I always hoped he'd be quiet during the installment of the current exciting novel. One of my favorite storytellers was Antonia Ridge, so I am pleased that her stories, first published in 1958, are still in print. After fifty years, *Woman's Hour* still airs daily on BBC4 and has its own website. The topics now include subjects never discussed in the fifties, such as divorce, single motherhood, sexual techniques and abortion. But basically the pattern is similar, a mix of newsy items and an ongoing novel. I wonder if there are enough stay-at- home-mums in England to sustain the program, or do workingwomen listen secretly on their electronic gadgets during business meetings.

Back to Birmingham

One evening in the autumn of 1956 Peter came home from work with terrible news: his boss, Tom King, had been killed in a tragic hunting accident over the weekend. Tom was head of the Medical Research Council (MRC) dental unit at King's College Hospital and it was the custom of the MRC to close units following the death or retirement of the principal investigator. Peter was of course aware of the temporary nature of MRC Units, but since Tom King was a healthy man in his forties, he did not give it a thought. In addition Peter had his own Nuffield Research Fellowship, funded for three years. However, a fellowship was of no use without a lab to work in! Peter was given three months notice to vacate his space, since the Unit would be closing down. There were few opportunities for a person with Peter's qualifications: a dental degree as well as a Ph.D. in histochemistry. What little dental research was going on in British dental schools at this time was mostly of a clinical nature, not basic science. The situation was quite different in the USA, where PhD level dentists were in demand in well-funded, research-oriented dental schools. Indeed, in the US, a Ph.D. was pretty much a requirement for anyone aspiring to a senior position in a prestigious school of dentistry.

While Peter mulled over the possibility of applying for a position in the USA, he was offered a temporary job at the University of Birmingham – my alma mater! Having little choice, he accepted, and in the winter of 1957 we moved into a furnished flat in Edgbaston, a suburb of Birmingham, in the same street (Rotton Park Road) where

I had lived with my family during World War II. We were quite close to my parents, who, having sold their house, now lived in one of the new post-war apartment buildings. Having my parents nearby, and being reunited with some of my old friends from the Refugee Club were about the only good things about our yearlong stay in the midlands. Alan was still a baby, but I think Gregory appreciated having grandma and grandpa around. My father took him to visit the factory where he worked to watch the amazing new process of injection molding: powdered plastic was put into a machine at one end and, lo and behold, combs (or curlers or coat hangers) shot out at the other end and dropped onto a conveyor belt.

Gregory missed Broadbridge Lane and his little friends, and was bored playing by himself in our backyard. As his 4th birthday present my parents enrolled him in a local nursery school, which was much appreciated by all of us. I took him there on the back of my bike every morning, and he loved both the ride and his mornings in school.

The basement flat we lived in was dark, damp and chilly – but the rent was affordable. Moisture condensed on the brick kitchen floor, and at night I had to be careful not to step on the slimy slugs that came out of the cracks and slithered across the moist floor. A young Spanish couple, with a baby the same age as Alan, occupied the adjacent flat. We had rather different lifestyles: whereas our boys were served a "high tea" and were in bed before 8pm, Carlos, the little Spaniard, took his main meal with his parents around 10pm and enjoyed the same exotic, spicy food that they did. By the time they finally quieted down around 1am, we were exhausted, and it seemed like minutes before Alan woke up at dawn, demanding his early morning bottle. Our neighbors, on the other hand, complained that our boys made too much noise in the morning, waking poor little Carlos! We reached a few compromises but never became friends. Our landlady, Frau Scheuer, like me a German-Jewish refugee, was a friend of my mother's, which is how we got this flat. She defended our right to hang laundry out to dry in the back yard against the complaints of the very posh lady next-door, who maintained that this was inappropriate in an upscale neighborhood, and that it spoiled her view. She was even more upset about Alan (aged about

14 months) running naked under the sprinkler on warm summer days and she once called the police. A young officer responded, and, far from making an arrest (? for indecent exposure) had fun playing with the boys. The lady closed her shutters with a bang, and never bothered us again.

A Convent for Gregory

We had rented out our bungalow in Smallfield and, on our return, found everything in order, except for dark greasy stains on our sofa and armchairs, where the tenant's head had rested. Gregory was nearly 4 ½ years old in the autumn of 1957, too young by six months to attend the local elementary school. Since he had enjoyed his nursery school in Birmingham, we enrolled him in the Infant School (ages 4-7) run by the Franciscan Mission Sisters of the Convent at Copthorne, a village in West Sussex, about five miles from Smallfield. Peter was now seriously considering emigration to the United States, so all our arrangements were of a temporary nature.

Serious schoolboy. Gregory, Fall 1957

Gregory was proud of his school uniform, consisting of gray flannel shorts, white shirt, striped tie and a dark green blazer embroidered with the school crest. A green "mac" (raincoat) and natty school cap completed the outfit. For the first week of school I rode with Gregory on the nine o'clock bus to Copthorne and picked him up again at three o'clock. It was a long day for a four-year-old and, although he seemed to like his classes, he was tired and cranky when he got home. He hated the mid-day school dinner, consisting, according to him, of " tough meat, potatoes and *lots* of cabbage". Gregory told us that he could see the big field full of cabbages from his classroom window, and was despondent at the thought of having to eat his way through them. The nuns grew all their own vegetables as well as beautiful flowers in the gardens surrounding the Convent

After Gregory got used to riding the bus, I just walked him to the bus stop at the end of Broadbridge Lane, and made sure he had his two pennies (one each way). Then Alan and I waved good-bye as the big green bus carried him away. At the Convent bus stop one of the nuns met the little pupils.

Gregory's teacher was Sister Bonaventura – he pronounced it Bonaventure (rhymes with adventure) – and he learned a lot from her in the 18 months that he attended the Infant School. The children were taught to read and write (print) little stories, and they did a lot of arithmetic. The latter consisted of adding, subtracting and memorizing multiplication tables. Gregory would recite 2x2=4, 3x2=6 etc ad nauseam, along with passages from the catechism, quite incomprehensible to both of us. I gathered that he had some arguments with Sister B. regarding the role of God. On being told that God had made everything on earth, he remarked that this was not true; he himself had seen that *everything* was made in his grandpa's factory in Birmingham. Moreover, having helped his dad sow peas and beans, he also doubted Sister's view that God made all things grow. "I think you have to water them," he said.

Sister was not unduly worried about our little skeptic, realizing that he would be leaving the school well before it was time to prepare for first communion. But Gregory told me that some of his classmates said he would go to a nasty place called hell, and he wondered where that was. "Maybe in America?" He must have heard us discuss that country. "Absolutely not," I said, "America is more like heaven, and they eat lovely soft meat there, called hamburgers and drink sweet orange juice every day."

Meanwhile Alan, now a toddler, behaved quite differently from his brother. Gregory's favorite toys during his first and second year had been his building blocks, with which he constructed precariously balanced towers, and he now worked with more complex wooden construction sets, and later a metal *Erector* kit. He was very patient and persistent; constantly improving and rebuilding collapsed structures.

Alan, on the other hand, had only one use for building blocks: they were hurled to the furthest corners of the room, hopefully hitting something to make a resounding "clonk". The louder the better! When all the blocks were scattered around, he would clap his hands happily and expect someone (usually me) to gather them up, so he could repeat the performance. We bought him some small rubber balls, which he loved, but *every* object, including finger food, was a potential missile for him, to be thrown vigorously and with amazing accuracy at a target of his choice. This feat was accomplished only with his left hand, no matter where I placed the object. Had I been acquainted with baseball, I would have recognized a deadly left-handed pitcher in the making. And indeed he became just that about seven years later. Another talent he seemed to possess, even as a crawling baby, was the ability to keep track of many small objects: Like most young children Gregory and Alan enjoyed collecting horse chestnuts (called "conkers" in England) in the autumn. Each boy stored his hoard of shiny red-brown nuts in his own pail or shoebox. Predictably, to Alan they represented potential missiles and were soon scattered, while Gregory liked to string his conkers together in long chains, after Peter skillfully drilled holes through them. Before going to bed at night, Alan went through a ceremony of putting his conkers to bed in their box, and would not rest until *every single one* was retrieved from under the bed or wherever they were hiding. I have no idea how he knew exactly how many he owned – but he did!

Driving School Adventures

Around this time (1957) the German government announced

that reparations would be paid to Jewish refugees who had been deprived of access to public education in Germany. To claim this money one had to fill out many forms and submit them to a law firm specializing in reparations. I had to prove that my parents had spent money on my education in England, and calculate exactly how much. In theory, the higher the level of education a refugee attained, the higher the cost – and the higher the compensation. So I thought that, since I had a Ph.D., I should be getting *a lot* of money. I fantasized about buying a car, maybe not a Rolls Royce, but something really nice.

Well, I was quite wrong! As a Jewish refugee girl, I had been awarded a full scholarship to King Edward's High School for Girls in Birmingham from 1939 to 1942. Thus, no money could be claimed for my high school education. So what about my University education? Tuition at British Universities was nominal for both undergraduate and graduate studies, so even including fees and expenses for books and lab supplies, my claim did not add up to much. I forgot all about the matter, but a year or so later my lawyer informed me that I had actually been awarded a modest sum. After legal fees were subtracted, it was just enough to buy our first car: a Land Rover. This feisty vehicle was about 10 years old, and had been used by a doctor friend (Jimmy Newman) to make house calls in rural areas. He assured us that it would cruise over ploughed fields, ford rivers, negotiate steep and muddy lanes, in fact it was ready to go *anywhere at any time*. Actually all I had envisaged were trips to Gregory's school, to the shops in Horley and maybe an occasional picnic.

Peter and the boys were delighted. On rainy days Peter now *drove* to Horley Station in comfort, instead of bicycling, encased in his oilcloth poncho and leggings. Sure, the Land Rover leaked, but not too badly. A black plume of smoke issued from its exhaust pipe, evidence of its taste for oil. And on frosty nights Peter drained the radiator, which was too leaky to retain antifreeze. At weekends we went on trips around Surrey, Sussex and Kent, including Tonbridge, Peter's birthplace, which helped me appreciate this beautiful part of England.

For me, there was one downside to owning a car*: I could not drive!* Indeed I had never been interested in acquiring this skill.

Tree dwellers: Alan, Peter and Gregory. Summer 1958

Little boy and big Land Rover. Smallfield, 1958

But now, with the prospect of emigration to automobile-obsessed America hanging over me, I felt the time had come to get behind the wheel. At Peter's urging I enrolled in the Horley Driving School, and was soon on my way around the countryside with the owner (and sole instructor), a Mr. Snyder. He was a spooky little man with shifty eyes, slicked down black hair and a nervous tick. I disliked him at first sight. Although Mr. Snyder owned a nice school car with dual controls, I had asked him to let me use the Land Rover for my lessons, since I needed to learn how to cope with double-declutching[4] and two sets of stick shifts (one for the four-wheel drive mode).

The Land Rover had neither heating nor signals. One had to crank down the window to give hand signals at every intersection. I found it easiest to just leave my window open and dress accordingly: thick corduroys, my duffle coat and heavy boots with which to kick the stiff clutch and brake pedals. Mr. Snyder, in the passenger seat, kept one hand firmly planted on my knee and squeezed hard when he wanted me to brake. Gradually this hand crept higher up, and he suggested that I wear a skirt next time! Needless to say, I was too nervous to pay much attention to the road. One of the maneuvers I had to learn was a "hill start" – without rolling back even an inch. In order to practice this, Mr. S. took me to a secluded country lane, flanked with high hedges, where he got more and more amorous.

At this point I decided I'd had enough, and told Peter I was giving up driving – and why. I don't think Peter believed me. Terms like "sexual harassment" had not been coined yet, and if a "girl" attracted unwelcome advances, well, that was surely her fault. Peter pointed out that he had paid a non-refundable fee for a set of ten lessons and that, whereas Mr. Snyder might not be a very likeable person, I should ignore his behavior and concentrate on driving. Easier said than done!

I cut my losses and enrolled in the only other driving school within 10 miles. Mr. Andrews, a soft-spoken young man about my age, came to pick me up and we started from scratch. Every time he

4 A driving procedure used for a vehicles with an unsynchronized manual transmission. It can be difficult to master and, if not done correctly, the gears will "crash"… (from www.wikipedia.com)

moved his hand (perhaps to light his cigarette or blow his nose) I flinched and hit the brake. He asked me pull over and park.

"Now tell me, Mrs. Staple, have you had driving lessons before?"

"Well yes, Mr. Andrews, but only two or three," I stammered.

"Was your teacher perhaps a Mr. Snyder?"

"Yes! How did you know?" Mr. Andrews laughed.

"I have taught several young ladies who started with Mr. Snyder but dropped out. Now please relax. I am not like Mr. Snyder, and I will NEVER touch you."

He was as good as his word. Gradually I relaxed, and even began to enjoy myself. Under Mr. Andrews' gentle guidance I took control of the old Land Rover with all its complexities. On weekends, Peter took me for practice drives, with the boys bouncing around in the back. They had been told to keep very quiet, so as not to distract Mummy. Alan, about 2 years old was learning his colors, so at every traffic light he yelled excitedly "Mummy, light is blue, go, go!"

Finally I was ready for the Driving Test! Peter took me to the town of Reigate, where he and the boys had lunch while I set off on my Test Drive with not one, but two examiners on board. The older, portly gentleman introduced himself as the district examiner, who was making a surprise visit to monitor the testing procedure. He asked permission to ride along, and without waiting for an answer, installed himself in the back, while the local examiner sat in the passenger seat. I looked both ways, released the handbrake, signaled and took off. All went well. I gave correct hand signals, turned right, turned left, negotiated a roundabout, parked on a steep hill without rolling back, did a U-turn, backed into a narrow driveway – and finally got ready for a maneuver called "the emergency stop".

"Mrs. Staple, when I say STOP, we pretend a dog[5] has run into the road and you must stop as quickly and safely as you can," said the examiner. He directed me to a quiet street, and I could see him bracing himself. Remember this was 1958, decades before seatbelts.

5 The British, who happily hunt foxes to death, would give their lives for a dog.

"STOP!" he shouted. The Land Rover had powerful brakes, and I kicked the pedals hard. The examiner hit the windshield and the fat district man levitated from the back seat and almost landed in my lap. Without being told, I pulled over and waited for the gentlemen to regain their composure, hoping that I had neither killed the imaginary dog nor injured my passengers. "Jolly good show!" and "splendid brakes!" they exclaimed in unison. "Please return to the town hall, where your driving license will be issued." On our way home, I stopped by Andrews' Driving School and told my teacher the good news. He was delighted, and we shook hands, our first – and last – physical contact.

The very next day I picked Gregory up from school and rejoiced to see how proud he was as his classmates and the nuns gathered round to admire our ancient vehicle – and *me,* the mum-driver!

***Where is* Alabama?**

Great news! Peter received a job offer from the University of Alabama School of Dentistry in Birmingham: a tenure track position as Assistant Professor, effective Fall 1959, with a salary that was more than twice our current meager income. The way this came about was complicated and involved a chance meeting between an old friend of Peters, Gil Parfitt, then a professor of dentistry at the University of Alabama, and Jim Danielli, in whose department at King's College, London, both Peter and I had worked. Jim's recommendation was enough to induce Gil to talk Dean Volker into advancing this job offer.

Although I had been anticipating an eventual move to America, I was far from thrilled. I loved England and our little house in Smallfield, and the thought of being so far away from my parents and from my brother's family made me sad. Moreover, my visit to the United States a few years ago, wonderful though it was, had convinced me that, whereas I would like to explore more of this great country, no way would I want to *live* there.

"Where *is* Alabama?" I enquired.

"It's in the South," said Peter.

"You mean in South America?"

"NO, of course not, it's near Arkansas, I think."

We had heard of Arkansas (and even knew how to pronounce it!) in connection with the international publicity that Little Rock received during the 1957 school desegregation fiasco. This was not reassuring.

Peter got out the Times Atlas. "Look, *here* is Alabama, right next to Georgia." Hey, I knew about Georgia from *Gone with the Wind*! Although it was many years since I had read the book and seen the movie, the images of Atlanta burning were still vivid in my mind.

"I bet it's hot there; New York was bad enough, and this is further south. How about finding a job in Boston," I enquired hopefully, thinking of the gorgeous fall foliage I had seen on my train journey through New England. But Peter was pleased with the offer, and before long we found ourselves at the American Consulate in London, finalizing our Immigration Visa applications. This involved a physical, as well as an interview with the Consul for all four of us. Gregory and Alan, five and two years old respectively, were dressed in their best clothes and understood the importance of the occasion. When our turn came, we were ushered into the Consul's office, and found him in his shirtsleeves, lounging in a swivel chair, his feet on the desk, cigarette in hand, smiling broadly. He stood up, at least six feet of him, and greeted the boys first.

"Hiya, Greg and Al, good to see ya!" He squatted down to shake hands with them before turning to us. "Howdy, Pete and Joan, so you're off to Alabama?" He asked a few questions about Peter's job, seemed satisfied, and told us the visas would be available shortly. After wishing us the best of luck, he personally showed us out. A preview of casual, yet efficient, America!

The next task was to sell our bungalow. There were unexpected complications: plans were under way to develop the small airfield located at Gatwick into a world-class international airport. Gatwick was only a few miles from Smallfield, and it was uncertain at this time where exactly the new major highway, together with access roads would be located. For our little property the possibilities included acquisition by the highway authorities, being stuck high up on the edge of a ramp or, hopefully, being just far enough from the highway to provide easy access without the noise and fumes. Proximity to a major airport would also entail the deafening roar of jet planes, which had only recently come into use. Prospective buyers had to consider all this and, not surprisingly, were reluctant to make us an offer until more was known about the location of new roads. But since we needed the money, we were not in a position to wait until Gatwick Airport was built. Several would-be buyers did look at 13 Broadbridge Lane. They did not like the bright paint and wallpapers of which we were so proud, and wanted everything painted beige. They were also suspicious of the limited central heating we had installed. One lady worried about "the air being so dry that your bread-and-butter curls up," and another felt uneasy about a fire burning *all night* in the anthracite stove. The average English family was still used to living in a cold, damp house and lighting a coal fire in the sitting room on chilly evenings. We planned to depart in April 1959, leaving the bungalow in the hands of a capable estate agent.

Farewell England

My parents did not seem distressed by our decision to emigrate, or maybe they hid their true feelings from me, so as not to make leaving even harder. They had made two trips to New York to visit my father's brothers, Otto and Alex, and his sisters, Franzel and Martha, who were happily settled in the U.S. with their families. Papi, ever the optimist, promised to visit us soon and get acquainted with the South. He realized that having a car was very important in the U.S. and immediately ordered an export model Vauxhall Estate Car (station wagon) for us as a parting gift. Our Land Rover just about survived the winter. When the brand-new blue and white Vauxhall was delivered, all of Broadbridge Lane turned out to admire it. Although this vehicle would now be considered a "compact", it seemed very long, and I had considerable difficulty getting all of it into our garage. Driving it was easy, compared with the Land Rover, in spite of the fact that the steering wheel was on the left, so I decided to pick up Gregory from school and take the boys for a picnic in the woods. It had been raining, and the place where we usually parked was rather muddy, but we enjoyed our egg sandwiches, played hide-and-seek for a while and then got ready to drive home. The engine sprang to life, I accelerated, but the car did not budge! We got out and studied the situation: the rear wheels had sunk deeply into the mud. Being used to four-wheel drive, I did not even perceive this as a problem. Why didn't the car move? Gregory offered to push, while Alan said anxiously "walk home?" Neither prospect was appealing. Nobody was in sight. It was dusk and starting to rain again as we trudged out to the nearest paved road, Alan riding piggyback and Gregory, tired from his day at school, clinging to my hand. A car stopped for us, and the kind driver returned to inspect our car. He laughed "what made you park in this *swamp*, young lady?" He rocked the car back and forth to no avail. Finally we had to be towed out. I learned a lesson, not taught at driving school: a car, no matter how new or how pretty, is *not* an all-terrain vehicle. Stay on paved roads.

We spent Easter 1959 with my parents in Eastbourne, a final get-together about a month before our departure. Finding a hotel for all of us in this lovely resort town on the coast was difficult for reasons which seem ridiculous now. Mutti and Papi insisted on an "en suite" bedroom, but only a few luxury hotels boasted rooms with private bath; it was more usual for guests to share a bathroom down the hall. My parents eventually found a room to their liking but this upscale hotel did not accommodate children. So the rest of us stayed in a less luxurious, but more child friendly hotel, which tolerated kids on the premises – but did not go so far as to permit them to dine with their parents. A "High Tea" was provided for young children between 5 and 6 o'clock; dinner for grownups was served at eight. All these regulations made "togetherness" a little difficult at times. Nevertheless we all enjoyed ourselves and the weather allowed us to spend time on the beach, building sandcastles and doing all the usual "seaside" things. I did not realize then that I would never see my parents again.

A week before our scheduled flight to New York on April 9, 1959, the bungalow was almost empty: our favorite furniture was packed and held in storage, ready to follow us to Alabama, while the

A last reunion. Grandparents Sali and Selma Lorch with Gregory and Alan. Eastbourne, England, March 1959.

A last farewell, just before our departure to Heathrow Airport for the trip to the USA. From L to R: Joan, Alan, Peter, Robbie Lorch, Gregory, Walter Lorch with Baby Caroline, Janet Lorch.
Buck House, Iver, Bucks. April 1959.

rest was disposed of. The Vauxhall was ready to be shipped too, after transporting our suitcases to my brother's house at Iver, where we would spend our last week in England. But we could not leave 13 Broadbridge Lane before celebrating Alan's third birthday! All the neighborhood kids assembled and had a great time, racing around the empty house and sitting on the floor to eat birthday cake.

Meanwhile Diana informed us that while we were still welcome to stay with them, we should be aware that Janet (almost 12 years old) had developed chicken pox and had passed it on to her baby sister, Caroline. Robbie (just 10) had the disease a few years ago, so was not affected. We realized of course, that chicken pox was inevitable, but did not want to start life in a new country coping with this itchy condition. So we kept our distance from Janet and baby Caroline. When the great day came, Walter loaded the four of us plus plenty of luggage into his Rolls Royce; final snapshots were taken, hugs all round – except for the pox-infected girls – and off we went to London (Heathrow) Airport.

3. Life in the "Confederacy"

"Segregation in the South is honest, open and above board. Of the two systems or styles of segregation, the Northern and the Southern, there is no doubt whatever in my mind which is the better." Senator Strom Thurmond

"I'm Leaving on a Jet Plane..."

Non-stop transatlantic jet flights had only recently been inaugurated by Pan Am Airlines, so we felt like pioneers as we boarded the huge Boeing 707 in the late morning of April 9, 1959 at Heathrow's new Terminal 2. It took a long time to board the one hundred and eleven passengers, the most ever carried on one plane, but eventually the four of us were settled in our seats, feeling both excited and anxious, at least I did. Peter and I had flown before – he in a small fighter plane during WWII and I in a prop plane from Paris to London – but this was very different. We were packed in tightly in the center of the cabin, leaving very little room to move and no way to look out of the windows. The tremendous roar of the jets took us by surprise and before long we were airborne. Our seats were very close to one of the few toilets on board, where queues formed as soon as the seatbelt sign was turned off, and continued throughout the flight. I had brought games and puzzles for the boys, and they seemed to enjoy watching the passengers and especially the pretty "stewardesses", who brought us Coca Cola with *ice cubes* and salty peanuts – a first taste of America. In those days Pan Am required stewardesses to be beautiful, slim, single and young. Their retirement age was 32, and they wore military style uniforms, soon to be replaced by more seductive outfits designed by top fashion houses.

At lunchtime we were served chicken sandwiches made with very soft snow white bread, probably Wonder bread. I had seen such bread on my previous trip to the United States, but Alan was quite perplexed and, not recognizing the pale fluffy substance as something edible, he carefully picked out the chicken bits. Gregory bravely bit into his sandwich and promptly christened the material "mushbread". In the weeks to come, after we had settled into our American home, I started baking bread, because none of us got used to the "mushbread".

The flight took about 7 hours and was quite choppy towards the end as we circled over New York, awaiting permission to land at Idlewild (now JFK) Airport. We all felt queasy and Alan threw up just as we were landing. Understandably, he was upset, and was even more miserable after he slipped and fell on the way to the Immigration Desk. The official examining our Immigrant Visas welcomed us warmly and hoped we would be very happy in our new country. Alan took this opportunity to remark in his high pitched very English accent, "I wish I had *never* come to your country!"

I felt like sinking into the slippery floor, when the nice man came out from behind his high counter to see where this little voice was coming from. On spotting the diminutive new immigrant the man bent down, picked up the disgruntled boy and took him to the luggage slide to watch the bags come out. He even stopped the conveyer belt and allowed Alan to slide down the ramp.

"Now, Alan Staple, do you think you like America a bit better?" he enquired. Alan, a big smile on his tear-stained face, admitted that he did. And we all agreed we had come to a country of wonderful people!

My old friend, Lori Goldstein, had come out from Levittown to meet us. Lori and I had known each other in the 1930s in our German hometown, Offenbach, where we were members of a six-girl Kränzchen (little circle) who met every Saturday to play games and gorge on cake and hot chocolate. She drove us to a nearby hotel and we found that our London travel agent had booked us into a luxury suite of two interconnecting bedrooms. English hotel rooms are very small and rarely have private baths, but this was something else: the combined rooms with their *two* full bathrooms were larger than our bungalow in Smallfield. Each room had two enormous beds; I later learned they were called "king-size", although there is no royalty in the United States. In keeping with this metaphor, the price tag could be called "emperor-size"! The boys, tired and grumpy after the long journey, instantly revived, flung themselves onto the giant beds and bounced around wildly. Peter and I were speechless. Fortunately Lori had the presence of mind to persuade the hotel to cancel one of the rooms, explaining that we were poor immigrants from England, not aware of how big everything is in America. Then she helped me put the wild boys to bed. They were easily persuaded to have a warm bath in the large *pale blue* bathtub. All the bathroom fixtures were pastel colored, something we had never seen before. After reading a bedtime story, Lori returned to Levittown to cook dinner for her family. I am forever grateful to her for saving our sanity that afternoon. Peter and I set our watches back 5 hours and, realizing it was actually quite early, ordered a couple of hamburgers from room-service before falling into our king-size bed for our first night in America.

A Different Birmingham

The next morning saw us once more at Idlewild Airport, boarding a regular prop plane, which seemed quite small after the Boeing, en route to Birmingham, Alabama. This trip was accomplished in short laps, involving several stops, layovers and changes of aircraft. Since these planes did not fly at a high altitude we saw a lot of the country, which seemed vast, heavily forested and sparsely populated, compared with Europe. At each stop it got warmer and we were soon able to shed our English coats and sweaters. The friendly stewardesses, not quite as glamorous as those on Pan Am, treated us to Coca Cola, lots of ice cubes, peanuts and more "mushbread" sandwiches, as well as potato crisps, which they called "chips".

Finally we buckled up for the last landing: our new home town, Birmingham, named of course for Birmingham, England, where I had gone to high school and university. Apart from their major industries, steel and pig iron, I felt the two cities had nothing in common. We were met at the airport by a delegation consisting of Peter's new boss, Dr. Robert Teague, chair of the Pharmacology Department at the School of Dentistry, and his wife, as well as

Peter's old English friends, Gil and Muriel Parfitt. The latter took us to a small apartment, not far from the Dental School, which would be our home until we could buy a house. I had great difficulty communicating with the Teagues (they were true Southerners!), but immediately liked the Parfitts, especially Muriel, who had tried hard to make the apartment look like home, even having tea and home-made scones ready for us on our arrival.

While Peter started work almost at once, the boys and I explored Birmingham and surroundings with Muriel's help. I was pleasantly surprised at the beauty of the suburbs south of Birmingham, perched on an escarpment, which includes Red Mountain, so called because of the iron oxide rich red soil. The huge iron statue of Vulcan (only the Statue of Liberty is taller!) dominates Red Mountain. The Roman god of the forge stood with his arm extended, carrying a torch whose green light was visible for many miles. I later learned that the light turned red if there had been a fatal traffic accident in Birmingham.[1]

We had arrived at an ideal time of year: everything was in bloom. The heavily wooded hillside was covered with flowering trees and shrubs, many unfamiliar to us. I loved the snow- white dogwoods, interspersed with pink redbuds. The gardens (called yards here) surrounded the houses like parkland, without the interruption of fences or hedges, and were ablaze with spring flowers. Muriel and Gil lived in an area called Bluff Park, south of Red Mountain. They encouraged us to search for a house there, since there was a newly built elementary school nearby, as well as bus service to the Medical/Dental Campus downtown. Moreover, since the escarpment was 1000 ft. above the city of Birmingham, temperatures were considerably lower up there. Bob Teague lent us his little Nash car, but, being a new driver, used to a quiet rural area, I was intimidated by the volume of fast-moving *right* side traffic, and did not use it. Instead, I took the boys exploring on the city buses.

One day, on our way home from the beautiful zoo, we – or rather Alan - inadvertently caused a civil rights incident, worthy of Rosa Parks, whose defiance had led to the integration of buses in Montgomery, the capital of Alabama, four years earlier. We were

1 In 2000 the torch was replaced by a spear, going back to the original 1904 design.

boarding a bus, which was fairly full, and Alan tried to make a dash for the back, hoping to kneel on the bench facing the rear window. The driver was upset. I did not understand exactly what he said, but suddenly I remembered something Muriel had told me: buses, like most public places, are racially segregated. White people sit in front and colored people must sit in the back. Alan was breaking a law!

"Alan," I said, "please sit right here with Gregory and me."

"But I want to sit in the *back*! *Why* can't I sit in the back? I'm *going* to sit in back…" A tantrum was brewing.

"Alan, it is not allowed. Only *colored* people sit in the back."

"What colored people? I don't *see* any colored people!"

In fact the bus was packed with colored maids returning from work. At a loss what to say I waved at the crowd and told Alan to look around. A light went on in his toddler brain.

"Oh, *these* ladies (at least he called them ladies!), but they are not *colored*, they are *plain brown.*"

The crowd on the bus erupted in laughter and applause. A very large, very black "mammy" got up from the coveted rear bench, and made her way forward through the narrow aisle towards Alan.

"Y'all come sit with me, honeychile," she drawled, picking up the screaming little boy and clutching him to her ample bosom. She returned to the back, and placed Alan firmly on her lap. He stopped in mid-scream. Gregory and I breathed a sigh of relief. The driver, very annoyed at the delay, promptly started the bus.

Gradually we got used to segregation, but not without making many more mistakes. One concerned the public lavatories, quaintly called "Restrooms." They came in sets of four: *White Men* and *Colored Men*, adjacent to *White Women* and *Colored Women.* Gregory considered himself too old to accompany me to the ladies room, and decided to visit the *Colored Men's* restroom, remembering the pastel fixtures at our airport hotel. He was disappointed to find everything "plain white and rather dirty." Drinking fountains intrigued the boys – they did not exist in England. I don't remember drinking much water there, and certainly no ice water. Maybe England's cool damp climate was more conducive to drinking hot tea. Be that as it may, in Alabama we always stopped at drinking fountains. They too were

Segregation Signs in the South

Colored drinking fountain

Typical rest-room sign reads WHITE LADIES ONLY

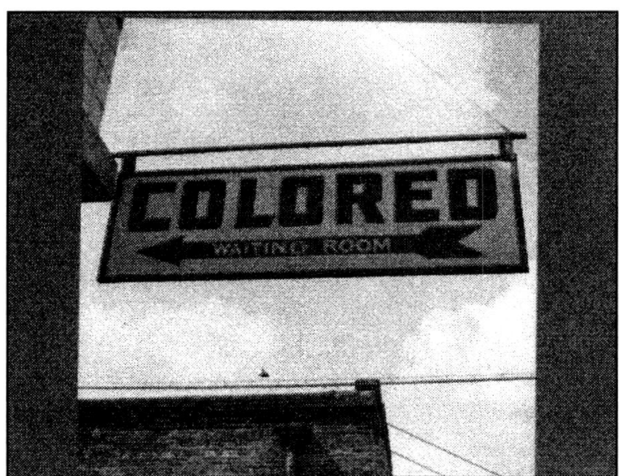

White waiting room at a Southern bus station

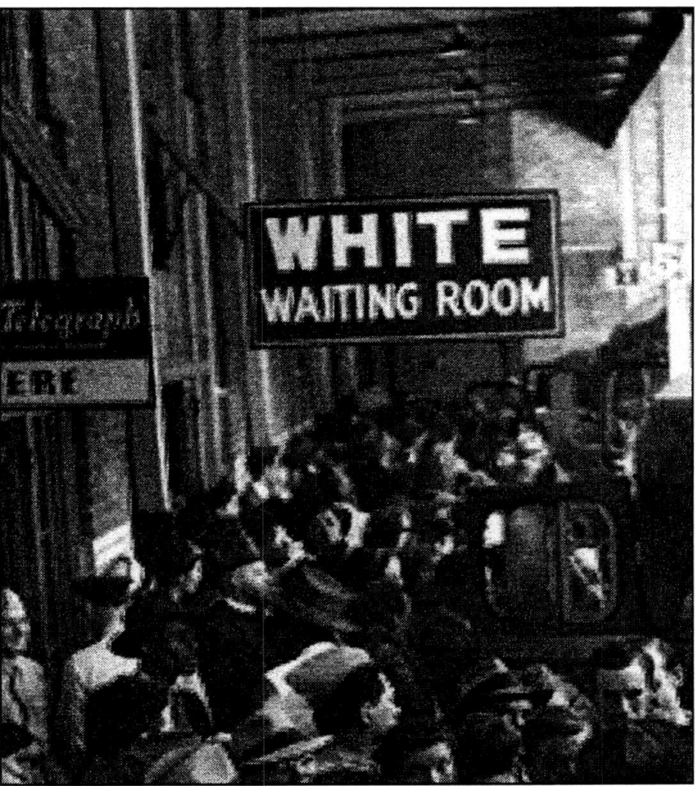

A Southern bus station sign

labeled *White* and *Colored.* On first spotting a pair of fountains, Gregory, proud of his reading skills, made a beeline for the *Colored* one, telling his little brother, he could make do with the *White*. Again a disappointment: both fountains yielded plain water. Prior to our arrival in Birmingham, our sons had never seen a person of color. Rural England was 100% white. Anticipating questions regarding the many colored persons we saw in the city, I told the boys that these brown-skinned people had originally come from Africa, a far-away country, where everybody had dark skin to protect them from the strong sun. I felt this was enough explanation for the time being. Sooner or later they would no doubt learn how the original Africans had come to this country and why whites treated them as inferiors.

At Home on Shades Mountain

One day our friendly realtor took us to see a vacant house she thought we would like. It was a bungalow (here called a ranch house, which sounds much more impressive) on a quiet street in a subdivision called Shades Mountain. I was now used to seeing rural and suburban streets, which looked like parkland: the houses were barely visible from the street, obscured by flowering trees and shrubs as well as dense woodland.

There were no sidewalks, and neither hedges nor fences separated the properties. I wondered how people knew where their "yard" ended, and soon found out that nobody was really sure, nor did they care. Unlike English suburbanites, the residents here seemed unconcerned about privacy. Kids on balloon-tired bikes, as well as assorted dogs, roamed freely across the properties. This looked like fun, but I later discovered some drawbacks as well.

As our realtor had predicted, we liked this three-bedroom ranch house on Darlington Street. The front door led straight into a spacious living room with beautiful hardwood floor, which extended throughout the house. At the back was a "kitchen-den combination", which had a window air-conditioner unit. A louvered glass door opened into the carport. Nobody here had garages. The master bedroom had its own bathroom, and there was a second bathroom off the hall. What luxury! The kitchen was fully equipped with built-in

Our house at 2122 Darlington Street on Shades Mountain
after a rare snowfall. Winter 1960

The Staple family at 2122 Darlington Street, 1961

stove and dishwasher, something I had never seen before, and there was even a separate utility room off the carport "for your washer and dryer," the realtor said. I was amazed to see all the closets and built-in bookshelves; really one needed very little furniture. Another feature that surprised us were the wire mesh screens on all windows. I assumed there must be a lot of nasty bugs here, and indeed I was right – more of that later. In England we put up with flies and even with wasps and bees. The house was priced within our range; we made an offer, and, within four weeks of our arrival in the United States we were owners of this luxury mansion.

Gil and Muriel had been out of town for a week and had cautioned us about aggressive realtors, and not to do anything rash during their absence. As soon as they returned, we took them to see "our" house, and waited with baited breath for their verdict. They approved our choice, and, although not exactly neighbors, we were only a 10-minute drive from each other. Peter immediately took steps to have our furniture and the car sent over from England. This would take about six weeks. To save the rent on our apartment, we decided to move into the house anyway, and "camp" until our stuff arrived.

I don't know how the neighbors realized we had moved in, but they showed up in force and overwhelmed us with true "Southern hospitality", bringing food and even toys for the kids. Our accent at first led them to suspect that we might be Yankees, maybe from Boston, which would not make us very popular. But once the word spread that we were *English,* they became even more cordial. When it became apparent that we had no furniture, they brought over folding cots, chairs, a card table, kitchen utensils and bedding. One essential item we had to buy immediately: a refrigerator. The kitchen had no larder or pantry, and daytime temperatures were already in the eighties, hot by English standards. To make matters worse, I was expected to drive to a supermarket to stock up with food, a big change from the daily deliveries we had in Smallfield. So, off we went to Sears Roebuck, who were advertising a Giant Appliance Sale, and offered a Free Gift of a case of coke to any buyer "For One Week Only." Our problem was, that we did not have enough money for the fridge (let alone for a washing machine that I secretly hoped to acquire). We explained the situation to a Sears manager and showed him an official letter from the Dean of the Dental School, confirming Peter's appointment and salary. But Sears were not impressed.

"You surely have credit *somewhere*," the manager said, "which firms did you do business with in England?"

We had to admit that we always paid cash, except for the utility companies. Moreover, we would not have been allowed to leave England, if we had outstanding debts. Then I remembered that I had paid our butcher once a week, and when I mentioned this, the manager's face lit up.

"Swell, so you *did* have credit with a merchant! Please have the meat market manager send a letter confirming this."

Peter and I had a good laugh when we visualized Mr. Collins, our portly village butcher in Smallfield, with his blue and white striped apron, as the sole merchant able to come to our rescue. We wrote to him, explaining the situation, and in due course Sears received a beautiful handwritten letter from Mr. Collins, confirming that, indeed, we had always paid our bills promptly in the five years that he had the pleasure of serving us.

Where Dean Volker had failed, Mr. Collins succeeded. We got a Sears Credit Card! Only our passports were more valuable. A big refrigerator, matching the built in appliances ("mushroom" was the in-color of the fifties) was promptly delivered, along with a case of 100 bottles of Coca Cola. This did not escape the notice of the neighborhood kids who came running over for a coke orgy in our carport. And yes, we bought a washer too, but saw no point in getting a dryer when we had a good clothes line already rigged up in the backyard.

Let me introduce you to some of the wonderful neighbors, who did so much to make our lives on Shades Mountain easier, and who became our good friends. Right next-door were Mr. and Mrs. Rucker, an elderly couple, who tried hard to explain some Alabama customs to us newcomers. Mr. Rucker owned a hardware store and kindly provided Peter with another essential item, a push lawnmower, "on credit". This kept the front lawn more or less neat, but of course not like an *English* lawn. Our back yard, which covered almost an acre, was so overgrown, that more drastic measures were needed before one could operate a lawnmower. Mrs. Rucker found a "yard man" for us, who labored hard to get the jungle under control, for very little pay. The first day the man reported for work was really hot and, not knowing any better, I invited the sweating guy into our air-conditioned kitchen to eat his bag lunch, have a glass of cold water and use the bathroom. He first declined, but then entered the house very reluctantly, and stood with his back to the louvered kitchen door, as if ready to escape. The phone rang and it was Mrs. Rucker. She sounded distraught.

"Joan, I saw the boy go into y'all's kitchen. Are you all right?"

She admonished me strongly that I must *never* let a colored man come into my house. *Terrible* things might happen to me! I calmed her down as best I could. Meanwhile the "boy" had already resumed his labors. No wonder he was reluctant to come in! If I had chosen to accuse him of assault, he'd be lynched for sure. Obviously I still had a lot to learn about Southern living. Next time the yardman came, I put a pitcher of water in the carport for him, and hoped he'd find a suitable "restroom" somewhere in the woods, rather than in our backyard.

All the boys who came over to play with Gregory and Alan had the last name of Adams. Eventually I figured out that Bill, Jerry and Charlie came from the house across the street, while Blake and Will lived a bit further away. They were not related. All were between three and eight years old. The parents of the threesome were Bob and Trudy Adams, who had adopted the brothers two years ago from an orphanage and were doing a fantastic job trying to reverse the trauma of institutional living. Bob was chief photographer of the Birmingham News and often used the neighborhood kids as subjects for his weekend mood pictures. Blake and Will belonged to Ruth and A.B. Adams, a radiologist. They had a sister, Enid, who never came out to play, because little girls had to behave like "young ladies". They wore pretty dresses with voluminous starched petticoats, and stayed indoors with their dolls.

It was wonderful the way the neighbors looked after us newcomers and I soon found out that they also cared for each other, without being intrusive. Some of my neighbors took turns taking an old woman shopping once a week, and I became part of that roster. I don't know how old Mrs. Shaup was, but to me she seemed very ancient, a shriveled, wrinkled little person, who lived alone in an equally ancient house on a dirt road. She told me that she had lived here long before there were any other houses and that she and her husband grew corn, beans and scuppernongs. Her garden was now a wilderness, but the scuppernongs remained, having spread all over her property. In case you don't know what scuppernongs are (I didn't!) I must introduce you to this very southern fruit, actually a variety of large Muscatine grape. It was known in the time of Sir Walter Raleigh and was the first wine grape in North America. A 400-year-old vine still exists in the little town of Scuppernong, NC.

Going shopping with Mrs. Shaup was an adventure. She always forgot at least one item and we often went all the way back to the supermarket to get it. While I drove, she told me stories of the old days on Shades Mountain, which made it all worthwhile. As summer progressed she worried about who would pick her scuppernongs in the fall, and the boys rashly said, "**We** will, Mrs. Shaup!"

"And will y'all make grape jelly and wine?" she enquired.

"Yes, ma'am, we sure will"

When the grapes were ripe, Gregory rallied all the boys he could find and we picked the pungent fruit, which did not grow in large bunches, but in clusters of four. I had no idea how to make grape wine, but I did make a lot of scuppernong jelly, which I shared with Mrs. Shaup. We also picked her apples and made more jelly.

Not long after we moved in, we had visits from two local clergymen, one Baptist, the other Methodist, who asked which church we belonged to. I made the mistake of telling them the truth, namely that I was Jewish, my husband was Church of England (called Episcopalian over here) and we did not belong to *any* church. After that they practically camped on our doorstep and vied with each other to get us to join their respective churches. At the time Peter and I did not understand the important part the churches played in the social structure of Alabamians (maybe of all Americans?) and that it was unthinkable for anybody *not* belong to a church or synagogue. Before very long we were made aware of the consequences of having un-churched children – but more of that later.

A few blocks from Darlington Street was Shades Mountain Elementary School, a brand-new building, surrounded by acres of red dirt – it had not been landscaped yet. One day in early May I strolled over there to register Gregory, who was almost six years old, for school. I had brought along his excellent report cards from the Copthorne Convent. The principal welcomed me warmly, and expressed surprise that this little boy had already attended school in England. He told me that at his school, children started first grade in the fall after their sixth birthday. There was no kindergarten. He suggested that Gregory be tested to decide whether he would best fit into first or second grade, and added that we might as well wait till fall, since school was nearly over for the current year. It was my turn to be amazed: were they about to *close* school in *May*? Yes, indeed, they closed just before Memorial Day and would open again "after Labor Day", which, I had learned from my previous visit to the U.S., was a very important date in September. So, what did kids do during the three long hot months of summer? Well, I was about to find out.

Neighborhood boys enjoying coke. Gregory and Alan are in from at left. Birmingham, Alabama, May 1959

Great excitement: our furniture was coming! The neighborhood gang gathered in anticipation and cheered as the big van approached our driveway. The moving company had hired some colored men, who got busy unloading, while the (white) driver sat under a shade tree, smoking and drinking coke. It was nice to see our belongings again after nearly three months. Nothing was broken, and everything fitted in nicely.

"Where is your TV, ma'am?" inquired Charlie.

"Yea, and your radio and toaster and all that stuff?" chimed in Jerry.

"They don't have electricity in England," explained Bill, the oldest, "not even lamps, I guess they use candles."

Gregory defended his country: "*Of course* we had electric light *and* a toaster *and* a vacuum cleaner, but we didn't bring them, because the plugs wouldn't fit."

I tried to explain that English appliances worked on 220V, while here 110V was the norm. However, we never owned a television set, nor did we buy one now. As a result, when the Adams boys were playing at our house, and it got near four o'clock, there was a general exodus – they all ran home across the street to watch "Leave it to Beaver". Not surprisingly, Gregory and Alan followed their new friends. Great! For an hour or so there was peace and quiet.

The day after the furniture came Mrs. Rucker enquired whether her boy had been helpful, and I suddenly recalled that I had gratefully accepted her offer to send "her boy" over to help. I did not even know she had a boy, I presumed he might be a teenager.

"I'm not sure, Mrs. Rucker, there was such a commotion, what does your son look like?"

"Ah don't mean ma son, its ma *boy* Ah sent over – *there* he is" and she pointed to a gray-haired colored man who was pottering around her yard.

Of course! "Yes, ma'am, your boy was *very* helpful, thank you so much for sending him over."

"Y'all are welcome, he's a *good* boy, been with us going on thirty years."

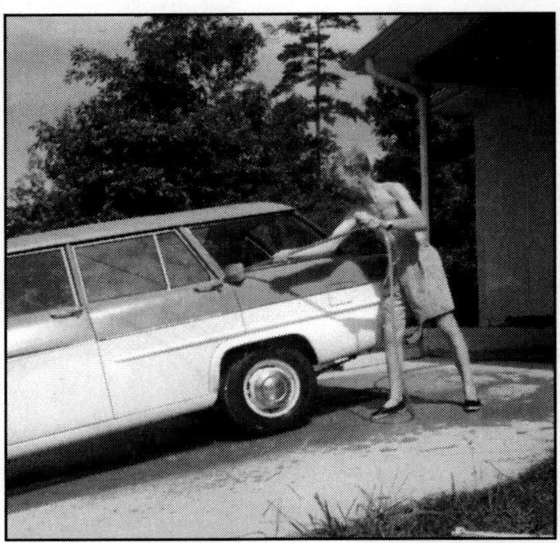

Peter washing our blue and white Vauxhall after it arrived from England. Summer 1959

The furniture in place, Peter got a ride to Mobile to pick up our beloved blue and white Vauxhall, which had made the long voyage across the Atlantic. Rejoicing all round:

"Look at that *cute lil old station wagon,*" the neighbors exclaimed. So much for our brand new Estate Car, the biggest vehicle on Smallfield's Broadbridge Lane. Indeed it looked small in our carport, but all the kids wanted a ride in it.

Our first trip was to the supermarket, and I took four year old Charlie along to help me identify foods that he and the rest of the gang might eat for lunch. Both Trudy and Ruth Adams had assured me that all kids love peanut butter-and-jelly-sandwiches, so I shouldn't go to any trouble. Alas, although I had eaten peanuts (on the plane!), I could not visualize peanut *butter*. No problem. Charlie zeroed in to an aisle in the huge market, and pointed out rows of peanut butter jars and all kinds of jams and jellies. But it had to be *grape* jelly (also unknown in England) and he identified the needed jars quickly by their pictures. He also threw a package of bright pink meat he called "baloney", a jar of "Miracle Whip" and some pickles into the cart. A loaf of Wonderbread completed our purchases; we checked out and headed for home. Lunch was ready. The Adams boys loved it. Not so Gregory and Alan. I admit it took some getting used to.

A Southern Summer: Boys, Bugs and Other Critters

One of the delights of early summer evenings on Shades Mountain was watching the fireflies. We soon found out that our neighbors had their evening meal much earlier than our English dinnertime, and by seven o'clock all the boys were out there, calling for Gregory and Alan to join them. The brief dusk almost over, it was soon pitch-dark and the lawns sparkled with tiny flickering points of light – the "lightning bugs". Equipped with jelly jars, the kids hunted these elusive insects and nobody went to bed without their little night-lights. First thing in the morning they released the bugs, perhaps to be caught all over again.

Once the sun had set, temperatures often dropped below 80°F, and everybody came outside, to sit in carports or screened porches.

In the distance we could see Vulcan's torch, usually green[2], and the red-orange glow of the coke furnaces downtown. Conversation was sometimes difficult because of the deafening chorus of cicadas and tree frogs, which seemed to continue most of the night. The children, having spent the hottest part of the day in tepid swimming pools, now roamed around happily or played informal games of baseball under bright lights.

Not all insects were as friendly as the fireflies; in fact most were distinctly unpleasant. Ants were everywhere, invading our kitchen and even the rest of the house. The little black ones could perhaps be avoided by having a spotlessly clean floor, but even the tiniest crumb served as a banquet for hordes of them. The big carpenter ants on the other hand went after anything made of wood. More threatening were the termites, which could eat up your house in no time, so we were told. We signed up with an exterminator service, and were soon visited by two different men: a termite specialist and a guy who dealt with ants and, most important, searched for black widow spiders, which secrete a highly toxic venom. Gregory and Alan were fascinated by the "bug men" and followed them around. Like most houses in our neighborhood, we had a shallow basement, about three feet high, called a crawlspace. It had a dirt floor, and was accessed from outside through a sort of trap door. Only the furnace inspector and the exterminators ventured into this mysterious cave. It was strictly off-limits to children.

"Don't you *ever* go into the crawlspace, boys!" 'Mr. Bug' warned.

"Why not?"

"The black widders will *kill* y'all, yessir."

In my Zoology courses I had never paid much attention to the arthropods, although one of the professors at King's College, London was an internationally known expert on ticks and had a vast collection of these creatures, neatly pinned on framed white cardboard. But now I began to take an interest. One day I spotted a beautiful orange and black grasshopper on the front lawn. It was about the size of a rat and I approached it cautiously, hoping to

---

2 At that time Vulcan's torch changed to red when there was a traffic fatality.

trap it for further examination, if I could find a jar large enough to contain it. Gregory and Alan admired it, but our neighbors showed no surprise.

"Just a grasshopper, ma'am, ruins your plants, lots of 'em around, stomp on it - hard!"

Before long both boys developed an itchy rash around their ankles and especially in the groin. They scratched incessantly, causing the sores to become infected. I suspected some exotic disease and, after consulting Trudy Adams, took the kids to the local pediatrician. Trudy explained that only such a specialist would see children, there were no "family doctors" here. Moreover, the doctor would *charge* for his services. Being new immigrants, our health insurance, provided by the University, was not in effect yet, and there was no National Health Service.

To our amazement, people often asked us whether we had left England in order to get away from "socialized medicine", which surely was something Peter, as a dentist, was strongly opposed to. Having figured out that by "socialized medicine" they meant our National Health Service, we replied emphatically that, far from wanting to get away from it, we were indeed hesitant to come to a country, where so many citizens were uninsured and got minimal or substandard health care. However, the School of Dentistry assured Peter that his faculty position included health benefits for the whole family. I was – and still am - puzzled by people who happily send their children to "public schools", i.e. government supported schools, yet are opposed to a similar system for health care. As I write these memoirs almost fifty years later, "socialized medicine" is still anathema to most Americans, in spite of the fact that certain sectors of society do receive federally funded health care, notably the armed forces as well as senior citizens and the indigent. The United States is the only developed country where millions of citizens, including children, are uninsured and unable to pay for needed treatment and medications. Michael Moore, maker of the 2006 documentary *Sicko,* and a tireless proponent of national health insurance, suggests it's time we dropped the demonized term "socialized medicine" and instituted "christianized medicine." I think "humanized medicine" would be better, yet one has to be careful in a country where benign terms like humanism and liberalism have acquired an evil aura.

Back to our private pediatrician: he took one look and informed me that the boys had “chiggers”. It sounded ominous. Was it slang for “chigroes”? And what were they anyway? Not surprisingly, another “bug”, or rather the larvae of tiny red mites that attack the skin. Peter brought us a microscope from the lab, so we could see the “red-bugs”. They were pretty, but very irritating. The doctor told us to wear long pants, long-sleeved shirts, socks and shoes, and to sprinkle sulfur on our clothes. Of course nobody did this. But one piece of advice made sense: *never* sit on the grass! I had noticed that people here did not have picnics on the lawn, as was the custom in England. There were picnic tables everywhere and one sat on benches. Now I knew why! But you should always check *under* the bench for snakes before sitting down.

Other insects new to us were the “noseeums”, minute invisible midges that came out in hordes at dawn and dusk to torment us with their bites. My survey of Alabama wildlife would not be complete without mentioning the ticks. Every evening at bath time I examined Gregory and Alan carefully, paying special attention to their heads. Later on, our longhaired dachshund Foxy, whose ears hung down to the ground, was an added challenge. Finding ticks was not too hard, but removing them was tricky, especially from the scalp. If you pull off the tick carelessly, its head gets left behind in the skin, causing infections. Urban legend has it, that you should hold a burning match close to the tick, which makes it release its hold. Maybe so, but you also lose hold of your boy (or dog), who will run away screaming. I had been wondering why all the local boys’ hair was cropped to an inch or so, which made them look so ugly. Now I thought I understood the reason: tick control!

Actually I was quite wrong. Their hairstyle had nothing to do with ticks. The boys actually *liked* their “brush cuts”, and it didn’t take long for our sons to clamor for a visit to the barber, whence they emerged looking like mini-convicts. To complete the “new look” they soon lost their rosy English complexion and acquired the pallor common to Southern children. Not only were insects and their allies out to get us, some plants were dangerous too. We learned the hard way about poison ivy: leaves of three, time to flee!

Alan and Gregory in their packing-case playhouse in our backyard. Birmingham, Alabama. Summer 1959.

Gregory converting packing case into a playhouse, Summer 1959

In spite of all those hazards and the unrelenting humid heat, the Shades Mountain boys played outdoors all summer, and seemed to be having a great time. The plywood packing case, which had contained our furniture, was now established among the pine trees in back of our house and became in turns a fort, playhouse or overnight camp. Whereas in Smallfield the kids had played "Cowboys and Indians"(neither of which had ever existed in England!), here the fight was between the Yankees and the Confederates. Our first year in Alabama (1959-60) marked the centenary of the War Between the States. There were many commemorative ceremonies and re-enactments, and confederate flags were ubiquitous. I knew virtually nothing about this war, which is called the Civil War in the North, but once Gregory started school I shared his history books and became more enlightened – or perhaps indoctrinated. Meanwhile I handed out ice water to the sweating little "soldiers", armed with noisy cap guns and plastic replicas of confederate rifles. I guess it is natural for little boys to fight (no wonder the girls stayed indoors!) but unfortunately males never outgrow this predilection, with disastrous results worldwide.

I mentioned that we had to pay for medical care now, so I was mortified when, one morning, I noticed a lump in my right armpit. I was ignorant of breast cancer, but thought any lump should be investigated. Peter took me to the University Hospital, where a surgeon decided that he would remove the small tumor, rather than bother with a biopsy. He considered Peter a colleague, and assured us he would not charge for his services. Thus I spent a few days in the hospital, which was an interesting experience. The first thing I noticed was that racial segregation seemed to stop at the hospital door. Inside, the patients lined up in the hallway on gurneys, were male and female, colored and white. I also noticed colored nurses' aides and maids, but later learned that colored doctors were barred from visiting their patients here.

The atmosphere was much more relaxed than that of an English hospital. The surgeon strolled into my room casually, without a retinue of nurses and residents, and actually removed the stitches himself. The tumor turned out to be a benign fibroma, but needed to be removed to prevent pressure on the underlying nerves.

I was unable to move my right arm for a while, so Peter had to do some of the housework, including hanging the washing on the line. As a result, a canary yellow dryer joined our beige washer in the utility room. Why yellow? Peter explained that it was on sale at Sears and he could not resist it! We also acquired a maid, Mae, who arrived on the bus early in the morning and did whatever was required throughout the day – all for $4 plus "carfare".

Alan, after being left alone with Mae, informed me that he would teach her English, since she spoke only "African", which he could not understand. Yes, I had told him that colored people had come from Africa, and he probably imagined a fairly recent arrival. Gregory, not to be outdone, offered to teach Mae how to read and write. Alas, neither project was successful – on the contrary. Before very long Alan, and to a lesser extent, Gregory adopted local speech patterns. I did not find this as disturbing as the thought that, along with acquiring a Southern accent, they might adopt the prevailing attitude towards colored people, especially after I overheard Alan referring to our maid as "the nigger".

Alan helping our maid clean shoes in our carport.
Summer 1959

We celebrated Gregory's sixth birthday (May 23rd 1959) a week after the actual date, in order to have a party at the Homewood recreation area, a nearby municipal pool with adjacent park and picnic tables. The pool opened for the season on Memorial Day, the last Sunday in May. Gregory's present was a bright red bicycle (from Sears of course), and before long Gregory was able to join the gang of boys riding around the quiet streets. It was great to see that he already had lots of friends. Unlike in England, most of the little kids here were already good swimmers, and I soon arranged swimming lessons for our boys.

We settled into a summer routine suitable for the climate and the 12 hour day/night cycle: we got up well before sunrise and I finished all household chores including cooking, before setting off to the pool for the morning. When the boys got bored with playing in the water, we went to the public library, which was air-conditioned. Gregory was an avid reader and Alan enjoyed looking at picture books. Lunch was followed by a long nap.

Peter usually took the early morning bus downtown to allow me the use of the car, and we picked him up from the Dental School at four o'clock. I dreaded this trip, not so much because of the rush hour traffic, but because of the daily thunderstorm, which arrived without fail at just this time. These tropical storms involved torrential rain, reducing visibility to zero. Most cars pulled over and waited it out, so we sat there listening to the hailstones crashing on the roof (probably pitting the paint), accompanied by the rumbling of thunder. Brilliant flashes of lightening relieved the darkness. I think the boys enjoyed it – I did not! As suddenly as the storm had started it was over. Steam rose from the wet pavement, shrouding the cars. Undaunted, we continued on our way.

"What took you so long?" Peter would say. "Let's get home and have some tea."

And he meant a pot of *hot* tea, ignoring the local custom of imbibing gallons of sweet iced tea.

Independence Day was our first American holiday and it was great. There were so many new things to enjoy: succulent charcoal grilled steak, Southern fried chicken with black-eyed peas, catfish and hushpuppies, fried okra, corn on the cob and – most miraculous of all – watermelons! They were huge; we could not believe these red monsters were edible. Watermelons were only eaten outdoors, and you tried to spit the seeds as far as possible. After the cookouts, everybody had fireworks. It was all great fun, and even Peter, staunch Englishman that he was, refrained from bemoaning the loss of the colonies.

I felt there was one thing missing from our happy family: a dog! As readers of the first volume of my memoirs will remember, I grew up with dogs and considered them my best friends. I no longer felt I wanted four children; the thought of being pregnant and coping with a baby in this heat, and without an efficient health care system, made that decision an easy one. Peter concurred: our financial situation was not as dire as it had been in England, but an additional family member would certainly strain the budget. And the boys agreed that a puppy dog was a much better idea than a baby sister!

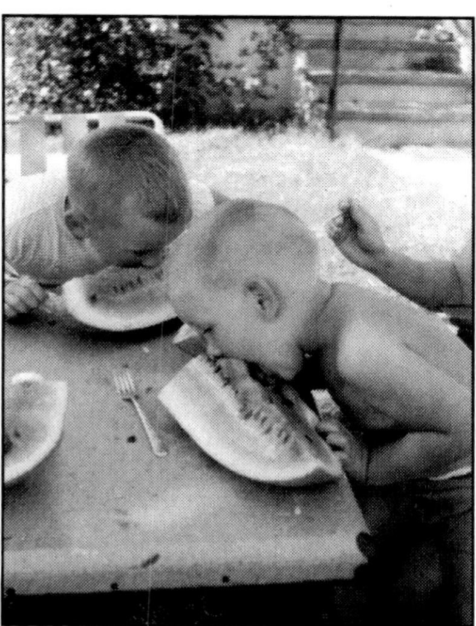

Our crew-cut sons enjoy their first water melon. July 4, 1959

So Fritzi, a beautiful red-brown longhaired dachshund pup, purebred from German stock, joined us. We loved the dog, but not his name and changed it to Foxy, because he really looked like a little red fox. Foxy romped around the neighborhood with the boys and the Adams' boxer, Ms. Dee. Peter built him a doghouse, which the boys painted white and green. Although I had much experience in training dogs, I found Foxy difficult and stubborn. One of his bad habits was particularly hard to break: he liked to chase cars. Actually not many cars came our way, but still it was a dangerous habit. I tried various techniques, including sitting on the porch with Foxy on a long leash and choke collar, waiting for a car to approach. As soon as Foxy made a dash for the car I pulled sharply on the leash. Unpleasant no doubt, but he was undeterred. So I tried another form of aversive conditioning. Again Foxy and I sat on the porch, but this time I had the garden hose ready. As he darted towards the approaching car, I hit him with a strong jet of cold water. Or did I? Oh no! I had hit the driver instead. I will not repeat the man's comments as he tried to cope with a yapping dog and a car full of water.

Foxy never learned about cars. He also turned out to be a racist. He hated our nice maid, as well as the yardman, growling fiercely as soon as they arrived. Once, stopped at a traffic light next to a car with a colored driver, Foxy went crazy on the passenger seat, spitting venom at the man out of the car window. This became even more embarrassing after we moved away from the segregated South.

About a year after Foxy joined our family, we acquired a cat. It happened like this: The Faculty Wives Club – an organization that, among other social activities, concerned itself with welcoming new faculty members, informed us that a British professor, a gastroenterologist, was arriving, and would we please help him and his family settle in. We were delighted to pass on some of the Southern hospitality we had experienced, and looked forward to the newcomers. That's how we met John and Jean Balint, who became life-long friends. I rented an apartment for them on a short-term basis, so that they would have time to look for a house. They did not actually come directly from England, but had lived in Baltimore for a year. Their son, Peter was about ten years old and his sister, Penny, was a little older than Gregory. Penny's most treasured possession was a tortoiseshell kitten, and she was heartbroken when she found out that the apartment I had rented for them did not permit pets! Everybody was very upset, so I immediately offered to take the cat until the Balints could move into their own house.

I had never had a cat in my life and wondered how this would work out. Well, I need not have worried: the boys were delighted, and even Foxy adored the lively little creature, which we called "Pussy Balint". Whenever possible, Jean brought Penny and Peter to visit, and the kids became good friends. The Balints soon found a house in Bluff Park, not too far from us, so we were able to continue our friendship. Pussy Balint went back home, and we missed her sadly, so when an old lady, who lived alone in our neighborhood, was suddenly taken to hospital, leaving a house full of cats, I took one of them, a Siamese, we called Leo. He (she?) was a beautiful animal, not particularly intelligent, but very affectionate and cuddly. The old lady died, but all her assorted cats found homes.

Before long another cat joined us in a strange way: on a chilly St Patrick's Day, as we were going for a walk in the woods, Foxy suddenly rushed down to a little stream, barking excitedly, and came back dragging a small black and white animal, which he deposited at my feet. I thought it might be a badger – but no, there are no badgers in Alabama. It was in fact a very wet and bedraggled kitten, its hind legs tied together with rope. Bits of rope on its front legs suggested that they had been tied too, but the kitten had managed to free them. We were appalled. Who would do such a horrible thing?!

Well, of course we took it home and nursed it back to health. While Leo was somewhat hostile, Foxy allowed "Patrick" to sleep in his basket, licked him tenderly, and kept him warm. Odd behavior for a male dog, I thought, but was grateful. Soon Patrick grew into a fine longhaired tomcat; we had him neutered, and he became a beloved member of the family.

Disaster Strikes

During the four months of our residence in Alabama we had kept in touch with our families in England as best we could. Transatlantic phone calls were possible, I think, but extremely expensive, and rarely used. We corresponded regularly by airmail, sending photos and pictures the boys had drawn. Best of all, we recorded messages on a tape recorder that my brother Walter had given us as a farewell present. This was still a new technology at the time, and the machine was the size of a carry-on suitcase with

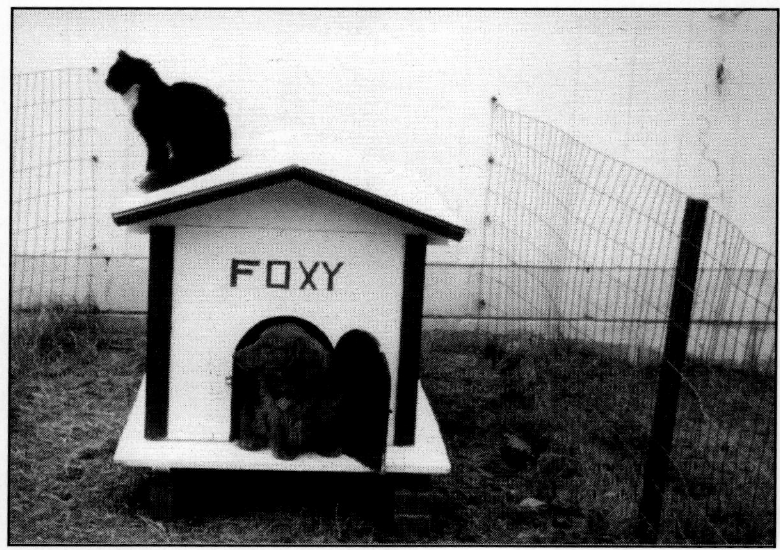

Patrick sitting on Foxy's house. 1961

Joan with Leo and Foxy, Birmingham 1963

reels of tape to match. We not only taped our own voices but also typical sounds of the South: the local radio programs, complete with rapid-fire, incomprehensible commercials[3], the soft accents of our neighbors, the deafening evening chorus of cicadas and the raucous morning serenade of the mockingbirds.

We sent these tapes to my parents in the "old" Birmingham, and to Walter and family in Buckinghamshire, so they could share our lives to some extent. My parents loved the tapes, and, in turn sent the boys little presents and photos they had taken on a recent trip to Italy. They had sold their house and moved to a spacious apartment, still in the suburb of Edgbaston, where we had lived as refugees during the war. My father, who had retired after his 70th birthday, bought a new luxury car, a Bentley, and enjoyed "motoring", as it was called in England. He was in excellent health, and Mutti had made a pretty good recovery from her stomach cancer surgery a few years ago. A young German au pair girl, Ingrid, lived with them to help with household chores.

Then one day in early August a sad letter arrived from Mutti. She told us that Papi had a car accident and was in hospital suffering from concussion, many bruises, and a broken ankle. He had a head-on collision with a wall. After being in a coma for several days, he recovered consciousness, and told investigators that he was unable to avoid the wall, since the steering wheel had locked. The insurance company, after examining the badly damaged Bentley, found that, indeed, the power steering was faulty. Papi continued to suffer from symptoms of concussion and was severely depressed, mourning the loss of his beloved new car, although Bentley promised to deliver a replacement vehicle immediately. He wrote to me himself, saying that he hated the hospital and hoped to be back home soon. His ankle was stabilized and, at his request, he was discharged home, in spite of continuing depression, which, it was thought would clear up once he was back in familiar surroundings.

One of Papi's best friends was his second cousin, Dr. Willy Mayer-Gross, "Uncle Willy," who had come to my rescue at the Maudsley Hospital years ago. He had moved from Scotland to take up a position at the University of Birmingham, where he was now

---

3 Commercial radio did not exist in England, only the BBC

Professor emeritus of psychopharmacology. Willy was a frequent visitor and, both as a friend and a psychiatrist, strongly advised that Papi be admitted to another hospital or a nursing home until his mood improved. Antidepressant medication was not available yet, so there really was no treatment for clinical depression, other than ECT (electro convulsive therapy). But Papi flatly refused to be hospitalized.

What happened next is not entirely clear to me. Early in the morning on August 29, I received a Western Union Telegram stating,

Papi, Mutti passed away. Will phone later. Walter.

This was read to me over the phone, the caller asking me to sit down before she delivered the message. I did not know what to make of this, and assumed some error. Was it possible that Papi suddenly got worse and died? But what about Mutti? That evening Walter called and told me that, after Papi's sudden death, Mutti had taken "a handful" of sleeping pills and fallen into a coma. The hysterical au pair girl called him immediately, but by the time Walter got to Birmingham – a 100-mile drive over often winding country roads, which he completed in less than two hours – Mutti was dead. He was too distraught to provide further details, and I did not piece together the whole story of this disaster until a few weeks later when Uncle Willy wrote me a long letter.

My first reaction was to fly to England immediately. But both Walter and Peter dissuaded me. Since my parents were dead, there was absolutely nothing I could do in Birmingham. Walter was making all funeral arrangements, and wanted to shield me from further trauma. Thus, I never saw the local newspapers, which apparently had gory detailed descriptions and photos of the death of two respected Birmingham citizens. My parents are buried in the Jewish section of the main Birmingham cemetery. According to Uncle Willy, what had happened was this: After spending an evening with my parents, Willy was very concerned about my fathers' condition and decided to arrange for a full-time psychiatric nurse to be with Papi, starting the following day. But it was too late. Very early the next morning Papi left the apartment and made his way to the fifth floor of the building from where he accessed the roof. He jumped off the roof. Mutti and Ingrid were awakened by police and asked to identify the body. My parents' personal physician was on the scene and gave my mother the sleeping pills to calm her down. After taking all the pills she returned to the apartment and collapsed.

By the time she was found it was too late for resuscitation because, with only a small part of her stomach left after her cancer surgery, ingested material would go directly into her intestines to be promptly absorbed into the bloodstream. Willy mentioned that, since Mutti's doctor must have been aware of her medical condition; he should not have provided what was *for her* a lethal dose of narcotic. Indeed much later, at the coroner's inquest, the physician was severely censored, and temporarily deprived of his license.
Nevertheless the coroner's verdict was suicide, not accidental death.

Willy ended his letter by saying that he blamed himself for the course of events. He should have taken action earlier. I was told that he never recovered from the shock and was a broken man until his death the following year.

The rest of this summer is a blur in my mind. I do remember that I was sweating day and night, and often nothing seemed to matter except trying to keep reasonably cool. It was hard to explain to Gregory and Alan, then six and three years old, what had happened. They had been aware that Papi had a serious auto accident because something went wrong with his car, and they realized that he was injured. So we now told them that he got worse and died.

"What about Mutti? She was not in the car, was she?" they wanted to know. The boys accepted our answer that she died of a broken heart. Gregory was concerned about the safety of riding in a car, and for some time Peter did elaborate "inspections" of our Vauxhall , assuring the boy that everything was in good order.

Much later that year, Walter sent lists of our parents' possessions, asking me to choose what I would like shipped to Alabama. Thus we acquired some rugs and paintings, including a pastel portrait of me at age two and, my favorite, an oil painting of snow covered mountains lit by the setting sun, which now hangs in my bedroom. Walter and I split our parents' beautiful white and gold Rosenthal dinner service, as well as the engraved silver, which had been wedding presents in 1913, each of us taking twelve place settings. My mother's jewelry was mailed separately, insured at probate value. Sadly, it never arrived and numerous inquiries failed to retrieve the package. Peter received Papi's Leica camera. He developed the film found in it, which contained the last photos taken of my parents.

My parents, Sali and Selma Lorch on vacation in Italy. July 1959. This photo was found in Papi's camera after their untimely death one month later.

Strangely enough it took me quite a while to realize that my parents were gone forever. A few letters still arrived, weeks after their death, and of course we were not accustomed to seeing each other frequently. But eventually, when it hit me that I was an *orphan*, I felt sad and lonely in this strange country. Our neighbors and many new friends, especially the Dental Wives (spouses of Peter's colleagues) rallied round and went out of their way to make life easier for us. They brought us casseroles and invited the boys to cookouts and pool parties.

Bob Adams' mother, who lived in a little house in the woods nearby, explained to Gregory and Alan that she was now their grandma, and they must visit her often. In addition, I was comforted by the myriad of letters I received from people who had known and loved my parents. Some came from former refugee children to whom my parents had opened their home, and from many others who were grateful to my father for mentoring and supporting them, including his former secretary in Germany, Gretel Seelmann (the late Frau Kaiser).

Life Goes On

With the proximity of Labor Day, Peter was busy preparing his classes for the start of the Dental School semester, while I got Gregory ready for Shades Mountain Elementary School. For most parents this involved buying socks and sneakers (kids went barefoot all summer) and "back-to-school" clothes, as well as the usual school supplies.

Alan clamored to go to school too, and I persuaded Corinne Ray, the owner of Shades Crest Kindergarten, to start a group for three-year olds. My neighbors advised me to keep Alan home until he was at least four, since he would get bored with the place, but he was so keen to go, that I ignored their advice.

A week before classes started, Mr. John Edwards, the principal, scheduled tests for Gregory, to help us decide in which grade he should be placed. To the amazement of the school administration, Gregory qualified for third grade. I was not surprised. After all, he had attended Copthorne Convent, where the nuns taught him "the three Rs" and, thanks to the Birmingham Public Library, he had kept up his reading during the long hot summer. He loved to climb trees, and would sit high up on some shady branch absorbed in his "chapter book". In contrast, local six-year-olds were just starting their first school experience. Gregory was a bright little boy, but hardly a child prodigy. Peter and I agreed with Mr. Edwards that Gregory should be admitted into second grade.

He was a year younger than his classmates, but adjusted well to this very different school environment. His teacher, Joy Thomas, who had been to England, was a charming young woman, and very understanding. One day she asked him to wear his English school uniform, which he did proudly, although it was much too hot for the sweater and blazer. But when asked to bring an English flag for "show and tell", we could not find one, nor could he describe it. English schools do not display flags, and there was nothing comparable to the Pledge of Allegiance, which he soon recited for us, solemnly placing his right hand over his heart. He also sang a song to the tune of the British National Anthem "God save the Queen" but with new words that sounded like "my country teessothee". We had no idea what it meant. All this display of patriotism seemed strange to us. In England loyalty to the Queen (rather than the flag, which is, after all just a piece of cloth) was taken for granted. But here, in a young country, populated by relatively recent immigrants, constant reminders were appropriate.

One Monday Gregory came home from school looking miserable and tearful.

"Everybody hates me," he proclaimed.

What had happened that morning seems rather trivial – but here it is: while taking attendance on Monday mornings, Miss Thomas asked each pupil whether s/he had attended Sunday School. Homerooms that achieved 100% attendance were awarded a "star" by the principal, which was prominently displayed on the door for all to see. It turned out that Gregory was the only child who gave a negative answer to this question, thus preventing his Homeroom from getting the much-coveted star. No wonder his classmates were upset! Obviously religion – in addition to patriotism - played an important part in American public schools. Somehow, I remembered learning that, unlike in England, there was a separation between church and state over here. Maybe so, but not in Alabama. Perhaps I should have been alerted by the fact that Gregory brought home slips of paper with a daily bible verse, which he struggled to memorize every morning while chewing his Wonderbread toast, made palatable by lots of butter and English marmalade.

"I gotta learn this, in case Miss Thomas calls on me; she picks on somebody every morning."

"Do you understand what this verse means?" I enquired,

suspecting that a sentence plucked at random from the Old Testament made no sense to our unchurched son.

"No ma'am, nobody cares about that, you just gotta *say* it."

I did not pursue the matter, but pondered how I could prevent a repetition of the Monday morning roll call debacle.

Peter, born and baptized into the Church of England, had attended a Quaker boarding school and was attracted to that denomination. I was raised in a liberal German- Jewish family, but became an agnostic sometime during my University years. Neither of us had attended any religious service since leaving school.

"I pledge allegiance..." At Bluff Park Kindergarten, Birmingham, Alabama. September 1960. Alan is in the middle.

In spite of the efforts of the visiting Baptist and Methodist ministers, we did not intend to join *any* church or synagogue, yet were interested in providing some form of ethical/moral education for the boys. There was no Ethical Society in Birmingham, nor did Secular Judaism exist at that time – at least not in Alabama. But we had heard of the new Unitarian Church in the beautiful suburb of Mountain Brook, to which several of Peter's colleagues belonged, including the Dean of the School of Dentistry, Joe Volker[4].

One day, I was surprised to receive a request to visit a second grade classroom at the Unitarian Sunday School, and show the children some protozoa and algae under the microscope. Somebody there seemed to know that, before becoming a fulltime mother, I was a biologist, working with amoebas. I was rather ignorant of what goes on in a School, but did not think it included lessons in biology.

Well, the Unitarians were certainly different, as I was about to find out. Peter managed to borrow a microscope, and I collected some pond water with little creatures to show the church school pupils. This was part of a class called "Miracles Abound"; the topic was the natural world and evolution, as well as creation myths from various religions. I found the children excited about their studies, and obviously happy to attend this class, where questions were encouraged, and memorizing bible verses did not exist. To make a long story short: we enrolled both Gregory and Alan in the Unitarian Church Sunday School. We even attended services, at first because it was simpler than driving the kids back and forth, but soon because we enjoyed it. Rev. Alfred Hobart's sermons were fascinating, and we could relate to the principles embraced by this church, where people from diverse religious backgrounds were welcomed and respected. In fact the only thing that prevented me from becoming a member was the word "church".

Unitarians are not traditional Christians, and believe neither in the divinity of Jesus nor in the trinity, but I still balked at the idea of belonging to a "church". Apparently I am not alone in this: a number of Unitarian (now Unitarian Universalist) churches deliberately call themselves "societies" or "fellowships". We made many friends at the church, one of whom (Jackie Mazzara) I still correspond with almost 50 years later. And yes, we did eventually become members and both Peter and I taught in the church school.

In addition to my involvement with the Unitarian Church, I became active in the Parent Teacher Association (PTA) of Shades

---

4 Dean Joseph Volker, Ph.D., DDS was founder and president of this Church, now the Unitarian Universalist Church of Birmingham. He eventually became President of the University of Alabama.

Mountain Elementary School. Public schools in Alabama were not supported through property taxes – in fact there was no property tax – but were financed directly by the state. However, since this was a poor state, the public schools scraped by on very little funding. I was told that the colored schools in downtown Birmingham were very primitive, but in the more prosperous white neighborhoods parents pitched in and subsidized their schools. Ours was a largely middle class white neighborhood, and I soon found out that without the active involvement of parents – mostly mothers – this school would be unable to function. The mothers volunteered their skills through the PTA, and worked at the school as teachers' aides, librarians, school bus drivers and telephone operators. We parents paid for such essential services as the telephone, library books, and breakfast for indigent pupils, and even toilet paper, which was doled out sheet by sheet on request. Some of the kids from rural areas did not come to school because they had no shoes. The PTA provided shoes (and other clothing as needed).

I noticed that there was no school nurse. When a boy scraped his knee in the gravel-covered yard, a teacher had to take time out to provide first aid and comfort. I decided to do something about that, and was promptly appointed "Health Chairman" of the PTA. As such I established a First Aid Station, appropriately equipped and staffed by volunteers, some of them former nurses. A public health nurse, who visited area schools periodically, taught me how to test children's vision and hearing. When I detected a child with problems I notified the parents, but only "poor" children could attend the public health clinic. Fortunately it was not my job to decide who was eligible. Mr. Edwards often told us how grateful he was, and that he could not run his school without us ladies! I sometimes wonder how such a system could function nowadays, when most women work outside the home. Eventually I did so well, that I was nominated for the office of statewide PTA health chairman. I declined this honor, and with it a chance to have tea in the governor's mansion with Lurleen Wallace, Alabama's first lady, who became governor after George Wallace's death.

One day, an announcement made at a PTA meeting caught my attention: volunteers were urgently needed at the Well Baby Clinics downtown, especially at the colored clinic. I was interested in public health, went into the city to investigate, and was immediately hired at the colored clinic. It was a cheerful, well-run place, where mothers could bring their babies for checkups and needed immunizations. Latania, the colored nurse in charge, was indeed very busy and in need of helpers. She welcomed me and assigned me the job of registering the mothers, mostly single teenagers, and their babies. Sounds easy? No way! I did not understand a word the girls said. Most were unable to spell their names and, when asked to sign the register, just made a cross. Latania, who easily communicated with me as well as with her clients, switched me to a different task, which she hoped I *could* do: taking the babies' temperatures.

I had the mothers all lined up with babies on their laps, bottoms up and diapers down. Equipped with a bunch of rectal thermometers, I made my way down the row of smooth baby bottoms, which ranged in color from glossy black to – yes – pink. I concentrated on my assignment of identifying any babies with raised temperatures (who would not be eligible for shots that day), rather than wondering about the origin of the many light-colored bottoms in this, supposedly strictly segregated society. These young women were proud of their babies and had obviously dressed them up for the clinic visit. The little girls had ribbons and beads in their wispy black curls. There was much laughter and socializing, and new babies were admired – especially those palest in color. This was of course way before the time of "black is beautiful".

In the waiting room, another volunteer showed "educational" movies. A typical episode depicted a middle-class white couple, the pregnant young woman relaxing in her rocker on the shady porch. The husband comes home from work and urges the mom-to-be not to get up.

"You must rest, honey, I can fix dinner."

He then serves her a delicious meal on a tray. The voiceover told the audience that a pregnant lady needs a lot of rest and a good balanced diet. To the assembled girl-mothers this was absolutely hilarious. The room rang with laughter, waking some of the babies who promptly began to howl.

I continued to work at the clinic one morning a week, while

the boys were in school, and gradually got better at communicating with the mothers. Latania asked me to recruit more volunteers in my neighborhood, but I did not succeed. Some of my neighbors in fact volunteered at the *white* baby clinic, but could not bring themselves to go to the black one. "Why not?" I asked. They had a compelling reason: they could not take directions from a colored girl, no matter how well qualified. And some just felt they could not "handle the picanninies".

I had noticed by now that not all colored people were poor – there was a beautiful suburban neighborhood, not far from Mountain Brook, where middle class colored families lived. So I asked Latania whether she had found any volunteers in that area.

"No ma'm," she said, "the folks up there don't want nothing to do with us poor niggers downtown."

There was one big event that fall: the first successful launch of a lunar rocket, Luna 2, which was a prestigious accomplishment of the Soviet space program. Unlike Sputnik 2, it did not have a dog on board, for which I was grateful. I remember that all of us were sitting outside on the evening of September 14, 1959 trying to spot Luna, when our concentration was rudely disrupted by a salesman, who stopped by our house. What was he selling? Funeral plots! Against the background noise of the cicadas, he filled our ears with the importance of buying a family plot in a beautiful area, limited to "upper-class white citizens", which was filling up fast. He handed brochures to the boys ("pretty angels", Alan commented) and was still talking fast when Peter managed to escort him to his car. I wondered whether he would be selling burial sites on the moon before long.

A Great American Institution

No matter how hot it was, the neighborhood boys played outside. They fought "the war between the States", they played informal games of baseball, or they just goofed around. But as August progressed, they turned their attention to football. This was not the football so popular in Europe – here called soccer – but something completely different. It involved a melon-shaped ball and much rolling around on the ground. Adult conversation also turned to college football, and I soon learned that this was an extremely important topic. How would our team, the *Crimson Tide*, fare this season? Would their famous coach Paul "Bear" Bryant (then in his second year at 'Bama) lead them to more spectacular victories? Would they *ever* beat Auburn? Friends and colleagues were appalled that we had never attended a football game, and I got the impression that this was equivalent to never going to church, of which we had also been guilty.

To remedy this situation, Peter's chairman, Bob Teague, presented us with four tickets to a home game of the *Crimson Tide* against the *Auburn Tigers* at Legion Field. We did not appreciate it then, but this turned out to be a historic game – the first time in six years that 'Bama beat their formidable old rival, a victory that led to their playing in a Bowl game! It was November and still quite warm, so we were glad to have seats under a shady canopy, a prime location, no doubt very expensive. The National Anthem was sung with great fervor, and the players trotted onto the field. They were the biggest men I had ever seen, all of them white[5], but with black smudges painted on their faces, maybe to make them look even scarier. The game began.

Peter and I had *no* idea what was going on; the action bore no resemblance to soccer – or to anything else we had ever seen. The huge football players gathered in tight clumps at intervals, then rushed off in all directions to ram into each other with enormous force, leaving some guys sprawled on the ground. But they were obviously prepared for this violence, wearing a sort of armor under their colorful football jerseys, big shiny helmets, and cages over their faces. The melon-shaped ball spent a lot of time hidden under a pile of players, yet suddenly it would soar through the air towards one of the goals, causing a paroxysm of excitement in the crowd around us. Gregory and Alan were soon jumping up and down and yelling "GO BAMA". Thanks to all the informal games on our front lawn, they seemed to understand something about football.

---

5 "Bear" Bryant recruited his first black football player in 1970, seven years after the racial integration of the University of Alabama.

Frequently the game came to a standstill, while the little referees in their striped outfits (like prison uniforms) were yelling at each other, so I had plenty of time to look around the bleachers. Something odd struck me: everybody except us was dressed up in his or her Sunday best! Most men wore dress shirts, if not ties, and the women wore their pretty "fall cotton" dresses and hats. The scene was reminiscent of the Epsom Down horse races in England. Nobody had thought to prepare us for this, so we showed up in shorts and T-shirts, as we did for other outdoor events. Again the analogy with going to church struck me: maybe American football *was* a sort of religion. The excitement generated here was similar to that at tent revival meetings that we had an opportunity to witness in later years.

At last the giant players marched off the field. It seems we were winning – everybody was happy. Was it finished? No way! It was half time, and the bands took over. Young men in elaborate uniforms, equipped with glittering wind instruments and beautiful drums, marched around the field, forming interesting patterns and making a cheerful noise. There were also groups of beautiful girls dancing around and twirling sticks overhead. I liked all that a lot better than the football!

We got our cokes and hot dogs, and walked around the stadium. The boys had spotted a pair of policemen, and stopped to gaze at them with awe. They had big *guns* in holsters on their hips! One of the cops smiled at them.

"Y'all never seen a gun before?"

"No, sir, only toy guns," Gregory whispered. Alan was speechless for once.

"Is that so! Well I'll be glad to show y'all."

He proudly demonstrated his pistol – just like in the movies. It was one of the highlights of their day, second only to the *Crimson Tide*'s victory over the *Auburn Tigers*. They won 10-0! The crowd went berserk, the applause going on forever, it seemed. We were exhausted, but it was well worth it. Thus ended my first and last American football game.

American Holidays

One day in October Gregory informed me that Halloween was coming soon and "you gotta make me a costume and buy lotsa candy 'cause everybody is going trickatreating."

"Yesm'm, me too!" Alan chimed in. "And we gotta carve a jack-o'-lantern."

As always, I had to consult my good neighbor, Trudy Adams, for clarification, since I had *no* idea what they were talking about. It seemed that all the kids would wear costumes and masks to school on October 31st, and in the evening they would walk around the neighborhood to beg for candy. Trudy advised me to keep it simple, make sure the masks didn't cover the boys' eyes, and have good flashlights available. I did not excel at sewing costumes, or anything else for that matter, but found that one could improvise with the aid of cheap accessories available at the five-and-ten-cent store. Peter balked at stocking up with candy to distribute. "A *terrible* idea, their teeth will rot away", he complained. To pacify him I made and wrapped popcorn balls and bought little packages of raisins, which the kids seemed to like.

When the great day came, the excited boys could hardly wait for dusk, and stood ready in their costumes and masks, a white-sheeted ghost and a black devil, shopping bags and flashlights in hand. Peter accompanied Alan, Charlie and little Will Adams, but Gregory ran off into the dark with a gang of lurid characters. It was my job to sit on the well-lit porch, flanked by our two artistically carved pumpkins, and hand out the goodies to a never-ending assortment of apparitions who ran by, shouting "trickatreat!" and "thank you, ma'm." They were very polite and well behaved. When the boys returned, they emptied the contents of their overflowing bags onto the carpet and squatted down to admire the huge pile, which was a mixture of tiny candy bars, popcorn, candy-apples, raisins and nuts. We threw out anything unwrapped, and then the boys traded until each got their favorite treats. They ate a few pieces and generously offered Peter and me "whatever you'd like," Most of the loot was saved, and lasted for weeks to come. At that time nobody worried about possibly poisoned homemade cookies or

Halloween 1961: Alan

Halloween 1961: Foxy

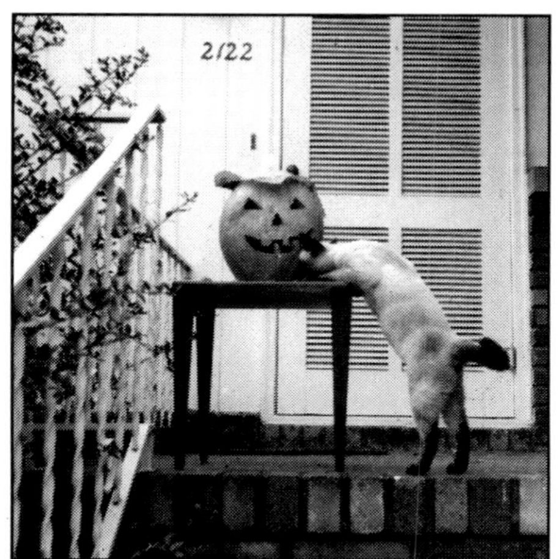

Halloween 1961: Leo

razor blades in apples. It was all a lot of fun. But I was glad it only happened once a year.

It seemed we had just recovered form Halloween, when a new holiday loomed on the horizon This time Gregory (our link to the New World) announced that he needed a pilgrim hat to celebrate Thanksgiving, and was looking forward to a feast of turkey "and all the trimmings". Alan seemed well informed too; he was an Indian, decked out in a colorful feather headdress he had made in nursery school. He showed us how to make cute little turkeys out of pinecones, toothpicks and cranberries. It was nice to think that the pilgrims had such a warm reception from the indigent population. Nobody mentioned that this auspicious beginning eventually led to the massacre of "Indians' as well as buffalo, when the immigrants "settled" the West. Well, we enjoyed our turkey and, whereas I did not relish pumpkin pie, I added one more American food to my favorites list: cranberry sauce. Cranberries (not grown in Europe) reminded me a little of the tart *Preiselbeeren* served in Germany, but they had a unique flavor. The weekend after Thanksgiving we combined all the leftovers in a big cookout, the last of the season. It was still warm enough to sit outside and we enjoyed the glowing fall foliage as we walked in the woods in nearby Oak Mountain State Park.

Immediately after Thanksgiving, Christmas decorations appeared on all the houses, and carols replaced the bland piped music in the stores. Whereas Halloween and Thanksgiving were new to us, we thought we knew all about Christmas. I was grateful that the Unitarian Church taught the kids not only the legend of Jesus' birth but also explained the winter solstice and the Jewish festival of Hanukah. I had never seen Christmas decorations on a scale displayed in our neighborhood – and indeed all over Birmingham. There were sleds drawn by teams of reindeer on the roofs of houses, and brightly lit angels and stars all over the place. Nativity scenes appeared on front lawns, while colored blinking lights framed doors and windows. And of course elaborately decorated Christmas trees and figures of Santa Claus (called Father Christmas in England) – as well as live bell-ringing Santas – were ubiquitous. Our friends and neighbors were planning big family parties, and we felt somewhat lonely, not having any family to celebrate with. So we decided to spend Christmas in Florida, where warm beaches beckoned.

But before taking you to Florida, I must mention two more holidays that came as a surprise to us: the first was Valentine's Day. Although it has existed in England since the Middle Ages, Valentine's Day was strictly associated with lovers, who sent each other romantic notes, often anonymous, and of course roses and chocolates. What was new to us was the idea that little kids would distribute Valentines – and not just to their best friends, but to *everybody.* Trudy Adams suggested that I buy two bags of little Valentine cards at the five-and-ten cent store for the boys to take to school on February 14th. This worked out fine: Gregory and Alan came home that day bursting with love and goodwill, with their backpacks stuffed full of similar cards, received from each of their classmates. They counted and compared cards, and even suspended, for at least an hour, their brotherly squabbles. Both boys had made beautiful cards for Peter and me, which they proudly presented to us. I kept these annual offerings for many years – probably until we began receiving similar works of art from our grandchildren. I suspect the greeting card industry has managed to spread the "Valentines for all" custom to England and other European countries by now, hopefully using recycled paper.

Easter did not take us by surprise, but Mother's Day did. I do not remember this being celebrated in England, but here it was a big deal. Again, I was presented with beautiful handmade cards, and for that one day the boys fell over themselves to be helpful. Peter took us out for dinner, a rare event, and told us of the ancient English custom of Mothering Sunday. On that day, which was the fourth Sunday in Lent, live-in servants (mostly young girls) were allowed to go home to visit their mothers. But this tradition bears no relation to American Mother's Day. I don't remember Father's Day being celebrated; maybe the business community had not discovered its potential yet.

Fun on Darlington Street, Shades Mountain, 1962*

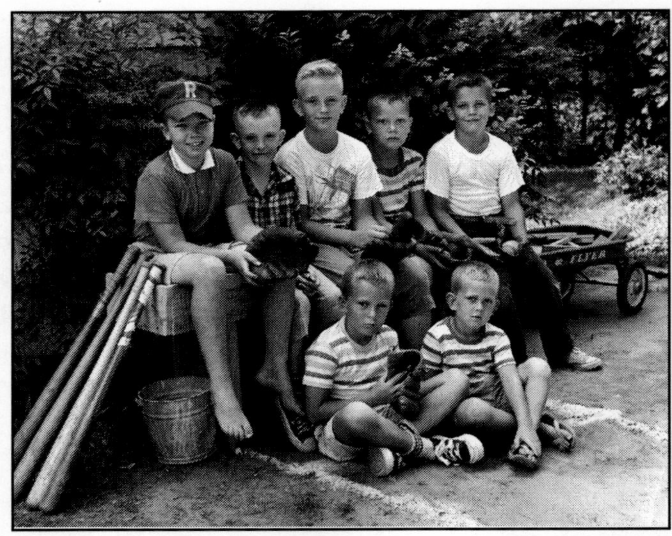

A rest after baseball. Gregory and Alan are in front

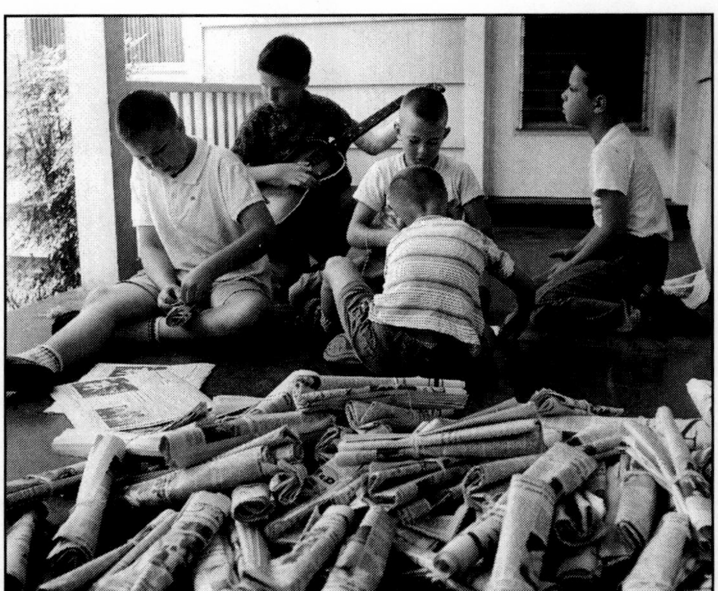

Rolling newspapers on Adams' porch

Football practice

Football practice

*The photographs on this and the previous page were taken by Robert Adams, staff photographer at the Birmingham News.

4. Traveling with Kids

"Travel and change of place impart new vigor to the mind." Seneca

Christmas in Florida

Since we had no extended family to celebrate with, we decided to head south to Florida, where, we were told, beautiful sandy beaches awaited us. A road trip, so routine for most American families was something quite new to us. Although distances in England were miniscule compared to those in the U.S., it was difficult to travel with children, who were not welcome in most hotels and restaurants. In fact, the Brits tolerated dogs better than young kids. Our neighbors assured us that we would not encounter any such problems here. There were modest motels everywhere along the highways and beach cabins with kitchenettes could be rented by the week at very low cost, since December was still off-season in North Florida.

So we piled boys, beach stuff, Christmas presents and Foxy into our little station wagon, with its new blue and white "Heart of Dixie" license plates, which matched its paint, and off we went, heading south. We spent the first night in Florida's capital city, Tallahassee, in a small motel, which had a shuffleboard court. The ground was covered with frost, which did not prevent the boys from playing this new game, while I explored the old town with its huge live oak trees hung with Spanish moss. On our road trips we developed a very traditional (sexist?) division of labor: Peter was the driver and in charge of car maintenance. My job was to plan the route, act as navigator, keep the boys entertained, make sure that we found a shady picnic area with clean restrooms and space for walking Foxy; and had plenty of food, drink and ice in the insulated picnic box. In late afternoon we would approach a pleasant motel with swimming pool, not too far from the highway –but not too

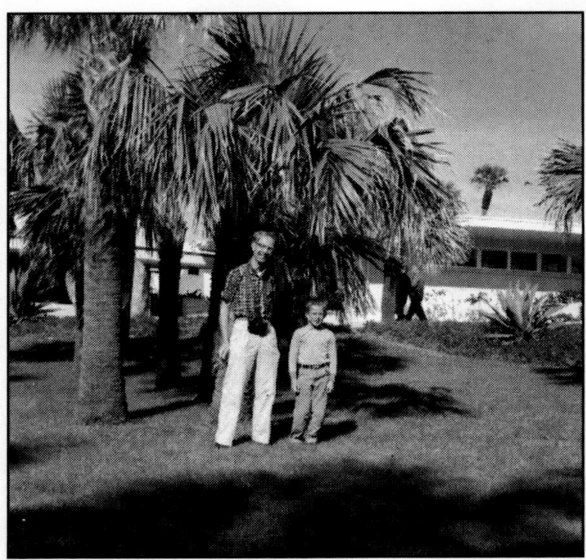

Peter and Gregory in St. Augustine, Florida
Christmas 1961

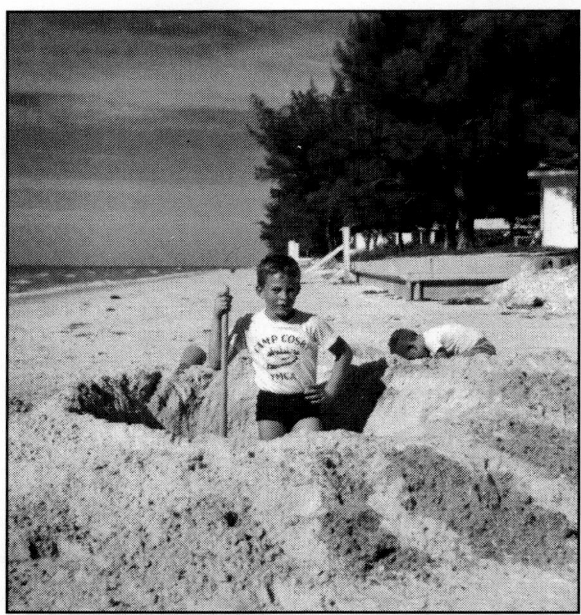

Gregory on the beach at St. Augustine, Florida
Christmas 1961

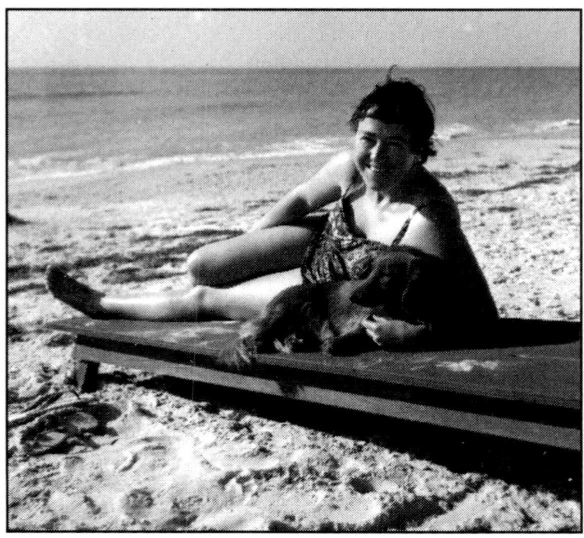

Joan and Foxy on the beach at Boca Grande
Christmas 1962

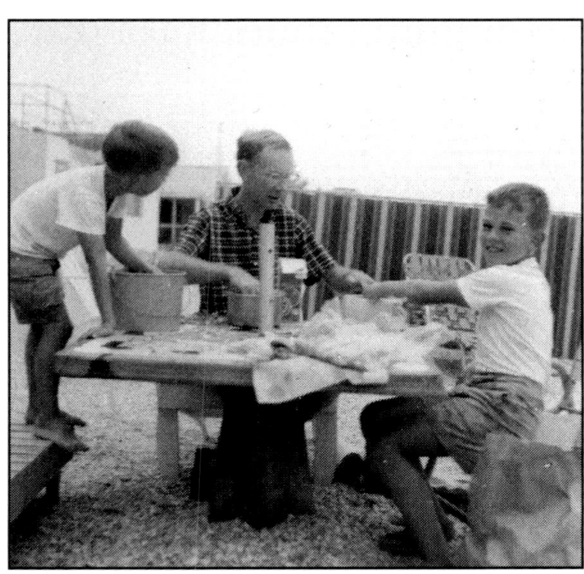

Alan, Peter and Gregory sorting shells at Boca Grande
Christmas 1962

close either – with a restaurant nearby. We always carried a toaster and a jar of English marmalade, without which breakfast would be unthinkable. Before long Gregory, who was fascinated by maps (and still is!) helped me plan our trips.[1]

We got pretty good at "car games", such as spotting state license plates, cows, horses and, at this time of year, Santa Clauses. Even so, the boys got bored at times, and started to poke Foxy to make him restless. Next we would hear, "Dad, Foxy needs to get out, let's stop right now!"

Since there were no multi-lane highways at that time, it was usually possible to turn into a quiet lane and let the three of them run around for a while. We had no car radio, let alone a tape deck, and of course no air conditioning.

We spent our first Christmas in the oldest town in the United States, St. Augustine, which was settled by the Spaniards in the sixteenth century, long before the pilgrims landed at Plymouth Rock. The narrow cobbled streets fascinated us, as well as the clip-clop of horse-drawn carriages. There were interesting museums, which helped us understand American history, but my three guys liked the car museum best. They also loved exploring the ancient Spanish fort (San Marcos), made of indestructible coquina limestone, which took thirty years to build.

We found a housekeeping cabin on the beach and settled in for the week. The weather was bright and sunny, but not particularly warm, so we pretty much had the beach to ourselves. At night temperatures dropped to near freezing, and the little gas heater in our cabin did not work. It was all very English, but since this was supposed to be *warm* Florida, we complained to the owner. The elderly man, who had recently retired and bought these cabins, had no idea how to turn on the heat. While we waited for a service man to come (small chance on Christmas eve!), Peter, who loved to fix things, found the pilot light and got the heater going. He restored heat not only to our cabin, but also to all the others in this establishment. The landlord was overjoyed.

---

1 Over thirty years later, in the late 1990s, Gregory spent some years creating original maps of the world's telephone traffic, and coined the word "Telegeography". The company he founded can be visited at www.telegeography.com

"Stay as long as you like, Mr. Staple, I wouldn't dream of charging you!" he exclaimed. "And here are coupons for the restaurant."

So we enjoyed a free Christmas week in St Augustine. Both boys had asked Santa for Confederate rifles. Thus Christmas Day found them marching up and down the deserted beach, shouldering their rifles and singing Dixie songs. Foxy, however, was not happy: there were prickly plants at the edge of the beach, and after one painful encounter with this exotic vegetation, he insisted on being carried everywhere.

After some inquiries, we learned that this part of Florida was usually quite cool in December. One had to travel further south to find warmer beaches. On this and all subsequent trips, we were amazed at the sheer size of our new country. We resolved to get used to traveling greater distances, perhaps by driving at night when the boys would be asleep. Peter even considered letting me take turns at driving, but discarded that idea when he became familiar with the navigator's responsibilities. However, next year we would surely make it all the way down to the Florida Keys! Actually we never did. There was too much to see and explore on the way.

One of the many beautiful places we visited was Cypress Gardens in central Florida. I don't know which was more impressive there: the lush tropical vegetation or the young women, attached to large kites, which rose up into the air, looking like great colorful birds. Other girls, dressed as Southern belles, strolled among the huge cactuses and poinsettia trees. In complete contrast to this sunny world were the spooky cypress swamps for which the park is named, and the dark tunnels formed by ancient banyan trees. We kept a close eye on the boys and especially on Foxy, as they explored the boardwalks, since alligators were lurking in the dark water, immobile like statues, yet ready to leap out at any time.

Another interesting place we visited was Homosassa Springs. From the "Fish Bowl", a floating, submerged observatory, we watched thousands of fish in the crystal clear water, and were eye to eye with the placid, cow-like manatees.

In our quest to get further south we found ourselves one Christmas Eve on the Gulf Coast somewhere between Fort Myers and Naples on what looked like a causeway to nowhere. I loved the Florida causeways and bridges, especially the bridge across Tampa Bay. To be completely surrounded by sky and water felt like sailing, but without the choppiness. This particular causeway "did not exist", according to Gregory, meaning he could not find it on our map. I couldn't identify it either, and conceded that we were lost.[2] After some grumbling ("you *never* know where we are"), Peter decided to continue, since it was late afternoon and we needed a place to stay. Night comes suddenly in the South, the sun disappears into the ocean and within a few minutes it's pitch dark. Eventually we spotted a sign "Boca Grande", and realized that we were on Gasparilla Island, where the road came to an end. There seemed to be only one hotel here, a majestic old luxury resort, no doubt way beyond our means: the Gasparilla Inn. It was too late to drive back to the mainland, so I braved the reception desk at the venerable resort, and inquired whether there was perhaps a modest motel on this island.

The Gasparilla Inn lobby was awe-inspiring, with opulent antique furnishings, a huge chandelier, tropical plants and thick carpets, the aura of a five-star resort. The receptionist, who introduced himself as Robert, was gracious and sympathetic. He stepped out from behind his desk and inspected our little station wagon with its ragged travel-weary occupants. Foxy, with his paws on the windowsill actually wagged his tail and "smiled". Robert confirmed my impression that this was the only accommodation on the island and yes, it was an "upscale" resort – "the best in Florida since 1913". Guests were required to dress for dinner and neither children nor dogs were accommodated in the main building.

"But", he said, "we have one vacant cottage, a last minute cancellation, and your family is welcome to stay there over the Christmas holiday."

He named a surprisingly reasonable price. Having really no choice, we agreed, and were immediately shown to our "cottage", which turned out to be bigger than our house in Birmingham, and furnished with understated elegance. There was just one snag: the cottage had no kitchen.

"You may dine at the Inn; we will supply a tie for you, Sir, if

---

2 We were in fact on the causeway to Gasparilla Island, completed in 1958, too new to be on our map.

you should need one."

Fortunately Peter had a suit coat with him, and I always packed one skirt, so we were all set. Needless to say, the meals were superb, especially the Christmas dinner.

At the tip of Gasparilla Island is Charlotte Harbor, which at the time, was a major phosphate port. The train brought in phosphate, and the loaded railroad cars were transferred directly to huge freighters to be shipped all over the world. Peter, a great railroad fan, was fascinated by the harbor. He and the boys spent most of their time watching the freighters, as well as the oil barges on the Intracoastal Waterway. There was also a long pier and a marina for sport fishing vessels, where one could watch tarpon being weighed and measured. I had *never* seen fish that big (they grow up to 8 feet and can easily weigh 300 pounds), and wondered how anybody could catch such a monster with a fishing line. Apparently it takes great patience; you have to hang on for hours, until the hooked fish is worn out and gives up the fight. Although the proud fishermen usually released the exhausted giants back into the gulf (tarpon are not edible), many of the traumatized fish did not survive. I did not like this "sport", and found the phosphate port too dusty, so I spent most of my time in Boca Grande on the sandy beaches, collecting the great variety of shells, and socializing with some of the guests at the Inn. They were mostly family groups, who had been spending Christmas at the Gasparilla Inn for generations. From their accents I judged that they were "Yankees", and indeed most had come from New York or New England. None were from the South, which surprised me.

Evenings were most beautiful at the old (1890) lighthouse, from where we watched the sun slip into the ocean. Sitting on our porch was not so pleasant: we had to wear hats to protect us against the incessant bombardment by seagulls – the only hostile creatures on this charmed island. Altogether it was a memorable Christmas, and our last in Florida. The following year would see us in snowy Buffalo.

To the Mountains

Just as we went in search of warm beaches for our Christmas vacations, so we looked for somewhere to escape the heat in summer. Unwilling to drive great distances, we ruled out “the north”. We reasoned that it was surely cooler in the mountains, and the obvious area to head for was the Southern Appalachians, especially the famous Smoky Mountains National Park. I gathered maps, and brochures with glowing descriptions of cottages in shady groves, where one “slept under blankets”. This advertising slogan sounds quaint in our era of “climate controlled” rooms and cars, but to us it conjured up visions of peaceful nights without noisy fans blowing hot humid air around our sweat-soaked beds.

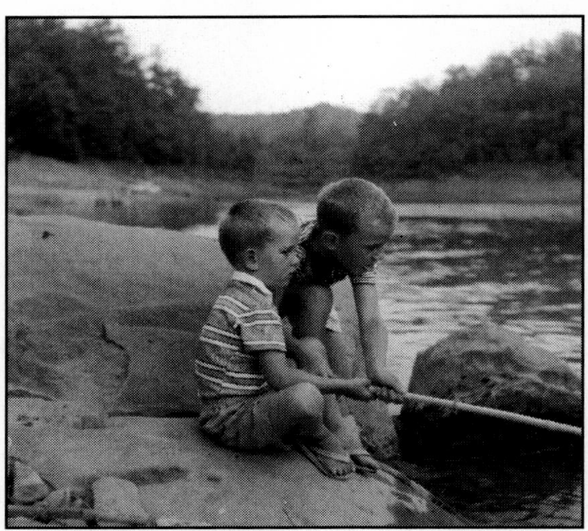

“It's biting…!” Gregory and Alan fishing near Franklin, NC. Summer 1961

On the recommendation of friends, we booked a housekeeping cabin near Franklin, North Carolina, and were delighted with our choice. The well-equipped cabins, shaded by maple trees, were lined up along a crystal clear, fast flowing creek, stocked with trout. We traveled through the night this time, which had certain advantages: sleeping boys, cooler air and less traffic. But of course Peter, who, as usual, did most of the driving, was dead tired when we arrived in

Franklin, and collapsed into bed – yes with blankets – while Gregory, Alan and Foxy were full of energy and ready to explore. I sent all of them out to play in the creek, while I got the cabin organized and cooked breakfast.

It turned out, that this shallow creek provided endless entertainment – one could fish for trout, pry wriggling "crawdads" out of their rocky hiding places, build dams and collect pretty stones. Nearby was a delightfully cold pond for swimming, and lots of blackberry bushes, just ready for picking. Mrs. McNish, our landlady, gave us a set of jelly jars, and the boys picked so many berries, that I had to make jam, although I vowed I was "on vacation". I remember stacking the jars in a box on the roof rack, keeping my fingers crossed for their safe arrival in Birmingham. Another vivid memory was of Peter standing in the stream, casting for trout, and trying to fend off a wasp. Instead of the pesky insect, he hit his glasses, which flew off into the fast-flowing creek. The boys thought this was very funny, but we all spent hours in an unsuccessful attempt to retrieve the glasses.

Not far from Franklin were the gem mines, where visitors could dig for rubies, rhodolites, garnets and sapphires. Mr. McNish, always a source of useful information, warned us to beware of certain mines, which were "salted" with worthless imported stones or even bits of colored glass, so we only patronized the "all native" mine recommended by him. Prospecting for gems was hard work – it still amazes me what people will do on a "restful" vacation. After a slow dusty drive on bumpy dirt roads, we reached the mine, which was really just a hollow of typical Southern red dirt, where long wooden troughs with running water, called flumes, had been set up for sieving the soil. The procedure was a follows: After paying an entrance fee, we parked on, hopefully, firm ground, perhaps under one of the scarce shade trees. Then Peter was equipped with two tin pails and a shovel. The idea was to fill the pails with soil to be carefully screened, using the wire sieves provided. To spot gemstones, it really helps if you know what you are looking for. Obvious? OK, but not easy. Fortunately Peter seemed to have some knowledge of gems, acquired during his war service in Burma, and taught us to identify sapphires, rubies and garnets, all of which came

Peter carrying pails of "red dirt" to be scanned for gemstones. People in back are washing and sifting soil at the flumes. Franklin, NC. Summer 1961

Foxy finds a cool spot at the gem mines near Franklin, NC. Summer 1961

in a variety of shades and shapes. Visits to gem shops and the Gem Museum (in the old Franklin jail) also helped.

The boys and I sat on the low wooden bench at the flume and did the sieving; while Peter kept us supplied with soil, bearing in mind that, in addition to the entrance fee, you had to pay a modest sum for each filled pail. If you needed help, there were brawny teenagers around, who would fill and carry your pails (for a not-so-modest sum). You might think sitting in the sun, screening and washing soil is a dreary way to spend your day, but actually it was exciting, even addictive. Any minute you might come across this big ruby, worth hundreds of dollars! Alan was particularly good at spotting gems and picking them out of the debris with his nimble little fingers. Our hopes were kept high by frequent finds of lesser stones, which we carefully washed and stored in empty film boxes.

Meanwhile Foxy was content to bury himself in the mud, only his face protruding, rather like a furry alligator. Since the soil was the same red-brown color as his coat, I did not realize just how filthy he was until he got into the car. We returned to our cabin tired, but happy. Our hoard of little gems was counted, sorted, and admired by neighboring guests for the rest of the day, and the boys couldn't wait to go back for more. At the end of the week Peter took some of the stones to a gem-cutting shop in Franklin to have them prepared for mounting in a ring. Did anybody ever find "that huge thousand dollar ruby"? Probably not. But one of our cabin neighbor, who sold his finds to a gem-shop, made enough money to cover the cost of his family's vacation.

Twenty-five years later, when I started teaching annual Elderhostel[3] courses at Highlands, NC, Peter returned to our old haunts. The dirt road was now paved, and there were shady picnic areas, restrooms and gift shops galore. Canopies for all-weather operation covered the flumes. Visitors were not allowed to dig – attendants provided soil of *their* choosing. Peter still enjoyed it, although he admitted that the old aura of adventure was lacking.

Not far from Franklin is the Nantahalla National Forest with its beautiful waterfalls, conveniently lined up on US 64. "Dry Falls," where you could walk behind the falls without getting wet, intrigued the boys. But usually we managed to get soaked anyway; it was part

3 Residential courses for Senior Citizens

of the fun. The first real mountain Gregory and Alan climbed was the Wayah Bald (just over 5000ft), a good "beginners' mountain" with a fire tower on top, from where one had wonderful views of several states. On subsequent visits we ventured into the Smoky Mountain National Park and "conquered" such peaks as Clingman's Dome (6643ft), the highest peak in the Smokies. A paved road leads to the top from the Newfound Gap parking area, so it is not exactly adventurous. But after admiring the panoramic views, we walked on the nearby spruce scented Appalachian Trail, and I like to think that the boys acquired their love of hiking on these early explorations. Most young kids get bored just walking along a trail, so we tried to make it more exciting by playing various games. Much of the time we did not see the boys because they were "Indians" lurking in the dense forest, ready to pounce on us at intervals. But Foxy *always* knew their whereabouts, no matter how silently they tried to stalk us, so we did not worry. When the going got rough we had "treasure hunts", dropping incentives (Hershey kisses were popular) along the trails to keep the kids going.

Black bears were (and still are) common in the Smokies. On the main road across the mountain "bear jams" sometimes developed, with traffic backed up for miles because a bear family had chosen to browse in a nearby clearing, or to sit in the middle of the road, so drivers stopped to look at them. Foolish visitors – we included – got out of their cars to take pictures, and even fed the bears. This is of course quite dangerous, and the Park Rangers have long since put a stop to it.

Another interesting place we visited on our summer travels was Lookout Mountain near Chattanooga, TN. Although the mountain is not particularly high (about 2000ft), the views are spectacular, encompassing seven states. But what really fascinated the boys, especially Gregory, was the museum, which contained a large interactive diorama of the Battle of Missionary Ridge (1863) in which Ulysses Grant defeated the Confederate Army. Gregory had a large collection of model soldiers and never tired of reenacting various battles of the War Between the States. At gift shops (which we tried, in vain, to bypass) he was always on the lookout for particular soldiers, maybe a Union lieutenant or a Confederate cavalry officer, to add to his collection. These toy soldiers were beautifully crafted in either metal, or plastic, and were fairly expensive even then. Gregory's collection would now be worth thousands of dollars, but he eventually lost interest and I gave them away.

As you drive on the highways of Southern states, whose beauty is marred by the ubiquitous advertising signs, two slogans are inescapable: SEE RUBY FALLS and VISIT ROCK CITY. These signs appear at regular intervals, even on highways hundreds of miles from the attractions. They are often painted on old barns[4], and we soon added "counting barn signs" to our car games. I vowed we would bypass these tourist traps – but eventually we succumbed. Ruby Falls, 140 ft. high, is truly a geological wonder, located in a huge cave inside Lookout Mountain; it is said to be the world's largest underground waterfall. It was certainly worth seeing and I enjoyed it more than the battlefields. As for Rock City – it was fun walking on the swaying suspension bridges connecting the rocks, but not as unique as the underground waterfall with its surrounding stalagmites and stalactites. And the best thing was, that we could now travel past the painted barns without hearing, "Dad, **when** are we going to Ruby Falls/Rock City? **Today?"**

We Visit England

It was time to go home! Yes, Peter and I still thought of England as "home." Not so, our sons, now eight and five years old. In their speech and behavior they seemed no different from their Alabama contemporaries. Perhaps not surprising: the two years in Birmingham, which seemed short to me, represent almost half of Alan's and one third of Gregory's life. We booked flights on Icelandic Airlines (*Loftleidir*), the cheapest transportation available, and stopped visiting the barber, so that the boys' crew cuts had time to grow into a more acceptable style for England. The jet-prop plane refueled in Reykjavik, but although there was a lengthy layover, we were not allowed to leave the airport. Instead, we were offered a huge meal at 2a.m., not my favorite dining hour, and plenty of time to go shopping for Icelandic goods, mostly very heavy sweaters. The boys were fast asleep and I remember dragging them to the

4 I read there are 900 signs still in existence.

Alan, Gregory and Joan on Dartmoor in Devonshire, July 1962

The boys at Haytor on Dartmoor, Summer 1962

Alan, Joan, Caroline (Wink) and Walter Lorch in Iver Bucks, July 1962

Walter and Diana Lorch on the beach near Bideford, Devonshire, Summer 1962

airport lounge, where they continued to sleep until it was time to re-board. To our surprise we found the plane's engines running, the propellers whizzing around while we dodged under them to enter the cabin. Apparently there had been a problem starting the engines, so the crew hand-cranked them, and hoped they wouldn't stall again. Well, they didn't, and we made it to Shannon Airport (Ireland) and from there to London's Heathrow. We were happy to be met by my brother, Walter, in his Land Rover for the short trip to "Buck House" in Iver, Bucks.

Diana, my sister-in-law, came running out to embrace us all, welcoming her "Yankee nephews". The boys stopped in their tracks:

"Aunt Diana, we are NOT Yankees!" they exclaimed in unison.

In England, all Americans were referred to as Yankees, and of course Diana could not know that the term "Yankee" was anathema to her "Southern" nephews. Hearing their protest, she simply assumed they still considered themselves to be English, and we left it at that. I was not about to launch into an explanation of the War Between the States and its ongoing consequences.

Janet and Rob were young teenagers, while Caroline (nicknamed Wink) was a toddler. We settled into the guest flat in the "annex" and the first thing we noticed was how *cold* it was. At least it seemed so to us, normal English summer temperatures being some twenty degrees lower than in Alabama. The boys put on their flannel-lined jeans and sweatshirts, refusing to take them off even in bed. Diana brought over a small electric heater from the main house, and filled hot water bottles for our beds.

Another thing we noticed was the long hours of daylight. Diana, a strict disciplinarian with kids, did not appreciate Alan's refusal to go to bed because it wasn't dark yet. He waited in vain for the moon – and the lightning bugs – to appear. Eventually he fell asleep on the floor, and never saw "the dark", remarking the next day, "in England they don't have the sun, nor the moon". Well, we soon adjusted to all that and enjoyed visiting old friends and taking the boys sight-seeing in London. While we drove around in our rental car, remembering to keep to the left, the boys frequently shouted that we were "on the wrong side" or "on the sidewalk", since the road was so narrow. We did all the tourist things, visiting the Tower of London, and taking a cruise on the Thames, where the captain allowed Gregory to steer the boat for a while. During a visit to Peter's sister, Betty, and her family in Kent, we explored the ancient castle at Rochester. All that history was probably lost on the boys, they preferred chasing the pigeons and playing hide and seek among the ruins.

Although I still had friends in the "old" Birmingham, I did not include a trip there, because I felt I would miss my parents too much. As you may remember, they died in August 1959, just four months after we left England. They are buried in the Birmingham Jewish cemetery, but I had no interest in visiting their graves, preferring to remember them alive and well, as they had been during that last Easter weekend we spent together in Eastbourne. While staying with Walter and Diana, I tried to find out more details regarding Papi and Mutti's sudden deaths, but they refused to discuss the subject.

Walter had booked rooms for all nine of us at the lovely old Portledge Hotel near Bideford in Devonshire for the first week in August, which included both Diana's and Janet's birthdays. It is usually very warm and sunny there, however, that year was an exception, and I don't think we "Americans" ventured into the ocean. I suggested to the manager that he might light a fire in the big fireplace, which graced the hotel lobby. It would make the evenings cozier. He readily agreed that it would, but then explained patiently:

"You see, Madam, it is not the *custom* to light a fire in August. In Scotland, they would indeed do so, but not here in Devon."

"It's rather chilly though, don't you think?" I ventured.

"Oh yes, Madam, it is *unusually* cold for this time of year, but we do not light fires in August." Irrefutable British logic, I guess.

Perhaps to make amends, the manager offered to let "the American boys" sleep in a tiny bedroom adjacent to the boiler room, which was really cozy.

"It's actually a maid's room," he said apologetically, "our guests would not care for such a stuffy bedroom."

Well, the boys liked it, and so did Perry, Walter and Diana's

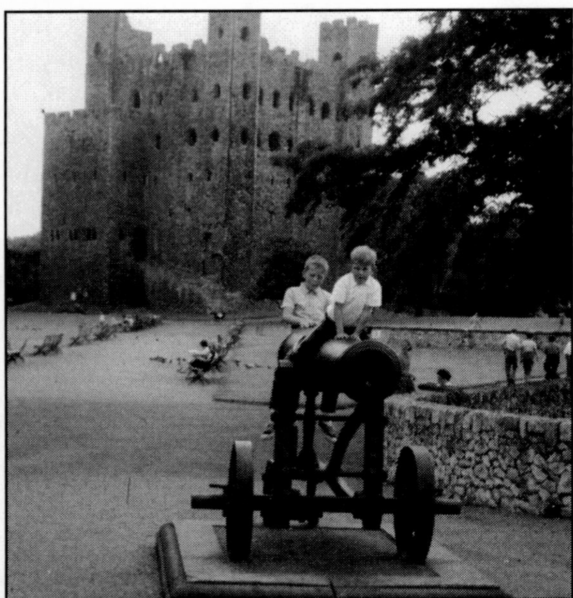

Visiting the ancient castle in Rochester, Kent, Summer 1962

Outside Buckingham Palace, Summer 1962

black retriever, who chose to sleep with them, filling the little room with a salty-damp, doggy aroma. The hotel laid on a fine birthday celebration. Janet, now sixteen, was a rather moody teenager, no longer very interested in family vacations. But Rob was happy, spending his time driving the Land Rover back and forth on the hotel's long private driveway. Little Wink tried hard to persuade her cousins to jump into the chilly waves with her, but to no avail. Alan eventually joined her and the dog in the warm puddles left on the sandy beach, as the ocean receded at low tide.

Peter and the boys at Granny Staple's house in Chudleigh, Devonshire. Summer 1962

Before returning to Buck House, Peter and I took the boys to visit their grandmother in Devonshire, staying at the lovely little guesthouse run by Peter's cousins, Anne and Elizabeth Hallett. I think Granny Staple enjoyed her grandsons in small doses; she showed them her garden and took them for walks in the village, largely inhabited by old people. Using Bovey Tracey as a base, we drove up to Dartmoor, where the boys could run wild, climbing on the rocks, and chasing sheep and wild ponies. It was a wonderful end to our "tourist" trip to England. Peter and I had mixed feelings about returning to Alabama, but Greg and Alan were anxious to get home and tell their friends all about it.

Gregory and Alan admiring Granny Staple's roses.
Chudleigh, Devonshire, Summer 1962

5. Moving North

"Segregation was not just a law, it was an ethos, a tradition, an informed practice that demanded conformity of all citizens." W. Edward Harris in *Miracle in Birmingham,* Indianapolis, IN 2004, *p.86*

"Segregation now…Segregation forever"

"So *why* can't we go to the pool, Mom?"

"It's *hot*, Mom"

"Yea, and its after Memorial Day, what's going on?"

Good questions, but not easy to answer. It was May 1962, and our summer refuge, the municipal pool in Homewood Park was closed. "Well then lets go to the Library, where it's nice and cool", Gregory suggested with resignation. The Birmingham Public Library was closed too.

The underlying reason was the same: the park and the library were restricted to white residents, as were virtually all public facilities in Alabama. But times were changing: months ago (September 1961) Federal Judge Hobart Grooms had ruled that public parks and recreation centers must be accessible to everybody. The Federal government no longer tolerated Alabama's State Laws regarding racial segregation, and Birmingham had been ordered to integrate these facilities, along with public schools and the University. It had been a long time coming, yet the city government had made no preparations and was not about to comply. Their response was to close the facilities "temporarily", perhaps hoping the problem would go away.

So did we swim that summer? Sure, we did! A few weeks after its closure, Homewood pool reopened as a private club. I have no idea how this was done. We filled out an application form, which included a question regarding race, paid a modest fee, and were accepted as members. We also swam and hiked at the beautiful Oak

Mountain State Park, which no longer barred colored residents, but I don't recall ever seeing a dark-skinned person there. Only white sunbathers, trying to get "a nice dark tan".

It is not my intention to launch into a history of the Civil Rights era, fascinating though it is, and much has been written on this subject.[1] But I will provide you with just enough information to understand what was happening in Birmingham during the early sixties, and why we decided, albeit reluctantly, to move north in the summer of 1963.

Birmingham had a Commissioner type of city government, consisting of three Commissioners, all dedicated to preserving the "Southern way of life". Best known was Eugene "Bull" Connor, Commissioner for Public Safety, a strict segregationist, strongly supported by Alabama's new Governor, George Wallace, who was elected by a landslide in November 1962. Connor and Wallace objected vigorously to all "federal meddling". But not all area citizens approved of racial segregation. There was a strong and vocal minority of progressive white businessmen, who realized that Birmingham's poor image was largely due to its non-compliance with Federal laws. Birmingham was steadily losing population, and business suffered as firms relocated their regional offices elsewhere. These forward-looking residents were well aware that another Southern city, Atlanta, Georgia, had adjusted well to the impending changes and was already on the way to becoming the vital business and cultural center it now is.

A lot of Birmingham's problems were due to the inflexible attitude of "Bull" Connor, and many residents felt that the only way to get rid of him was to eliminate the current city government. Hence a plan was developed to replace the Commissioner government with a Mayor-Council one. With the help of the Chamber of Commerce, the local Bar Association and much politicking, this was accomplished, and on April 12, 1963, Albert Boutwell, a former state senator, considered a "moderate", was elected mayor of Birmingham. The

---

1 A useful account of the events in Birmingham can be found in *Miracle in Birmingham: A Civil Rights Memoir 1954-1965* by W.Edward Harris. Stonework Press, Indianapolis. IN 2004

A superb book on the civil rights era is *Parting the Waters: America in the King Years 1954-63* by Taylor Branch. Touchstone Edition 1989

date was critical, because it was only *two days* before "Operation C" hit the city. Thus "Bull" Connor was still in charge and, predictably, chaos ensued, when the nonviolent demonstrators were met with extreme force.

So what is Operation C? To understand this, we must go back a few years to 1960, when the Student Nonviolent Coordinating Committee, organized by colored students and known as SNCC, started sit-ins in order to integrate lunch counters at major stores, as well as parks, libraries and other public venues. The operation was based on Gandhi's theories of nonviolent action. Before long, white people from the northern states, many of them students, arrived by the busload to support the integration effort, and to assist in voter registration for colored citizens. These so-called Freedom Riders faced frequent attacks and much harassment by white Southerners; indeed their lives were at stake.

In Birmingham, a vicious attack occurred on May 14, 1961 (Mother's Day), when a busload of Freedom Riders arrived at the Greyhound Station and were beaten up by the Ku Klux Klan. Police eventually responded. Commissioner Connor explained that his officers were "at home with their mothers", hence the long delay. I found it interesting that, while almost 50% of the Freedom Riders were said to be Jewish, *Southern* Jews kept a low profile, fearing retaliation by the Klan. After all, they had to continue living here long after the Freedom Riders had gone back home!

The Mountain Brook Unitarian Church was actively involved in civil rights, and, although we had no colored members, faculty from Miles College, a traditionally black college in Birmingham, and from the nearby Tuskegee Institute[2] occasionally attended a service. This was of course illegal, and was a subject much debated by the congregation. The membership was torn between wanting to welcome all worshipers, yet not wishing to break a state law, which would endanger the church's very existence. We worried about our beautiful wooden building on Cahaba Road, only a year old, and far from finished. The Klan was obviously keeping an eye on us, and might set fire to the place at any time, so members of the congregation took turns to spend nights in church. Our minister, Rev. Hobart, who

2 Now Tuskegee University, a traditionally black college, whose first teacher was Booker T. Washington.

took a strong stand in favor of integration, was often harassed. One night, while he was out of town, the Klan burned a cross on his front lawn, terrifying Mary Aymer, his wife.

Ku Klux Klan members burning a cross. A similar event occured on the lawn of our Unitarian minister's house in Birmingham, AL in 1961. Photo courtesy of Library of Congress.

The rift within the congregation came to a head when, in 1961, the Church received a request from the Birmingham Council of Human Relations, which had both white *and colored* members, to hold their meetings in our building. Rev. Hobart and several other Unitarians were active members of the Council. I remember the debate of this issue very well – it was very contentious and went on for hours. Members in favor of permitting the integrated meetings felt this was *morally* the right thing to do, although a state law, albeit an unjust law, would be broken. The opposition did not necessarily disagree with this view, but were more pragmatic. They pointed out that the police would certainly raid such integrated meetings, and possibly shut down the church. If the Klan decided to torch the building, neither the police nor the fire department would respond. Do we really want to risk losing our church? Finally the vote was almost 2: 1 *against* allowing the Council meetings to be held in the Unitarian Church. Many members left the church in anger. Peter and I were new members, and did not really feel qualified to evaluate this complex situation, so we abstained. I hoped that very soon federal laws on integration would replace the old state laws, making the whole controversy moot. And eventually that happened.

A group active in civil rights asked me to participate in sit-ins, which were going on in the city to integrate lunch counters at department stores. It sounded exciting, and I agreed to try it. Sit-ins had been very successful in other Southern cities, notably Greensborough, NC. I remember getting instructions to go to Loveman's Department store at noon on a certain day. I would see several women there, both white and colored, and I was to sit down with them at the lunch counter. Each of us would order our lunch and eat it, without any social interaction. The objective was to demonstrate that it was *ok to sit next to a colored person.* Well – it really wasn't! First of all the waitress completely ignored the colored customers, while taking my order. Then two policemen arrived and asked all colored persons to leave. None complied. The situation was tense, and I was much too worried to eat my sandwich. The cops disappeared, but a rumor spread around the lunchroom that they were coming back with teargas. I'm afraid at this point most of us chickened out and left in a hurry – without paying. So much for my inglorious contribution to civil rights!

An interesting reflection on Southern culture was provided by the fact that, while white and colored persons would not *sit down together,* it was ok to have a snack at Sears lunch counters, which required you to *stand up* at a round tabletop. I noticed a similar situation at the public library, which, after it was forced to integrate, removed the cute little tables and chairs from the children's' reading room. Well, all the kids happily sat on the floor with their books, including an occasional colored child, whose mother was brave enough to come in. But I now hesitated taking the boys there because, rather than integrating the restrooms, the library *closed* them!

I think these traditions date from the days of slavery, when it was not acceptable for slaves to sit down with their master. I had also noticed that our maid, Mae, would never sit down with me at the kitchen table, although she gladly accepted a meal and would eat it standing up. When the weather was bad, I would drive Mae to the bus stop, only two blocks away, but uphill. She insisted on sitting in the back seat, another odd custom. Many of my neighbors picked up their maids at the bus stop early in the morning, and the procession of huge cars, driven by white housewives, with a colored maid in the back, looked weird to me – the reverse of having a Negro chauffeur!

Now to Operation C, scheduled for April 12, 1963 (Good Friday). This was the name given to the plan devised by Martin Luther King and the Southern Christian Leadership Conference (SCLC) to challenge the system of segregation in Birmingham. The "C" stood for confrontation, the strategy of peaceful actions, such as rallies, demonstrations and boycotts. Dr. King and SCLC wanted to attract national attention to the situation in Birmingham, and anticipated a violent reaction by Police Commissioner Connor. And indeed it was violent: "Bull" Connor ordered the police to disperse the peaceful demonstrators by using fire hoses trained on the hapless youngsters, most of them high school students, as well as to deploy snarling police dogs. Over 3000 people were arrested, and hundreds were thrown in jail, as was Dr. King himself. This is where, on Easter Sunday, he wrote his famous *Letter from a Birmingham Jail.*[3]

SCLC's objective, to attract national attention was achieved. Graphic pictures of Operation C appeared in the national press and caused a general outcry. Not so in Birmingham itself. The two local newspapers carried only brief notes of some "unrest" in the city. Personally I did not know what was going on until I got the New York Times on Easter Sunday! This may seem odd to 21st century readers, but keep in mind that we had no TV, National Public Radio did not exist yet, and I only listened to local news.

One of the criticisms leveled against Dr. King was the timing of Operation C. As I mentioned previously, the new city administration under Mayor Albert Boutwell had only been in office for two days, when Operation C struck. Why did King and the SCLC not give the new city government a chance to show that they would indeed integrate public facilities? King answers these criticisms eloquently in his *Letter from a Birmingham Jail* (April 12, 1963). He points out that, although Mayor Boutwell was a "much more

---

3 The cell, in which Dr. King was incarcerated, can be seen at the Birmingham Civil Rights Institute museum.

gentle person" than Commissioner Connor, he was nevertheless a segregationist. King goes on to say that:

"Freedom is never voluntarily given by the oppressor, it must be demanded by the oppressed. Frankly, I have yet to engage in a direct action campaign that was 'well timed' in the view of those who have not suffered from the disease of segregation... We must come to see with one of our distinguished jurists, that 'justice too long delayed is justice denied'."

Author James Baldwin put it more bluntly, when he said "all of Africa will be free before we can get a cup of coffee." Meanwhile Civil Rights Legislation at the federal level was still in the works. John F. Kennedy, who had made Civil Rights one of his major election campaign platforms, took office as President of the United States in 1961. But, disappointingly, the Civil Rights Bill did not come before Congress until 1963. In August of that year, Martin Luther King organized the famous March on Washington, where he made his much quoted "I have a dream..." speech. The Civil Rights Bill encountered many obstacles, and was still in Congress when Kennedy was assassinated in November of that fateful year.

President Lyndon Johnson finally signed the Bill into law in 1964. It is interesting, though not surprising, that voting on the Bill was not divided along party lines. With a few exceptions, representatives and senators from the eleven Southern states (former Confederacy) voted against it, while those from the North voted in favor. After signing the Civil Rights Bill, President Johnson is said to have remarked: "We have just lost the South."[4] The passage of the Civil Rights Act was responsible for far-reaching changes not only in the Southern states, but also in the United States generally. As I discovered after our move north to New York State, racial discrimination was not confined to the South. The Civil Rights Act mandated equal access to all public facilities, voting rights and employment opportunities, for persons of all races *and both sexes.* Howard W. Smith, a powerful Democrat from Virginia, who opposed integration, and had absolutely no interest in women's rights, had

---

4 By "we" he meant the Democratic Party, and indeed the South, traditionally Democrat, began to change its allegiance.

added the "sex" clause to the Bill's Title VII as an additional obstacle to its passage, a device that fortunately did not succeed.

Governor George Wallace "standing in the school house door" at the University of Alabama to prevent racial integration. June 11, 1963. Photo courtesy of Library of Congress.

Meanwhile, Alabama Governor George Wallace, who was elected on a platform of "Segregation now, segregation tomorrow, segregation forever" was as good as his word. He promised to "stand in the schoolhouse door" to prevent the admission of colored students to the University of Alabama, and indeed he did so, on June 11, 1963. As a result, President Kennedy federalized the Alabama National Guard and sent them, as well as federal marshals, to Tuscaloosa to enforce registration of the two colored students, who were brave enough to attempt enrollment. Looking back on this period I am amazed that Governor Wallace, a Democrat, could run a successful election campaign on a strong segregation ticket, while just 45 years later the Democratic party's black candidate, Barack Obama, was elected President of the United States!

Like most universities and colleges in the United States, the University of Alabama had federally supported programs. Most successful researchers in the sciences apply for and receive grants from agencies such as The National Science Foundation and/or The National Institutes of Health. The Civil Rights Act would stipulate that federal support could not be given to institutions in violation of the law. In practice this meant that researchers at the University of Alabama would lose their research grants if Wallace failed to integrate the school. There was much discussion of this dire prospect among Peter's colleagues, and some of the researchers started looking round for opportunities elsewhere. Peter had already taken steps to search for a another position, because he felt his salary was inadequate, and he was considering two offers from Dental Schools: one in Lexington, Kentucky, the other in Buffalo, New York. Thus the possible loss of federal grants was not his only reason to seek a change.

In addition, we were concerned about our sons' education, especially Gregory, who would soon be ready for junior high school. We realized that, whereas Shades Mountain Elementary School was fine, thanks largely to our active PTA, the high schools were really poor. They lacked funding for such essentials as well-stocked libraries, workshops, gymnasiums and sports facilities, and their curriculum was limited. One reason for the worsening school funding was Wallace's position of "separate but equal". In other words, while not integrating public schools, he would ensure that colored schools were equal in quality to white schools (which was certainly not the case). That meant finding funds to upgrade dilapidated colored schools, hence even less money for white schools. I was told that not only white, but also many colored residents were in favor of "separate but equal", especially colored educators, who feared that integrated schools would be staffed mostly by white teachers.

We were advised to put Gregory on the waiting list for Indian Springs School if we wanted a good education for him. This was an excellent (and expensive) day/ boarding prep school about 50 miles away, i.e. too far for a daily commute, but we did give it serious thought. Apart from considerations of formal education, I was uneasy about our sons growing up in this racist environment, which constantly reminded me of my childhood in Nazi Germany. Rightly or wrongly I identified with the colored victims. I couldn't help feeling threatened by the Klan, who indeed persecuted Jews as well as Negroes.

Peter strongly condemned racism, yet never felt *personally* threatened. As an Englishman, he and his ancestors had never been an oppressed minority. On the contrary, a hand-full of British colonials had ruled vast continents for generations, hence the self-confidence (some call it arrogance!) displayed by Brits.

I had one more reason for wanting to move north, albeit a minor one: the climate. I hated the long hot summers and violent storms. Our neighbors assured me that I would get used to it, but I don't think I ever did. Now the widespread use of air-conditioning has not only changed life in the South drastically, but has resulted in modern buildings, which are completely dependent on this technology. Climate control may well be a temporary benefit, as we strive to reduce our energy consumption in the twenty-first century.

Hard Decisions

After a visit to Lexington, KY, where Peter was offered – but eventually declined – a position, he flew to Buffalo, NY to be interviewed by Dean James English of the School of Dentistry at the newly organized State University of New York (SUNY). Peter was very impressed with Dean English's plans for the "new" Dental School and loved everything about Buffalo and its environment. No wonder: his hosts took him not only to nearby Niagara Falls, but also to Letchworth Park, one of the most beautiful State Parks in the eastern United States. The salary he was offered was about twice his current level, which sounded good, but of course the cost of living, especially heating, was much higher too. When Peter handed in his resignation, Dean Joe Volker offered to match SUNY's salary, pointing out that Peter had never *asked* for a raise. This had not occurred to him, unaware as he was of American campus politics. However, we had made up our minds to leave. Selling our house was not a problem, and we prepared to drive north in early August 1963, making the trip our summer vacation. There were a lot of sad aspects to our departure: I had so many good friends, both in our neighborhood and in the Unitarian Church, and I loved our house and the beauty of the surrounding hills. The blow was softened a bit by the fact that our close friends, John and Jean Balint, had recently moved to Albany, NY, where John had accepted a position as chief of gastroenterology at Albany Medical College. Being ignorant of the size of New York State, I thought we might not be very far from each other.

When we told the boys that we would be moving to New York State, Alan was uncertain where this was, but definitely did *not* want to leave his friends. Gregory, on the other hand, knew exactly what was involved, and was appalled.

"I don't want to go to school with Yankees, no ma'am!" he exclaimed.

"Nor me" chimed in Alan.

Foxy offered no opinion, but I was well aware of his habit of snarling at colored persons, who, I imagined would be our close neighbors in the north. I wondered how we could cope with our animals on an extended road trip. Foxy was a seasoned traveler, but the cats, Leo and Patrick, were outdoor creatures, not used to being confined to a house, let alone a car. So we decided sadly not to take them, and found good homes for both cats locally. When we told the neighbors of our plans, their immediate response was "*Buffalo*, you say? Y'all wont see your lawn from November to May, no ma'am."

"Why not?" I asked innocently.

"Because it will be under the snow, that's why."

On hearing this, the boys perked up.

"You mean there is *snow* in Buffalo, Mrs. Adams?"

"Yes, sir, *lots* of snow, almost year round, I heard tell."

Well, that sounded good to me too, and for the first time I began to look forward to the move. I loved snow, and had been skiing in Switzerland when I was a girl. We very rarely had snow in southern England, and here in Birmingham we saw snow just once. That was a momentous occasion. Although only about two inches of snow fell, schools closed and the hilly roads became impassable, as hapless drivers spun out of control, their cars blocking the street, while the men stood shivering in their white business shirts, pondering the situation. The kids loved it and started sledding down our sloping street on trays. Peter and Penny Balint even had a real sled, which was much admired. They, as well as our boys, still owned sturdy English leather shoes, while the local kids wore sneakers that soon got soaked. We built a snowman of course, which soon melted away in the sun – the whole phenomenon only lasted 24 hours. So you can see why the thought of snow endeared Buffalo to us, and made the prospect of moving less threatening.

During our four years in Birmingham I had kept in touch with my relatives in New York City: Aunt Franzel, my father's oldest sister, and her daughter Lotte, who had visited us once, and marveled at the differences in lifestyle between the South and the city she was accustomed to. I now wrote to tell them that we would be moving to Buffalo, and hoped that we would see each other more often. Aunt Franzel, the matriarch of the Lorch family, who knew everybody even remotely related to us, replied, telling me "you have relatives in Buffalo." That came as a pleasant surprise, so I immediately wrote a letter to "Cousin Pine" at the address my aunt had supplied. Her spidery handwriting was hard to decipher, and while I could not read the Pines' first names, I hoped that I got the address right. Before long a nice letter from Ellen Pine arrived. She offered to book a housekeeping unit in a motel for us, as well as look around for a suitable house to rent temporarily. She explained that her mother, Alice Kann, who lived in New York City and was a friend of my aunt's, was my father's second cousin. So Ellen and I are third cousins! We had met as children, at a big Familientag (Family Reunion) in Germany, which I vaguely remember, although I was only 6 years old at the time.

Well, I was actually beginning to look forward to Buffalo. Having relatives there would certainly make the transition to another strange city easier. Then an amazing thing happened: My former professor, Jim Danielli, with whom I had worked as a post-doctoral fellow at King's College, London, called me from *Buffalo*. Getting a long-distance phone call was thrilling in itself, but Jim's message was really exciting. It turned out that he, together with several colleagues and graduate students, had recently emigrated to Buffalo. At the invitation of Dean Dan Murray, he was establishing a research unit in SUNY's School of Pharmacy.[5] Jim had read in a university publication that Peter, who was his former Ph.D. student, had been appointed to a faculty position in the School of Dentistry,

5 Because of the scarcity of research grants in England, many eminent scientists left in search of "greener pastures". Jim Danielli was part of this "brain drain."

thus he realized that we were moving to Buffalo. Since he was in the process of writing grant proposals, he wanted to include me in his team. Yes, he was offering me a job! I was stunned. Having been a "stay- at- home- mom" for 10 years, I felt very uncertain about my ability to do any scientific work whatsoever. I had not kept up with the literature, in other words I was "out of it" – and I said so. Jim replied firmly that it was about time I did some work, and he would put me on his grant as a part- time research assistant starting January 1964.

We're on our Way

As planned, our much traveled Vauxhall station wagon left Shades Mountain in mid-August 1963 and headed north. The back seats were folded down and our luggage was on the roof-rack, thus leaving space for the boys and Foxy to spread out. No, there were no seat belts, let alone airbags! The temperature was in the nineties, and even with all the windows open, the car soon became like an oven. We took our time, exploring the states we traversed, trying to make a mini-vacation of the trip. I do not recall the exact route we took or where we crossed the Mason-Dixon Line, which separates the Southern states from the North. But we noticed the absence of "chain gangs"[6] so common along the Southern highways. These were colored prisoners in striped uniforms, shackled together in groups, performing maintenance jobs along the edges of the road. We could hear the convicts sing while they labored in the sun. The white guards, with their guns, would lounge on the grass nearby.

I clearly remember entering New York State from the west on Route 90 – the NY State Thruway. Wow – a four-lane highway! And the traffic! We had nothing like that in Alabama. It was indicative of things to come: Yankees seemed to live in the fast lane compared with Southerners. Before entering New York we had spent a night in Geneva, Ohio, a little old-fashioned beach resort on Lake Erie. How pleasant to be able to stroll on a beach and enjoy *cool* lake water in August. Then the weather turned gray and downright chilly (probably about 70° F) and the countryside became rather featureless.

6 Chain gangs were abolished in the sixties, but revived in 1995. I do not know if they still exist.

The only remarkable structures were the multitude of pylons and overhead wires everywhere as we approached the Lackawanna toll barrier. Ellen Pine had given us directions to a cottage-court style motel east of Buffalo. It was drizzling steadily when we reached our destination and the area around our cabin was flooded, suggesting that it had been raining for a long time. Everything about the place was cold and damp. Foxy jumped right into the nearest puddle but decided this was not the lukewarm mud he was used to, and quickly dried himself by rolling on the - fortunately mud-colored – motel carpet. Peter checked in while I started to unload the car, and the boys busied themselves looking for a thermostat in the hope of getting some heat into the place. Alas, the heating was not on – after all it was August! Just like in England, we "Southerners" felt miserable. No matter: there was a TV set in our cabin.

A call to the Pines cheered us up. They invited us to dinner at their house on Washington Highway in Snyder (a suburb) so we could get acquainted. It turned out that we had a lot in common: both Martin and Ellen were research scientists, working at Roswell Park Cancer Institute. Two of their three sons, Nat and Jay, were about the ages of Gregory and Alan, while Billy was still a toddler. Martin and Ellen had good news for us: a house just across the street from theirs had a "For Rent" sign – maybe we could get it! It was hard to find an *unfurnished* house for rent, and this landlord was very elusive. We literally took turns to sit on his doorstep on Washington Highway until we finally got hold of him. Yes, the house was still available and we signed a lease for one year with option to buy.

6. New Schools, New Jobs

"At work, you think of the children you have left at home. At home, you think of the work you've left unfinished. Such a struggle is unleashed within yourself. Your heart is rent." Golda Meir

At Home in Snyder

Our much-traveled furniture arrived and we gratefully moved from the motel into our rented house on Washington Highway in the village of Snyder. Names can be deceptive: Washington was not a highway, just a quiet tree-lined street in a suburb that had no doubt been a village fifty years ago. Snyder is within the town of Amherst, about three miles east of the city limits of Buffalo and the University campus. Our temporary home was a two-story brown-shingled frame house dating from the early 1900s. It had some beautiful woodwork and a few stained-glass windows, as well as hardwood floors and stairs. Yes *stairs,* something I did not have to cope with since we left our third floor walk-up flat in Kentish Town nine years before. Ranch houses were not so common here: we were told they would be more expensive to heat.

It was mid-August 1963, and time to register the boys for the nearby Harlem Road Elementary School, where Gregory was ready to enter sixth grade and Alan third grade. The principal, Mr. Davis, while looking over the boys' very good report cards, predicted that their grades would drop somewhat in their new school.

"Coming from England, you would not know this," he said, " Southern schools have a very low standard compared with New York State, but I'm sure your sons will soon catch up."

I put this down to the man's "Yankee superiority complex" and did not pass on the information. As it happened both boys were somewhat ahead of their Harlem Road classmates, but Alan encountered "communication problems". Having spent four of his seven years in Alabama, he spoke with a marked Southern accent, and his enunciation was not helped by the lack of front teeth. Nevertheless I was surprised when, one day at dinner, he said

"Guess what? Me and another foreign (!) boy were sent to the speech teacher today 'cause Miss Porcher says I don't talk good."

"So what did the speech teacher say?" I ventured.

"Oh, she knew right away that I come from the South, and she said not to worry about it."

The speech therapist must have had a word with Miss Porcher, Alan's home room teacher, because nothing more was said about the matter. Both boys soon adopted the – to our ears – rude manners and speech of Western New York. "Yea" and "Yep" replaced the Southern "yes, sir or ma'am," and I missed the friendly parting "y'all come back see us." I guess I had begun to like Southern gentility!

The University of Buffalo, a private institution, had recently been taken over by the State, and was now the State University of New York (SUNY), but everybody still called it UB. The new president, Martin Meyerson, had great plans and vowed to make UB the "Berkeley of the East". New faculty members, some very eminent, were recruited from all over the country and funding was lavish. Peter got himself a rusty old bike (he was warned that his nice Raleigh would be stolen!) and rode to the campus most days, allowing me to use the Vauxhall. So the boys and I explored our new environment, often with Ellen's help, until school started after Labor Day. Before leaving Birmingham I had read as much as possible about Buffalo, using the World Book Encyclopedia, and concluded that it was a beautiful city, with elm tree-lined streets and spacious parks designed by Frederick Law Olmsted. Architectural gems abounded, including several Frank Lloyd Wright houses. Buffalo's nickname was the "Queen City": It reigned over Lake Erie, whose pristine sandy beaches invited city dwellers to relax in the sun at weekends. Pleasure craft crossed the lake to the Canadian side, where the amusement park of Crystal Beach beckoned. And to top it all, spectacular Niagara Falls, one of the Seven Wonders of the World, was just a few miles away. I was looking forward to living in this city, with its famous Albright Knox Art Gallery, Kleinhans Music Hall and other cultural amenities. It would be a pleasant change from our life on remote Shades Mountain, and more stimulating for growing boys.

Yet here we were, about to settle in suburban Snyder. Why? First of all the rosy picture painted by The World Book was somewhat out-of-date. The majestic elm trees of Buffalo died of elm disease and had been replaced with young maples. Yes, the architecture was – and still is – remarkable in certain areas of the city, but there was also much urban blight and, just like in Birmingham, affluent white residents were migrating to the suburbs, leaving poor black citizens behind. Intruding four lane highways allowed the suburbanites to get in and out of the city fast, but degraded beautiful old neighborhoods and prevented access to the waterfront. The beaches were polluted and closed to bathers.

But what really deterred us from looking for a house in the city was the school system. Everybody we met, especially the realtors, told us "It's ok to live in Buffalo if you enroll your boys in The Nichols School." This was (and still is) the only secular private school in the city of Buffalo, an excellent boys'[1] school modeled on the typical English Public (meaning private!) School. Peter was educated in such schools, but we both felt our boys should attend American public schools. So – back to the suburbs which offered good schools, albeit in a cultural desert. Well, we reasoned, the kids can easily ride a bus into the city to visit museums, the zoo or the art gallery. Wrong again: just as in Birmingham, buses were scarce here, especially at weekends. Nobody cared about people who were too young, too old or too poor to drive a car, and this is still true over forty years later.

Back to the Lab

Once the boys were settled at Harlem Road School, which was easy walking distance from our house, I started to investigate my prospective job in Jim Danielli's new *Unit for Theoretical Biology* at UB's School of Pharmacy. Eleven years had elapsed since I left the Zoology Department at King's College, London, and metamorphosed from post-doctoral research fellow into full-time wife and mother. Readers of the first volume of my memoirs, *Chance*

1 The Nichols School is now co-ed

and Choice: My First thirty Years, will be familiar with my research, which I will briefly summarize here to help you understand my new projects.

After the completion of my Ph.D. in 1948, Dr. J.F. Danielli invited me to join him to study the relationship between the nucleus and cytoplasm in living cells. Our "guinea pigs" were one-celled organisms called amoebas, and we were particularly interested in "cytoplasmic inheritance", in other words: are there genetic determinants in the *cytoplasm* in addition to the known genes in the nucleus? Our initial experiments, published in the 1950s, involved the technique of nuclear transplantation, i.e. moving a nucleus from one amoeba into the cytoplasm of another by microsurgery.

We found that, indeed, certain characters could be passed on by *something* in the cytoplasm. It was not known at the time that mitochondria (and chloroplasts in plant cells) contain nucleic acids, in addition to the DNA in the cell's nucleus. In fact it was not known that DNA *is* the genetic material! Francis Crick, the co-discoverer of DNA, jokingly referred to this period in the history of biology as "B.C.", meaning "Before Crick".

Biology had been radically transformed during the years I was vegetating as a housewife, reading women's magazines instead of *Nature* and *Science*. Indeed I had missed out on the birth of the New Biology, as it is has been called, ushered in by the discovery of the structure of DNA by Watson, Crick and Wilkins in 1953. Since I was educated "B.C.", I was ignorant of molecular biology, and had a lot of catching up to do, which I did gradually, while working in the lab at the same time. Although my official starting date was to be January 1964, I spent time at UB throughout the fall, whenever I managed to get away from home.

Danielli had continued the study of cytoplasmic inheritance in amoebas with the help of several post-doctoral fellows, including my old friend and colleague Muriel Ord, as well as Shirley Hawkins. Neither was able to join him in Buffalo because their husbands did not want to leave London (yes, that's often the fate of married professional women!). However Jim brought two research assistants with him: Audrey Muggleton, his long-time technician, and Dr. Kwang Jeon, who had emigrated from Korea to London.

Equally important: he had brought over the amoeba cultures I had established at King's College in the late 1940s.

Other members of Jim's group included senior scientists as well as post-docs and graduate students, so altogether there were about 30 Brits at UB's School of Pharmacy. In 1966 Jim Danielli founded the *Center for Theoretical Biology* (CTB). This was an interdisciplinary organization with associated faculty members from 16 different departments at UB in addition to research associates, who were paid out of Jim's grant and had neither tenure nor fringe benefits. I belonged to the latter category, but I was so happy to be in the lab again that my low salary and lack of status did not deter me. Nor did it strike me as odd that *all* faculty members were male. The few women, referred to as "girls", were either researchers on "soft money"(grants) or technicians. Kwang Jeon decided to call our amoeba lab the *Cell Physiology Laboratory of the Center for Theoretical Biology* to give it an identity within this diffuse organization. Neither Kwang nor I considered ourselves *theoretical* biologists, but we joked that somebody had to do experiments, so that the rest of the team could theorize about them!

In 1967 the CTB moved out of the School of Pharmacy and into its own building, where we had plenty of space and, thanks to being on the concrete first floor, no vibration problems. While theoretical physics and theoretical chemistry were well-established specialties, biology was just beginning to acquire theoretical underpinnings. Jim Danielli was one of the pioneers in this field and editor of the new Journal of Theoretical Biology. At the urging of Tom Bardos, a professor in the School of Pharmacy, Dean Daniel Murray had obtained funding for the British group and established it in the Department of Biochemical Pharmacology. Dean Dan, as we called him, took an active interest in our work and often looked in to see how we were doing.

Having shown that cytoplasmic (or extra- chromosomal) inheritance existed in amoebas we now studied this phenomenon in more detail, injecting various fractions of cytoplasm into intact amoebas and testing the resulting clones for transmission of certain characters, such as antigenic properties and drug sensitivity. I will not burden my readers with technical details. If anyone wishes to know more, I would refer them to our published work (see appendix).

Most published papers, however short, involve months or years of experiments as well as collaboration between many people, from senior scientists to dishwashers. The latter are very important where amoebas are concerned because these organisms do not tolerate tap water, so everything has to be meticulously rinsed in several changes of double- distilled water. Disposable Petri dishes were available, but some of these early plastics were toxic, and we found that the amoebas grew best in Pyrex glass casserole lids made in nearby Corning, NY. When, to our horror, Corning Glass Works decided to discontinue this line in favor of opaque pastel-colored casseroles, we bought up their total stock of clear dishes, enough for the rest of my working life.

My vibration -free work bench, built of concrete, was located in a special temperature controlled cubicle, kept at 17° C (about 62° F), because surgery on amoebas proved to be virtually impossible at higher temperatures[2], a fact that I had not even noticed in England, where room temperatures rarely exceeded 65° F. So my working life was spent in this chilly, damp[3] box, hunched over the rough concrete bench, which chafed my knees. A fur-lined lab coat would have been nice, but in fact I made do with sweaters, wool leggings and fingerless mittens.

The first technician I hired did not last long in this environment, but eventually Lorraine Powers joined us. She proved to be wonderful, although she had neither a college degree nor any scientific background, or maybe *because* of that. She was a good housekeeper and mother, enjoyed washing dishes, and regarded the amoebas as her babies, to be fed, kept clean, and looked after. In case you wonder what amoebas eat, I will tell you that they are predators. By means of their pseudopods they engulf any living creature that happens to come their way. If the organism is too big, they will even "bite" off a piece. One of Lorraine's jobs was to grow certain ciliates (free-swimming one celled animals), called *Tetrahymena* as fodder for the amoebas. We had shelves installed in the cold room, and they were soon filled with Pyrex dishes stacked up to the ceiling. We

2 Amoeba cell membranes become more elastic and do not puncture readily above 60° F.

3 We installed a humidifier to reduce evaporation.

needed *a lot* of amoebas for biochemical work.

While catching up with the literature that had accumulated during my ten years of absence from the field, I was struck by how few researchers were using our technique of nuclear transplantation. Apart from Lester Goldstein's group at the University of Philadelphia and Alex Yudin's department in Leningrad, nobody did research similar to ours. Why should I care? Well, scientists like to see their work confirmed and extended by other researchers; it gives it credibility and stimulates progress. The main reason why our method did not become popular was its perceived extreme difficulty. This view originated with two eminent researchers, Robert Chambers and M.J. Kopac, both of New York University, who had attempted nuclear transplantation for years, did not succeed, and promptly declared the procedure to be "impossible". I find this attitude typical for many male researchers:

"I can't do this, therefore it can't be done."

Women tend to have a more humble attitude. They will say, "I can't do this because I am incompetent or clumsy, but if I try harder I might get it to work."

It took me many years to convince Chambers and Kopac that indeed nuclei *could* be transplanted successfully. Amoeba are about 0.1mm in diameter when rounded up, i.e. the size of a period on this printed page. To immobilize amoebas while they are being operated one holds them with a tiny glass hook in a small drop of medium. Then a thin glass probe is used to push the nucleus out of one cell and directly into another. If the nucleus touches the surrounding medium during the transfer it will be destroyed. The trickiest part was making the little glass hooks with an instrument called a "microforge".

For years I hoped that an easier technique of transplanting nuclei might be found, and one day in 1966 it actually came about, thanks to a chance observation. In an 1854 lecture Louis Pasteur, the famous French bacteriologist, said "Chance favors the prepared mind," and I often thought about that while slogging through mostly routine procedures in the lab. One day I was using a small pipette to pick up some amoebas, which were crawling on an agar[4] surface and noticed how difficult this was. The amoebas really stuck to the agar,

---

4 Agar forms a gel rather like gelatin. As amoebas crawl on it, the debris is left behind; it's like a drive-through car wash for them.

making it hard to dislodge them. A light went on in my head - hey, *this stuff is sticky!* Maybe I could operate on an amoeba *without the hook* by sticking it on agar! I shared the idea with Kwang and we set about putting it into practice, trying out different concentrations of agar smeared on microscope slides. It worked like a charm. No more tiny hooks to mess with. Using the agar method we could mass-produce any desired surgically manipulated amoebas in a fraction of the time it usually took. After we published this method, other researchers soon picked it up and our work was confirmed and extended in different labs.

A year later another chance occurrence, initially disastrous, led to a much more important discovery. But before telling you about it let's look at how Peter and the boys fared while I was in the lab.

"The Maid is Asleep in *My* Bed!"

Juggling work and childcare is of course commonplace nowadays, but it is still far from easy. Each family has to find its own way. Many mothers have to work outside the home for economic reasons; others, like myself wish to return to their profession, yet at the same time want to be perfect mothers. Well, it can't be done; one has to compromise. I decided to work part-time and hire a maid/housekeeper for the hours I was at work. Fortunately I was able to choose my own hours, and initially I worked three full days a week. Our first maid was a black[5] woman, called Arsie. The boys giggled about her name, but liked her, because she baked wonderful rich cakes every time she came, using a lot of eggs, butter and heavy cream. She had no recipes; it was all "in her head". Actually, like our maid in Alabama, Arsie turned out to be illiterate. Yet she had a driver's license! I don't know how she had managed to avoid the written test or how she navigated around town without being able to read street signs. But I was reluctant to let her drive the boys to after-school activities. When I came home from work, I found her busy cooking. The boys were "playing outside", but she had no idea where. Almost my total salary went to Arsie, not to mention the skyrocketing grocery bills.

5 Negroes then preferred to be called black, rather than colored, eventually this would change to African-American

Our next maid, Jenny, seemed all right for a while until one day Alan called me at work to report,

"The maid is asleep in *my* bed!"

I suggested that he wake her, but apparently he was not successful. By the time I was able to get home, Alan had gone out to play, Greg was still in school and, yes, Jenny, was snoring on Alan's little bed, dead drunk. That was the end of Jenny, although I must say she never touched our liquor cabinet, she brought her own supplies. At this point I changed my tactics: instead of working three full days, I worked five mornings, so I was home after school. At weekends Peter took charge, and I treasured those quiet days with the amoebas. As the boys got older I increased my hours and hired a woman to clean and wash twice a week. That woman was Helen Hoffman, who stayed with us for many years, and became a good friend. We share a birthday – June 13th – and Helen is now 94, still active and independent. She loved the boys and did not mind the chaotic state of their rooms. On the contrary: when Gregory, the messier of the two, eventually left to go to college, she felt positively deprived.

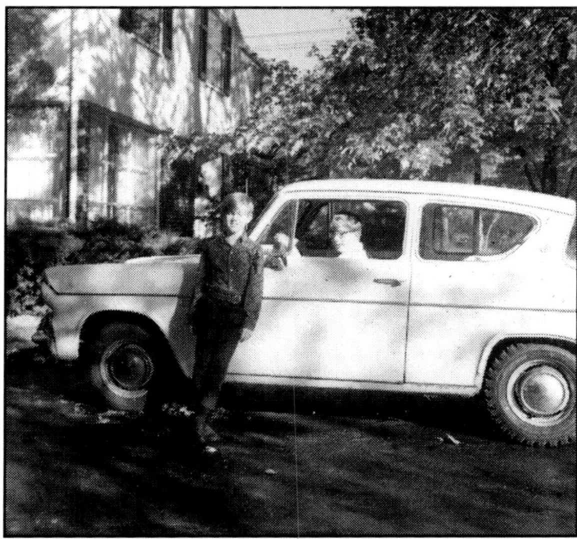

A car of my own: little "Angela". 1965

Childcare was just one problem; I also had to have transportation to and from UB. Having some money saved up, I took the big step of buying a car of my own which I called Angela. It was a tiny British Ford Anglia, used of course, but in good shape until its floor gave way, corroded from long winters of salted roads.

"But what do you do all day?"

I had vaguely imagined that as our sons spent more and more time in school, I would be free to devote myself to my work. Not so! It came as a surprise to me that mothers were supposed to be heavily involved with all sorts of projects such as baking cupcakes, watching Little League baseball games, attending band concerts and school plays. Greg, who had begun to play the piano in Birmingham, now switched to trumpet, for which his school provided lessons, and soon he was in the school band. His practice sessions at home were pretty noisy, but worse was to come!

Alan had started to play piano at age four, long before he could read. He accompanied me to Greg's piano lessons, where he sat quietly and listened. Then, when we got home, he reproduced whatever little piece his brother was working on. His tiny hands flew across the keys and I thought he really had a feel for this. But because he was left-handed, the accompaniment overshadowed the tune when he played. Alan begged to be allowed to have lessons too. After we settled in our home in Snyder, we found a left-handed graduate student from the UB music department, who sympathized with this little southpaw, and went along with Alan's taste for jazz and rock rather than sonatas. So far, so good – a great pianist in the making! I was wrong: one day Alan announced that he wanted to play a different instrument, *something louder than Greg's trumpet.* He found a big old kettledrum at a church sale and filled the house with happy noise. He really stuck with this one, graduating to a good snare drum and, eventually, to a full drum set with expensive cymbals.

When Alan was 11 years old he spotted an ad in the newspaper, which announced auditions at the Studio Arena Theater in Buffalo for a "little drummer boy" to play in the forthcoming production of the Gilbert and Sullivan opera *HMS Pinafore*.

"Please *please* take me to the audition, they want a boy *small* for his age who is a *great* drummer, that's ME!"

So off we went at the appointed time to find a long line of drum-toting boys, all eager to be in the show. Parents, mostly moms of course, waited patiently in the lobby all afternoon. Alan remained hopeful and, a few days later, he jumped with joy when Studio Arena called, offering him the part. Two boys took turns appearing in the opera and they shared the costume.

Alan had to be at the Theater four evenings a week plus some matinees, and he loved it all. He learned a lot about the stage, and soon both of us knew *HMS Pinafore* by heart. Peter, who had acted in Gilbert and Sullivan operas when he was a boy, took occasional turns driving our drummer boy downtown. I usually brought a book to read in the lobby, but sometimes I watched the show. It was on one of these evenings that something exciting happened: There is a lovely scene where the drummer boy crosses the drawbridge to the ship "drumming the captain on board". When the familiar cue tune started, Alan, followed by pipe-playing sailors, marched towards the bridge. To my horror the drawbridge did not come down – it appeared to be stuck in the open position! Alan could not see this, since the big parade drum slung around his neck obscured his view. I held my breath. The procession advanced in step to the music. *Seconds* before Alan reached the non-existing bridge one of the sailors swung him in the air and leaped across the gap. Alan never missed a beat and the show went on. I doubt that anyone in the audience noticed anything amiss.

Alan's love for drumming endured and he eventually played in a rock group with friends. I had a choice between driving Alan and all his equipment to rehearsals or allowing the group to play at our house. Since we had converted our in-house garage into a den, there was plenty of room for the kids to hang out. In summer the group practiced outside, after politely informing the neighbors, and making allowances for babies' nap times. Once the musicians were assembled on our lawn, I got out of earshot.

Coming home from the grocery store one day, I spotted a police car parked outside our house. The young officer was sitting in

Alan with his drum set, 1967

From the Amherst Bee. Winter 1968.

Alan H. Staple plays the part of the drummer boy in the Studio Arena's production of *H.M.S. Pinafore*. Alan is eleven years old and has been playing drums for about three years. A seventh grader at Amherst Junior High, he is a natural for the role, having been born in England of British parents.

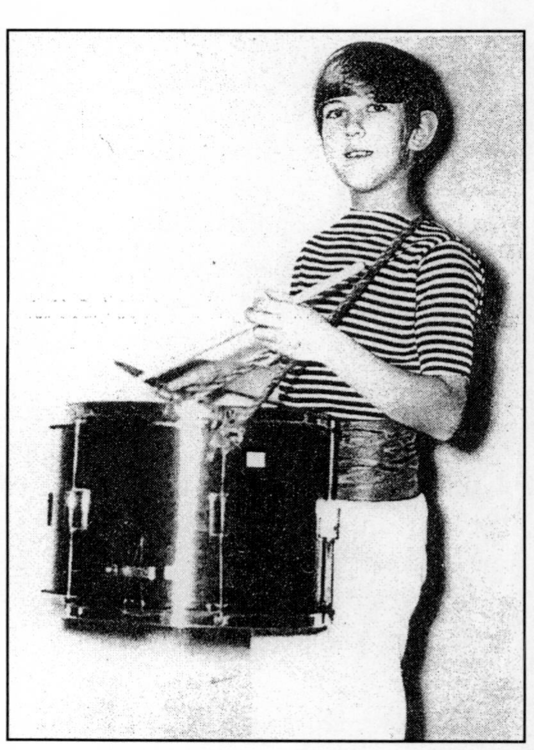

my deckchair, tapping his foot to the music, oblivious of my presence. During an interval I managed to get his attention and gathered that there had been some complaints from residents several blocks away, so he felt it his duty to pay a visit. But no law was broken. Mild clashes with the police were not uncommon. It seemed that being a longhaired teenager was by definition, undesirable. Once Alan was picked up by the "fuzz" simply because he was *running* along the sidewalk, and, by coincidence, there had been a theft in the neighborhood.

But when the teens decided to "party" at our house we had to keep a close watch. Older boys would bring in beer, and lounged around their cars in the driveway. Things could easily get out of control. Our days of "baby sitting" were not over! The youngsters did not stay put – they roamed around the neighborhood, preferably settling at a home where the parents were out. Greg and Alan were a year younger than their classmates, so they were often passengers in beginning drivers' cars, which scared me. Yes, they had curfews and usually observed them, occasionally calling to keep us informed of their whereabouts. But still I worried and I really hated Saturday nights.

Nowadays we hear about "soccer moms" and "hockey moms". In the sixties and seventies neither of these games were available to our kids. Baseball and football were "in". Fortunately our sons were not built for football, a game I hate. Gregory was not very interested in team sports, but enjoyed tennis. Alan soon became a fierce Little League pitcher, so Peter and I spent many evenings watching this – to me rather boring and long-winded – game. Alan was a born ball player: even as a toddler, he was able to catch and throw a ball with precision and, invariably with his left hand. He played ping-pong as soon as his head cleared the table and begged me to play tennis with him.

I was a mediocre tennis player and it wasn't long before Alan beat me, chasing me around our local school tennis courts, to the amusement of onlookers. One day a woman approached us on the court, introduced herself as Bea Massman, the coach of Amherst Senior High School's tennis team, and announced that "this boy" would one day be on her team.

"Miss Massman," I said, "Alan is *seven* years old!"

"Right," she replied, "high time he started tournament playing."

She found a high school student to be his personal coach, and before long I was driving to tournaments "to bring home the trophies," as Alan put it. So much for spending my summers in the lab! Peter, an excellent tennis player, was usually too busy to practice with Alan, but did occasionally take a turn at driving. My role at tournaments was to sit well back on the bleachers ("you make me nervous") and provide food and clean clothes. Like most of the tournament players, Alan had one favorite shirt, which he *had* to wear for finals. He fasted before his game, but would devour several hamburgers if he won. On the rare occasions that he was eliminated before the semi-finals, he was sad and ate sparingly. But he was never a bad loser. I watched with disgust the tantrums some of the boys engaged in. I saw one boy throw his racket over the fence onto a railway track after losing a set and his mother calmly replaced it with a new one. Alan soon got over his defeats and looked forward to the next tournament. He owned one racket.

Winners of a 12 and under tennis tournament. Summer 1968. Alan is on the left.

Alan stuck with drumming and tennis. Today, a middle-aged man, he plays in "father-son" tournaments with Justin, and the two of them make loud music together, Justin playing the guitar. Indeed Justin has his own rock group, so history repeats itself. Thus, looking back on my days as a "tennis mom" and band driver, it was all well worth it, even though it did nothing to advance my career as a scientist.

7. The Sixties

"If someone thinks that love and peace is a cliché that must have been left behind in the sixties, that's his problem. Love and peace are eternal." John Lennon

"The Times They Are A-Changing"

Before describing some exciting new developments in the lab, I will give you an idea of what was going on outside the confines of my chilly cubicle and our cozy home. It was 1964; the beginning of the turbulent decade usually referred to as "The Sixties", and the world has never been the same since.

What comes to mind when you think of the 1960s? For me the era evokes an old-fashioned illustrated Alphabet Book that children used to treasure, and it would look something like this:

A stands for Assassinations and Anti-War protesters
B is for the Beatles who revolutionized popular music
C stands for the Counterculture and for Civil Rights
D is for Draft Dodgers and for recreational Drugs
E stands for the Environment and Earth Day
F for the Flower Children and Free Love
G stands for the Generation Gap and Gay Rights
H is for the Hippies, Happenings and Hootenannies

We could go on like this through P for Psychedelics and the Pill, until we reach W for Woodstock and Women's Liberation.

One of the mottoes of the sixties turn-on, dropout youth culture was: "Trust no-one over thirty." Here I was, a middle aged woman over *forty*, yet I could not help being affected. There was much talk of a "generation gap". Yes, these youngsters *were* different. In the late fifties, just after the McCarthy era, I had been struck by how conservative young Americans were, but mistakenly attributed it to the fact that we lived in the Deep South, the "Bible Belt", where children were small replicas of their parents and aspired to become like them.

This had changed dramatically. Nobody who worked at a university or had teenage children could fail to notice this new spirit. Social taboos we had taken for granted were questioned and dismissed. *Why* should girls wear bras and uncomfortable pantyhose? *Why* should boys have haircuts? Didn't Jesus have long hair and a beard? Why should we study Latin and math rather than spend the time consciousness-raising or just loving each other? What is the point of grades? Let's attend a teach-in about Vietnam instead of taking that exam. What's wrong with sex? *Make Love not War!* And so it went. The topics ranged from the profound to the ridiculous, from gay rights to bra burning.

Over forty years have passed since this epic decade. That longhaired, bearded youth and his braless, barefoot girlfriend, wearing tee shirts tie-dyed in psychedelic hues, have turned into law-abiding citizens about to collect Social Security. Yes, it's over. In fact it's history, worthy of courses at high schools and universities, as well as carefully researched books.[1] But the spirit of that time has left its effect on our children's generation and, to some extent, on my generation. I agree with Bob Dylan's 1992 comment:

"People are still living off the table scraps of the sixties. They are still being passed around – the music and the ideas."

Has the influence of the sixties continued into the twenty first century? I don't think so. Contemporary kids seem to dwell in a virtual world dominated by electronic devices as essential to their social well being as their eyes, ears and vocal chords. They tend to live a "wired" existence, experiencing the world at second hand through signals delivered by flickering screens and chattering headphones. Texting has replaced person-to-person conversation and "friends" are images on *Facebook,* who leave inane messages on your cyber "wall".

Gregory was 13 in 1966, a freshman at Amherst Senior High School, and Alan was in sixth grade. The spirit of revolt trickled

---

1 For example Tom Brokaw's recent book *Boom! Voices of the Sixties NY*: Random House 2007

down to these youngsters from the rebel students at UB. They, too, demanded a loosening of rules. They resented the dress code and other irksome restrictions of school life. They stopped cutting their hair, and some of the older boys proudly sprouted beards. Away with chinos and button-down shirts: jeans (preferably torn and faded) topped by emblazoned tee shirts became the fashion. Socks and shoes were "establishment", barefoot was cool.

I remember one day getting a call from the assistant principal of Alan's school. Being in the middle of a tricky experiment, I resented the interruption, but our secretary had put the call through, thinking it might be an emergency. No, the administrator assured me, my son was in excellent health. The problem, it turned out, was his *toes*. They were visible to all through the straps of his sandals. Socks must be worn in school. I apologized.

"Any other pressing problems?" I gave up on my experiment and devoted myself to the distressed assistant principal, while making a mental note to supply the school with Peter's phone number, rather than mine.

"Yes, Mrs. Staple, one other thing: your son's hair is *beyond* shoulder length, very unsightly, *please* take him to the barber."

Alan's straight, fair hair would eventually grow to almost waist length before he graduated from High School at age 17. But it was clean and shiny. He shampooed it every morning, even though this meant getting up earlier, and bicycling to school with wet hair. For tennis practice and tournaments he wore a neat ponytail. My patience exhausted, I advised the educator to pay more attention to what was *inside* boys' heads, rather than what grew on top. And I hung up.

Remembering the ugly "butch" haircuts that the boys insisted on only a few years ago in Alabama, I took this new craze in stride, although there were certainly annoying moments. When friends came over to visit, I could never tell if they were boys or girls. Alan advised me to look at their feet (often bare), which did help a bit. And that reminds me of shopping for shoes: Buying well-fitting ski boots, always a difficult task, was made almost impossible until a perceptive store manager suggested we try a *boy's* boot.

"I hope you don't mind, but your daughter has rather wide

feet."

One day, while walking on the beach with Alan, a group of girls were giggling hysterically behind our backs. As they passed us I caught their comments: "Look at her – *topless*!"

Gregory lent me some of his favorite books, which I tried to relate to. I did not care for Jack Kerouac, William Burroughs and other "beat generation" authors, some of who, notably Allen Ginsberg, Robert Creeley and John Barth were actually here at UB. But I liked Ken Kesey, whose *One Flew Over the Cuckoo's Nest* was made into a hilarious film, which is still shown occasionally. And I really got hooked on Carlos Castanedo. Having previously read Aldous Huxley's *Doors of Perception*, I was familiar with the effect of psychedelic drugs. A psychiatrist friend of Huxley's, Humphry Oswald wrote, "To fathom hell or soar angelic, just take a pinch of psychedelic" thus coining a new term for the sixties.

But let's come back to Castaneda, whose books describe the author's travels in Mexico's Sonora Desert between 1961 and 1965 in the company of Shaman-Sorcerer Don Juan, who taught him amazing secrets revealed by the use of mescaline.[2] Castaneda's first book was originally written as a paper for a field archeology class at UCLA. Nobody seems to know whether Don Juan was a real person or maybe several persons. Perhaps Castaneda imagined it all. Be that as it may, I was fascinated by Don Juan's wisdom, and even now remember,

"Death is our eternal companion. It is always on our left at an arm's length. It has always been watching you. It always will until the day it taps you."

When I first read this I was in my forties; now, at 85, it seems more daunting, and I look over my left shoulder whenever the usual aches and pains of old age strike. I also remember reading Herman Hesse's *Damian* and *Siddharhta*, books written in Germany in the 20s, which became popular with the "hippy" generation who resonated to the recurring theme of the "quest for enlightenment". Hesse died in 1962.

A very different book that had considerable influence in the sixties was Harper Lee's *To Kill a Mockingbird*, published in 1960.

---

2 Carlos Castaneda. *The Teachings of Don Juan: A Yaqui Way of Knowledge* (1968) is the first of the series.

Being about the segregated South, it was of special interest to me, and this book opened up a little known world to Americans in the Northern states. It, too, was made into a famous movie, starring Gregory Peck , and has withstood the test of time.

But of all the literature of the sixties, I would rate Betty Friedan's *The Feminine Mystique* (1963) as most influential, not just in my life, but also in the lives of countless women – and men. Betty Goldstein (later Friedan), a 1942 graduate of Smith College[3], decided to survey her graduating class to find out what they were doing several years after graduation. It struck her that virtually none of these intelligent and highly educated women were pursuing a career, although they had great plans while at college. The typical graduate was married to a professional or businessman and was at home raising her young family. She loved her husband and her children, was financially well off and certainly should have been happy. Yet, as Betty discovered, these women were miserable. Almost 90% regretted their early marriage and failure to put their education to good use. After more extensive study, she found that the Smith alumnae were in fact typical of well-educated, middle-class women all over the United States. She called the "problem without a name" the *feminine mystique*.

It became more and more evident that educated women had difficulties finding appropriate employment, and once hired, they were consistently paid less than men in similar positions. A married woman was not considered "head of household", in spite of the fact that she most likely managed all household and childcare chores in addition to her outside job. The prevailing attitude was that married women did not really *need* the money, since their husbands supported them. So, did unmarried women get better pay? No, of course not: they were taking employment away from men, who were "heads of households". It all made no sense, since workers should be paid for the quality of their performance, not according to their "need".

Many educated women worked as volunteers in progressive organizations such as the civil rights and anti-war movements. What did they do? Typically they addressed envelopes, staffed the mimeograph machines and made coffee, while their male colleagues made policy and gave press conferences. The Women's Movement

3 A prestigious women's college in Massachusetts

of the sixties and seventies, sparked initially by Betty Friedan's book, exposed the prevailing sexual division of labor in society. One of its flaws was that it only addressed itself to the problems of middleclass, predominantly white women. Working class women and women of color felt left out of this movement.

In 1963 President Jack F. Kennedy established the President's Commission on the Status of Women, chaired by Eleanor Roosevelt, which clearly documented widespread discrimination against women. As I mentioned before, JFK, who was a fervent proponent of Civil Rights, did not manage to pass the Civil Rights Act in his lifetime. This event finally came about in 1964 under President Lyndon Johnson. Originally designed to eliminate employment discrimination against Negroes, it did include – as an afterthought – Title VII, which forbade discrimination in employment on account of sex. It took another eight years before Title IX was passed, which prohibited sex discrimination in education. Finally it became possible for girls to train for traditionally "male" occupations and to compete in well-supported athletic teams, something boys had always taken for granted. In 1973, about a year after Title IX, women's status in the sports world received a tremendous boost by the spectacular tennis match between Bobby Riggs and Billie Jean King. Riggs, a great tennis player and even greater male chauvinist, had always maintained that no woman could ever beat him. King accepted the challenge and, in a much-publicized match, beat him in three straight sets.

Various organizations to promote women's rights sprang up in the sixties, notably the National Organization for Women (NOW), founded by Betty Friedan in 1966, of which I became an early member. The term "feminism" was considered derogatory by many (including women!), perhaps conjuring up visions of bra-burning, man-hating females. I often heard women profess that they want better opportunities and pay, but – "Mind you, I'm not a women's libber." Extremists were certainly not representative of the Women's Movement, yet the press often picked up their negative view of motherhood – "they want to destroy the nuclear family." This sounds rather quaint in the 21st century, with the divorce rate at over 50% and a majority of city children growing up in one- parent (guess which one?) families. The "nuclear family" is the exception now, destroyed not by women, but by the irresponsibility of young men.

I did, and still do, consider myself a feminist, meaning that I strive towards *equal rights and opportunities* for both sexes. This is very different from aspiring to be "equal to men", surely an undesirable goal in view of the mess that men have made of world politics. The goal of feminists is best expressed by the Equal Right Amendment, proposed in 1972, which reads:

Equal rights under the law shall not be denied or abridged by the United States or by any state on account of sex.

This simple statement, which is intended to end *de facto* discrimination, has not been passed into law as yet, more than thirty years after the initial proposal.

Ruminations on Being Female

I have often been asked whether I *personally* experienced sex discrimination, so I will take a little "time out" from the sixties in order to discuss this question. Looking back at my childhood in Germany, described in detail in my first volume, *Chance and Choice,* I don't think I was restricted in any way by being a girl. All my friends were girls and I had a good time, not only doing traditional "girl things" but also roaming around freely on my bike, walking in the nearby woods with my dog Kuno, and swimming in the Main river. I learned to ski and hoped to go winter camping one day, although my big brother, Walter, told me that only boys could do that. Much to my elegant mother's distress I hated to dress up, but apart from that, being a girl wasn't too bad. I attended a co-ed Jewish school and thought of boys as rather silly.

After our emigration to England I attended a girls' high school, where we wore uniforms, so clothes did not play a big part in my teenage life. Nor did boyfriends. Academically, we girls did not compete with boys of course, and it was never suggested to me that girls could *not* become scientists, doctors or anything else they aspired to. All our teachers were "spinsters", highly educated women who had chosen a teaching career over marriage. I remember being very sad when my favorite history teacher had to leave the school in order to get married, and realized early that a girl had to choose between having a career or a family. This worried me, since I had vaguely thought of going to medical school, yet I also hoped to get married one day and have many children.

It came as a surprise to me that our medical school in Birmingham, England had a strict quota for female students, so only the most brilliant girls, chosen by the Dean, were admitted. But I did not give this much thought, and did not encounter sex discrimination during my undergraduate years at Birmingham University. Things were decidedly different when I was a Ph.D. student at Middlesex Hospital Medical School in London. This institution did not accept female *medical* students, but my professor, Samson Wright, smuggled me in as his laboratory assistant, simultaneously enrolling me at London University from where I obtained my doctorate. Suddenly I was in a virtually all-male world, not allowed to eat in the dining room or use any restroom in the building. Again, I don't recall being upset over this. There was another student-technician in the department, so the two of us joined the secretary for lunch at a little café across the street. We did not socialize with the all-male faculty or the medical students.

King's College, London, where I spent my post-doctoral years was co-ed at all levels and our department (Zoology) had some distinguished women faculty, one of whom eventually became a Fellow of the Royal Society – a very rare honor for women at that time. But even at King's the men had their own dining facilities, while we "girls" were relegated to a committee room to eat our sandwiches, provided no meeting was scheduled there. I noticed that, although all faculty members had doctorates, only the men were addressed as "doctor". As a newly minted Ph.D., I felt a little disappointed, but soon accepted it as normal. Many years later, when I was a new assistant professor at Canisius College in Buffalo, NY, and one of only a handful of women faculty at this Jesuit institution, my students addressed me as "Mrs. Lorch". This conjured up images of my late mother! If the kids wanted to "Mrs." me, I would be Mrs. *Staple*. At the advice of a more experienced female colleague, I wrote "Dr. Joan Lorch" on the blackboard at the start of each new course. Our students needed to know that, yes, women do get doctorates, and *you* could be one of them.

In the 1970s and 80s there were few professional women, and this was especially true in the physical sciences. If you asked a student to name three famous woman scientists, she would say "Madame Curie (yes, not Dr. Curie) and....well, I can't think of anybody else."

The contribution of women, not only to science and medicine, but also to literature and politics, was virtually ignored in history courses. And since it had been impossible for women to get published, their work was difficult to track, often appearing under their husbands' names or male pseudonyms. This was one of several reasons for the emergence of the field of *Women's Studies* on the academic scene. I was very interested in this development but also realized that, if I wanted to succeed in my career of teaching and research at Canisius College, it was not advisable to get involved in this controversial discipline.

Was there discrimination against women at Canisius College? Of course there was, but I did not always realize it, since, unlike State-funded colleges, Canisius did not have to disclose salary scales. When I started teaching in 1973 most of the women faculty were poorly paid part-time instructors. They were the equivalent of the research assistants in institutions like the Center for Theoretical Biology, where I had worked – paid by "soft money". i.e. grants, without fringe benefits or prospects of tenure. Of the few tenure-track women, none were full professors. I remember vividly a chance encounter with a senior woman faculty member, whom I met in the hallway during my first month at the college. She welcomed me, introduced herself and then said,

"Look at me, the oldest living associate professor!" I did not know what to say, but she continued, "Why do you think I am not a full professor?"

I had recognized her name and knew that she was a distinguished scholar, well known in her field. I remained speechless.

"I will tell you why", she paused dramatically, "It's because I don't have a *penis*!"

She went on her way, leaving me to ponder her words. She was right of course, but during the next 20 years the situation for women at Canisius, as at other colleges, improved greatly. We women spent thousands of hours on committees just to achieve equality of pay and status. With a few notable exceptions, the male tenured faculty resisted every attempt at change. But eventually it came about.

The Women's Studies Committee, which I initiated (*after* I had tenure!) did not concern itself so much with the status of women but rather with course material presented to our students. Our major project was to assure that all academic programs included the contributions of women throughout history and that all written material at the college used gender-neutral language. This was no small task in a traditionally all-male Jesuit college, which had only started admitting women students after World War II.

In the 1980s I developed *The Biology of Women,* a course for non-science majors, and also established a Women's Studies Program at the college. Long after my retirement, I am happy to say that both the course and the program (which grants a Certificate and a Minor in Women's Studies) are alive and well. I enjoy attending the annual Women's Studies Luncheon where awards are presented to persons who have made a difference in the lives of women at Canisius College. And these tokens of appreciation are known as the *I. Joan Lorch Women's Studies Awards*!

In most Western countries women have made considerable progress over the last forty years. More girls than boys graduate from high school, and female undergraduates outnumber males in most colleges *and* professional schools. There are female CEOs and college presidents – but not many. The "glass ceiling" has been cracked, not broken. Although NOW still exists, the Women's Movement is virtually extinct. Yet the battle for equality is far from over. I agree with Gloria Steinem, who has dubbed the Bush administration as one of the most hostile to women. Young women have forgotten the battles fought by their foremothers, from the suffragists of the early 20th century to the feminists of the 60s, just as young African Americans have forgotten the Jim Crow days. Let's hope they are justified in their optimism!

The Sad Sixties

Everybody remembers where he or she was when the news of President Jack Kennedy's assassination broke. Peter and I happened to be in our attorney's office in downtown Buffalo on that drizzly November day in 1963. The reason for our visit was a routine update of our wills, made necessary by our move from Alabama to New York State. It was not really a sad occasion, so we were surprised to find all the staff in tears when we entered the office. Attorneys, secretaries, custodians - all were clustered round a small black-and-white TV set. The news was so shattering that it took quite a while before anybody was ready to return to ordinary business.

The Rev. Martin Luther King, Jr. signing autographs after his speech in Buffalo, NY. Nov.9, 1967.

It was less than two years since JFK's inauguration, and the country was devastated. And this was just one of many sad events in that fateful decade. A few months earlier (September 1963), just after we left Birmingham, we heard of the bombing of the 16th Street Baptist Church, the largest black church in that city, that was the center of many civil rights meetings and demonstrations. Four black girls were killed and many others injured both in the bombing, and in the riots, which followed it. The Ku Klux Klan was known to be responsible, but it was more than ten years before some of the murderers were brought to justice. The last of the Klan perpetrators was convicted in 2002, thirty-eight years after the crime.

Not long after the Birmingham tragedy, black leaders Medgar Evers and Malcolm X were assassinated, and 1968 saw the violent deaths of both Martin Luther King and Robert Kennedy. After the jubilant beginning of the sixties and the prevailing optimism when JFK defused the Cuban missile crisis in 1962, it seemed like everything was falling apart. I was especially sad about the murder of Dr. King, whose philosophy of non-violence I greatly admired. We had taken the boys to meet Dr. King and to hear him speak at a concert hall in Buffalo about a year before his assassination. I also remembered his *Letter from a Birmingham Jail*, and his *I Have a Dream* speech made at the huge civil rights rally in Washington, D.C. in August 1963. If only he were alive to witness the nomination of Barack Obama, a black senator, as the Democratic presidential candidate, exactly 45 years later!

Meanwhile the Vietnam "conflict", so called because war was never officially declared, dragged on, tearing the country apart. Its history goes back two decades to the French Indo-China wars, of which I became aware only because I was working in Brittany in the early fifties. In the small town of Roscoff, where I spent some months at the *Station Biologique*, almost every family sadly missed a father or son who was fighting in "Indo-Chine". US combat troops were involved between 1965 and 1973, the exact dates are not clear.

Gregory was sixteen years old and a junior in high school in 1969, when the draft lottery for 19-year-old men was instituted. He was strongly opposed to the U.S. involvement in Vietnam, indeed to armed combat in general, and had no intention of fighting in this war, which had become more and more futile. He was active in the anti-war movement in high school, in the Unitarian Universalist Church, and later as a student at the University of Rochester. Before his nineteenth birthday he filed for conscientious objector status. This involved submitting an application explaining his objections, which had to be based on *religious* (not purely ethical or moral) grounds. With guidance and support from our minister, Gregory wrote an inspiring, superbly argued document in which he explained

Gregory. Buffalo, New York, 1971

Alan with his new bike on his 16th birthday.
Buffalo, New York, 1972

his beliefs in peace, freedom and human dignity. It never reached the draft board because Gregory drew a very high lottery number, and the conflict had ended before his group became eligible for the draft. But I hope he feels, as I do, that clarifying his beliefs was well worth the effort.

Contradictions

While the Vietnam conflict dominated the sixties, popular music centered on love and peace. Progress in space exploration, sparked by the Soviet's success with Sputnik, was phenomenal and culminated in Project Apollo's moon landing in 1969.

I did not follow the space race between the Soviet Union and the United States very closely, and sometimes wondered if the billions spent on this project could not be spent more usefully here on earth. But seeing two men actually walking on the moon was truly amazing. This was almost forty years ago and has never been repeated. However we now have space stations and are beginning to explore Mars. Space exploits no longer make front-page news, nor does the war in Iraq, which dominates the first decade of the twenty-first century and has many similarities with Vietnam.

In contrast to the space race with its rivalries and military overtones, the popular music scene was "groovy". Long before the sixties there were Woody Guthrie (*This Land is My Land…*) and Pete Seeger, whose *We shall Overcome* was adopted by the civil rights movement. Seeger's songs, such as *If I had a Hammer* and *Where have all the Flowers Gone* are still poignant today. Pete is in his late eighties and continues to sing! He, together with Ronnie Gilbert and the Weavers developed a whole new style of folk music, which preceded Elvis Presley, Bob Dylan and, of course the Beatles. I loved this music, especially John Denver as well as Peter, Paul and Mary, who picked up Denver's *Leaving on a Jet Plane.* But I initially had my doubts about the Beatles who took America by storm after their 1964 TV debut, and really defined sixties music. Nobody who had kids could escape the Beatles. Gregory and Alan played their records day and night and the car radio was always tuned to their songs. Eventually their music grew on me and I began to appreciate the genius of this group, who, unlike most performers composed all their own songs and lyrics.

Contemporary, i.e. twenty-first century pop music does not appeal to me. I do not like hip-hop; the rappers leave me cold, as do Madonna, Prince and Michael Jackson. It may be that I'm too old for this sort of thing, or the fact that, whereas the Beatles sang of love, the rappers' lyrics center on sex, hate and violence. And they do not leave me "feelin' groovy".

For me the "sixties" ended in 1973 with Nixon and Watergate, and, with one exception, I do not recall subsequent decades with the same clarity. The one national event that stands out for me was "Roe v. Wade", the Supreme Court's 1973 decision legalizing abortion. Although abortion had been legal in New York State for some time, this was the first federal law that made reproductive choice possible for women. In the last thirty-five years there have been numerous attempts to overthrow this law, and its future is not secure even now.

Winter in Western New York: *The Family that Skis Together, Freeze Together.*

Although we had the option of buying our rental house on Washington Highway, which was ideally located close to schools and just across the street from the Pine family, we decided against it. It was a dark old house, in need of a lot of renovations. Within a few months I had located a house for sale a few blocks away on Roycroft Boulevard, where lots of kids were playing on the grassy area that divide two one-way streets. The gray-shingled house itself was not remarkable – a "tract house" built, along with many similar houses, by a developer called Gennrich after WWII. But it had a big fenced back yard, where Foxy could roam safely, and five beautiful maple trees, which shaded the house and lawn. In fact they provided so much shade that Peter's efforts to grow a few veggies in our back yard met with little success. Coming from Alabama, I did not realize at the time that shade trees were not all that important here. Our maples grew into veritable giants during the 40 years we lived on Roycroft and their roots caused a lot of trouble in our sewer lines.

Alan spraying water on our skating rink, 1960

Peter with snow-shoveling crew. Gregory is in the middle, 1960

A snowbird? Gregory, 1968

Peter (masked against the wind) struggling with snow blower in our driveway, 1968

The owners, a family expecting their fifth child, were anxious to sell, as the three-bedroom house was too small for them. The interior was shabby and painted dark brown – "it doesn't show finger marks" – but the owner promised to clean and paint everything. At this point he broke his arm and, unable to keep his promise, lowered the price considerably, which enabled us to take possession right away and decorate the house in colors we liked. Greg painted his room bright yellow, he likes a lot of light, while Alan chose different shades of blue and thick "room darkener" drapes.

A very sad event marred the first month in our new home: Foxy somehow got out of the front door one evening and was hit by a car right at our corner, where police found his body. He was truly a member of the family and we all missed him. Since I was working now, I did not feel I could look after another dog, but eventually we acquired a purebred Siamese kitten, Candy Floss of Happy Acres, and I started breeding these fascinating creatures.

When Candy was in labor with her first litter, I kept Alan home from school to witness the birth. We marveled at the efficiency with which she bit through the umbilical cord, ate the placenta and licked each kitten clean while waiting for the next one. There were four kittens, looking rather like white mice. Candy was a "blue point", her mate a "seal point". The colored fur patches, called points, develop at about six weeks of age, leaving plenty of time for speculation regarding the exact color each kitten would be. I sold the kittens and those of subsequent litters and eventually had Candy spayed. She lived to the ripe old age of eighteen years and died peacefully in her sleep. I have not been without a Siamese cat for the last forty years.

We were excited about our first winter in Snyder, and the kids couldn't wait to see all that snow we were told to expect. Soon it was cold enough to make a little ice rink in the backyard by flooding the lawn. We hoped this would keep the boys entertained all winter. But just when they got proficient at skating the ice turned to slush! "Oh, it's the January thaw" the locals said. Fortunately there was lots of snow on the ground now, and we were advised to head for Chestnut Ridge, a county park about 15miles south of Buffalo, which offered free tobogganing and skiing. So the four of us, equipped with rental skis, started on this new adventure. I had learned to ski as a child in

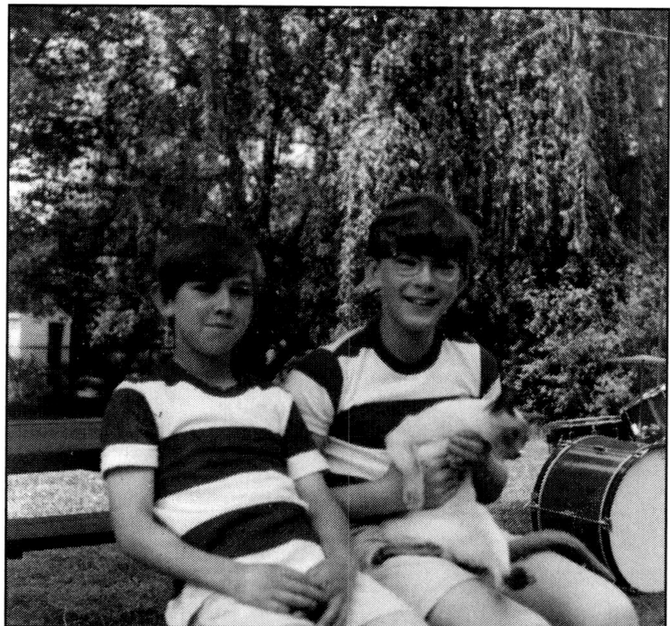

Alan and Gregory with Candy, 1967

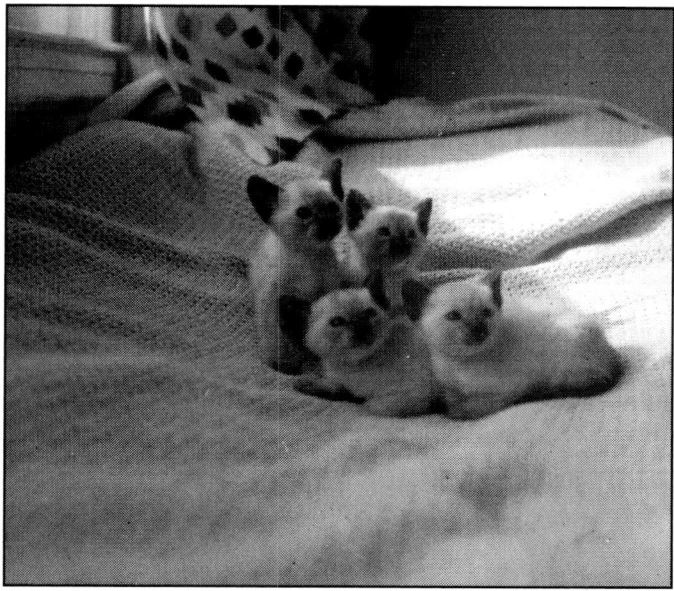

Candy's first litter

Switzerland and my body seemed to remember the basic techniques. Gregory and Alan soon learned to handle the rope tow and to "schuss" down the little slope. They loved it! But Peter did not take to skiing at all. I'm sure he felt silly lining up for the tow with all the kids, and spending a lot of time sprawled on the ground.

For the boys and me this was the beginning of our life-long love affair with skiing. The following year we could afford to ski at a better area called Glenwood Acres, where we took lessons. During the annual Presidents Day holiday we spent a ski-week in Vermont. It was incredibly cold at Killington, a huge ski resort spread over two mountains. An icy wind whistled around us as we sat huddled on the chairlifts and the ski patrol checked us periodically for the telltale pale spots indicative of frostbite. I remember nine-year-old Alan, hiding under the big poncho provided at the base of the lift, saying "Mom, just tell me when we get to the top." The instructors at Killington were excellent and both boys learned to ski parallel during that week. My progress was moderate, and Peter struggled bravely o

Gregory, Joan and Alan at Glenwood Acres, our local ski area. 1968

At the end of our ski week we were hooked. Well, *three* of us

were! Peter made a resignation speech to the effect that skiing was a) too cold, b) very dangerous, c) time consuming, d) too expensive and "just not my cup of tea." He returned his rental equipment and never skied again. From then on it was up to me: every weekend and holiday throughout the winter the boys and I got up in the freezing dawn, packed piles of sandwiches and loaded the station wagon for our trip south to "ski country", as Buffalonians call the area. I rejoiced when Gregory grew tall enough to load the skis on the roof rack, and when, at sixteen, he got his driver's license and took turns driving. He generously offered to drive Alan – and assorted friends – to the ski areas, so I could stay home and rest. It was a while before I allowed that. The roads were icy and treacherous and, well, I actually *enjoyed* our outings, although that may not have been obvious to the boys. They soon became expert skiers, while I remained a permanent intermediate. But all three of us had many fantastic ski trips over the years, both in the US and in Europe.

The sport of downhill skiing has changed tremendously since the 1930s when I first staggered around in Arosa (Switzerland) on my heavy hickory skis attached to hiking boots. New materials make it possible to use much shorter skis and the state-of-the art boots and quick-release bindings have made skiing both easier and safer. The primitive rope tows, which tore up our mittens, were soon replaced by T-bars and poma lifts. Now chairlifts and gondolas dominate the mountains. Downhill skiing has become a hi-tech and, not surprisingly, a high-cost sport. Then, in the early seventies, cross country (also called Nordic) skiing reached Western New York. This was a throw-back to the kind of skiing I did as a child - one literally walked across fields, "herringboned" uphill and skied down, using the "snowplow" to control speed as needed. But there were some big differences: modern nordic skis were extremely light, the step-in bindings simple and safe, while light aluminum poles replaced solid wooden sticks. Tired of crowded ski slopes, lift lines and noisy lodges, I gave this a try. It was hard work compared with downhill skiing but the constant exercise ensured that one rarely felt cold. I loved getting out into the quiet woods, where, instead of the hum of the lifts and the hissing of the snowmaking machines, the only sounds were the chirping of chickadees and the gentle swishing of skis.

Eventually I compromised: cross-country skiing at weekends to avoid the crowds, but downhill midweek, whenever I could get away. On fine days, when the snow was just perfect, I would skip work, take Alan out of school and “head for the hills.” Greg was in high school and able to get out with the school ski club in the evening. I tried night skiing but did not like the cold and the weird shadows on the snow.

So winters in Western New York were great. The kids were particularly happy when a snowstorm caused schools to close, but that did not happen very often. The winter of 1977 was an exception. A huge blizzard hit the Buffalo area on January 28 of that year and life came to a standstill as transportation ground to a halt. The city and some suburbs were paralyzed for 10 days. Snowploughs could not get through streets clogged by parked cars hidden under blankets of snow. Eventually Buffalo got State Aid and even Federal help as President Carter declared us a “major disaster area”. Fortunately Peter and I were home because Canisius College, where I was teaching, as well as the Dental School had taken the precaution to close early on that Friday.

Souvenir post card, showing the city.

Since I had this unexpected free and snowy afternoon, I

put on my cross-country skis and enjoyed the unusual experience of skiing along the deserted streets of Snyder. I decided to visit Ellen Pine, just a few blocks away. We had tea, chatted and casually watched the snow pour down, not realizing that a fierce blizzard was brewing. By the time I decided to ski home an icy gale force wind was blowing. Ellen's screen door flew off its hinges and took off. "I'll drive you home," she offered, but of course there was no way of getting her car out of the driveway. Her husband, Martin, was downtown at Roswell Park Cancer Institute where he worked, and we wondered how he would get home (He was trapped at Roswell for days!) Somehow I skied home, fighting the wind and snow all the way. These few blocks in a suburb were more challenging and scary than any mountain trip I remember! Ellen was worried and I promised to call her but by the time I got home the phones were out. The temperature had plummeted to well below zero F and the wind chill was arctic.

There was no way to get food for the next few days, but our refrigerator and freezer were well stocked. I would like to say this was due to my great foresight and planning, but actually it was just luck. There was no power outage in Snyder, but residents were asked to use natural gas sparingly. The national media, always happy to malign Buffalo, made the most of this blizzard. When communications were restored we had phone calls from all over the country, even from England, as friends were concerned about our welfare. Somehow this blizzard became an institution: there were souvenirs and postcards depicting mountains of snow with inscriptions like "I survived The Blizzard of '77". And to this day Buffalo holds an annual "Blizzard Ball" in February.

My Life Among the Amoebas

"Everything should be made as simple as possible but not simpler."
Albert Einstein

"Chance Favors the Prepared Mind"

At the end of Chapter 6 I illustrated Pasteur's perceptive observation with a little chance discovery of my own which led to a simplified method of microsurgery, and I hinted at more important chance discoveries to come. In the mid-sixties my colleague Kwang Jeon and I continued our study of the relationships between a cell's nucleus and its cytoplasm. As I mentioned previously, our work required large quantities of amoebas, which were grown (cultured) in Pyrex pie dishes and fed tiny swimming organisms called *Tetrahymena*. Our technician, Lorraine Powers, was in full charge of this "farming" operation. She enjoyed the largely routine work, declining to be trained for other tasks. One day in March 1966 Lorraine appeared very worried and told me that "her" amoebas were "not feeling good."

"What makes you think that, Lorraine?" I inquired.

"Well, they lost their appetite, they are just not eating much and they are not multiplying either." Indeed this was true. Their intended prey, the *Tetrahymena*, swam around untouched and eventually died, contaminating the culture medium. This was serious! What was going on here?

After examining samples of amoebas under the microscope, it became obvious that their cytoplasm was full of vacuoles (little sacs) stuffed with rod-shaped structures that looked exactly like bacteria. Each amoeba harbored between 60,000 and 150,000 of these tiny rods. Neither Kwang nor I had ever seen anything like that before. Sure, amoebas engulf anything in their path, including bacteria, by a process called phagocytosis, but whatever they gobble up is either digested or, if not edible, thrown out. What prevented the amoebas from digesting or discarding these presumptive bacteria? Searching the literature did not yield anything relevant. So, like perplexed clinicians anywhere, we did two things: we consulted experts (microbiologists), hoping they would culture and identify the invading bacteria, and meanwhile we treated our patients with hit-or-miss antibiotics. Nothing worked. Nobody succeeded in growing the parasitic bacteria outside their hosts – not even in a fresh mash of amoeba cytoplasm, and our consultants failed to identify the newcomers. As for the antibiotics - they did not affect the "bugs", but killed the amoebas.

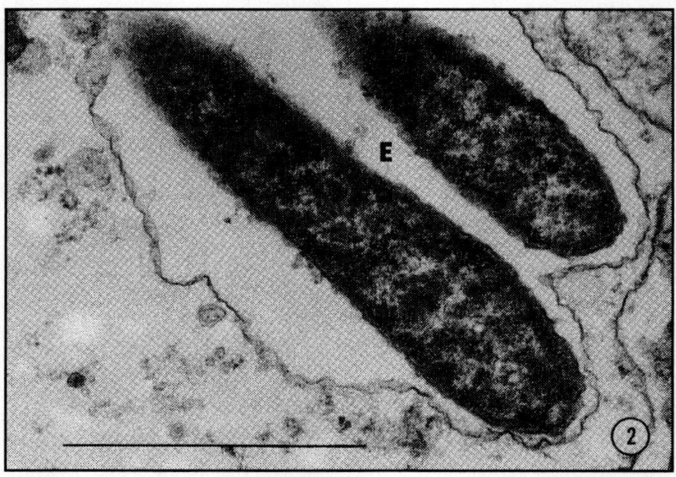

Two symbiotic X bacteria (E) inside an amoeba as seen with the electron-microscope. The line on left represents one thousandth of a millimeter. From a publication by Jeon and Lorch.

Thus we were faced with the sad prospect of losing all our cultures. Years of work and millions of amoebas down the drain? Well, not quite! Our boss, Jim Danielli, the perpetual optimist, who always expected the best outcome, and at the same time prepared for the worst, had instructed me to keep samples of all our different amoeba strains at home, just as we had done in England during WWII when there was a real risk of buildings being bombed.

"Why, Jim?" I complained. "It's a lot of trouble to culture amoebas at home, my kitchen is small, the boys and the cats might upset the dishes. We are not in England now, *the war is over.*"

"Just do as I tell you," he said. "Our building could burn down, student protesters might vandalize the lab[1], you never know." So I had kept duplicate cultures at home and – you guessed it – they showed no sign of the mysterious bacteria.

After a few weeks we noticed that some of the infected cultures in the lab seemed to be recovering under Lorraine's devoted care. Was this an example of "survival of the fittest" – a small minority of amoebas who happened to be resistant or were able to destroy their parasites? To test this possibility we kept a careful watch over these exceptional amoebas. Did they indeed get rid of the invasive bacteria? The answer was no! The bacteria were still there, albeit in smaller numbers, an average of 42,000 per amoeba. But their hosts were surviving and multiplying, *in spite of* their bacterial burden. Soon we had enough cultures of infected amoebas available to study this unique situation. These amoebas differed from the original cultures in a number of ways. Were we witnessing the origin of a new strain of *Amoeba proteus*? Could persistent infections cause speciation? And could a new species arise in a matter of *months* rather that thousands of years? These and other weighty questions churned around in our minds. The only thing we were sure of was that this chance observation, which seemed so disastrous at first, had to be followed up. We were on the brink of great discoveries!

Kwang and I now planned a series of experiments to exploit this unique situation. There was just one snag: Very few researchers are in a position to drop what they are doing and follow a whim or new observation. The amoeba group was committed to work on a specific project set out in Danielli's grant proposal and funded primarily by NASA[2]. This project was an ambitious one: we planned to "build" an amoeba from its constituent parts, in Danielli's words "cell synthesis." For a number of reasons neither Kwang Jeon nor I were thrilled with this plan, but our salaries depended on Jim Danielli's grant and "he who pays the piper calls the tune." By working long hours, we managed to continue the cell synthesis project - you will hear more (*much more!*) about this later - while at the same time investigating the infectious bacteria.

1 Animal rights activists did in fact invade labs, "liberating" rats and mice, which unhappily roamed the hallways and died in odd corners.

2 National Aeronautics and Space Administration

I want to emphasize here that unraveling the mystery of these infected amoebas became a long-term project. More than forty years have elapsed since the infection struck, but the work continues. The amoeba cultures, which I had established in London in the early 1950s from samples given to us by a Scottish nun,[3] had traveled to Buffalo, NY with Danielli's team in 1962. About eight years later Kwang Jeon and the amoebas moved to the University of Tennessee at Knoxville (UTK). There, with the help of graduate students and periodic visits from me, he continued the research. Kwang is now retired, but one of his former students, Tae Ahn, a professor at Seoul National University (Republic of Korea) has established our cultures there, and a new generation of researchers is hard at work. But I am getting ahead of the story.

Let's review the situation: In March 1966 unidentified rod-shaped bacteria had invaded our amoeba cultures, killing most of them. The survivors continued to harbor bacteria in their cytoplasm. Thanks to Danielli's foresight, we still had uninfected amoebas available, which continued to flourish in my home. We now posed the following questions:

1. What would happen if we transplanted nuclei from infected amoebae into uninfected cytoplasm and vice versa?
2. Can the infection be transmitted to the uninfected amoebas and is it still as virulent as before?
3. Is there *some* way we could get rid of the bacteria (without killing the hosts!); maybe a drug we have not tried yet or a change of temperature?
4. What would the "cured" amoebas be like?

In order to make it easier to communicate, we called the invasive bacteria, which nobody had been able to culture or identify, *X bacteria*. The strain of amoebas we were working with was called *D strain*, so we called the infected cultures the *xD strain*. I must introduce one more new word here: organisms that live inside other animals or plants are called *endosymbionts*. Thus the X bacteria are endosymbionts of amoebas. In fact they are *obligatory*

3 Sister Monica Taylor of the Convent of Notre Dame in Glasgow sent starter cultures.

endosymbionts, meaning they could not live independently of their hosts. The situation of one organism living in close association with another is called *symbiosis*. This was our new field of study: we had become *symbiologists*!

What did all this mean? Was there a precedent for this situation? To tackle the first question I brought some uninfected D amoebae from home to the lab, keeping them in a separate room from the infected cultures. Then I did nuclear transplantation experiments, replacing the nuclei of the D amoebas with nuclei from the (infected) xD strain. Surprise! These "hybrids" did not survive, i.e. *xD nuclei could no longer function in D cytoplasm.* In the relatively short time that the nuclei had been exposed to the bacterial infection something had happened to change them, making them dependent on the presence of the bacteria. Think about it! These bacteria were vicious pathogens; killing off most of the cells they invaded. Yet after a few months the surviving infected amoebas' nuclei could not function without the X bacteria. Control experiments, transplanting D nuclei into D cytoplasm and similarly xD nuclei into xD cytoplasm were successful. Also D nuclei could be successfully transplanted into xD cytoplasm, indicating that the established X bacteria no longer killed the newly exposed nuclei.

With regard to the second question – could we now infect regular D amoebas by exposing them to X bacteria? And if so, would most of these cells die, as had happened during the original "invasion"?

Yes, amoebas could be infected, either by letting them phagocytose (engulf) bacteria or, more successfully, by injection of bacteria into the amoeba's cytoplasm. The survival rate was good and the X bacteria soon established themselves at the level of about 42,000 bacteria per amoeba, as in the chronically infected cultures. We did not see the acute heavy infection experienced during the initial invasion, indicating that the X bacteria had lost their virulence during their long-term residence in amoeba cytoplasm. Thus, not only had the amoebas adapted to life with their symbionts, but the bacteria had changed drastically: they no longer killed their hosts, thereby assuring their own continuing existence.

In order to answer the third question – how to get rid of the intracellular bacteria – Kwang Jeon and I tried two more approaches: different kinds of antibiotics and different culture temperatures. Both had some success. Exposure of the xD amoebas to Chloramphenicol killed most of the X bacteria, while the amoebas survived for a limited time. The same could be achieved by culturing xD amoebas at 26° C instead of the usual 20°. The elevated temperature killed the bacteria, while the amoebas survived – temporarily. Why did these "cured" amoebas not establish permanent cultures? Had they become dependent on their symbionts? In order to answer this question, I injected X bacteria into the "cured" amoebas. Lo and behold they now flourished! There was no doubt that the established xD amoebas could no longer live without their bacterial symbionts, any more than the X bacteria could live outside their hosts.

The implications are profound: what we witnessed here was the emergence of a new strain of amoebas, which required the presence of endosymbiotic bacteria for its survival. Moreover the X bacteria, which must have been free-living at some time in the past, could no longer exist outside their hosts.

Readers who enjoyed (or endured) learning about cells in high school biology class may recall structures called mitochondria. Your teacher probably referred to them as "the powerhouse of the cell," and indeed they are concerned with energy metabolism. Mitochondria resemble bacteria in many ways, and cell biologists think that they were, at some time in the distant past, free-living bacteria that got engulfed by amoeba-like primitive cells. Somehow they resisted digestion and became endosymbionts and, eventually, required cell constituents (organelles). A similar story can be told about chloroplasts, the green, chlorophyll containing organelles found in plant cells, which enable plants to capture energy from the sun for the synthesis of carbohydrates, a process called photosynthesis. A byproduct of this process is oxygen, on which virtually all life on earth depends. Chloroplasts most likely evolved from tiny green organisms resembling modern cyanobacteria (chlorophyll-containing bacteria, formerly called "blue-green algae").

There are other examples of organelles, which most likely originated from primitive bacteria, and the subject has been much studied, particularly by Lynn Margulis[4], a professor at the University of Massachusetts at Amherst, who has spent most of her long professional life documenting the *Endosymbiotic Theory of Evolution*. The parallel of the evolution of mitochondria and chloroplasts with our X bacteria is inescapable. Margulis followed our work closely and was delighted to recognize it as the *only* known instance where the change from free-living pathogenic bacterium to required cell constituent has actually been observed, rather than implied.

Another eminent scientist who was intrigued by the X bacteria story is Lewis Thomas, former president of Memorial Sloan Kettering Cancer Center. Thomas was an unusually perceptive observer of the world of biology in the widest sense, and his monthly *Essays of a Biology Watcher* in the New England Journal of Medicine had a large following and were collected in several books. In his last book[5], *The Fragile Species (1992)*, he devotes a chapter (p.139-157), entitled *Cooperation* to the X amoeba story and its implications. Here is a brief excerpt of that chapter:

> *. . . Jeon and Lorch have extended the experiments (on xD amoebae) and discovered that the adaptive change in the amoeba nucleus, as well as the shift of the interaction from parasitism to symbiosis, takes place with remarkable speed. The whole transformation, representing on its face a small-scale model in evolution, can be brought about in as short a time as six weeks and after no more than sixteen generations of infected amoebae.*
>
> *This seemingly freakish event can be taken as a sort of biological parable, reminding us of what must have been one of the three or four most crucial turning points in the evolution of life on earth – the formation of complex, nucleated cells like ours, known now as eukaryotic cells,*

---

4 See for example *Symbiotic Planet: A New Look at Evolution* (1999), one of many books Margulis has devoted to this topic. She is still aggressively promoting her theory. On the same topic are Jan Sapp's *Evolution by Association: A History of Symbiosis (1994)* and his new book *Foundations of Evolution: On the Tree of Life (2009)*

5 Lewis Thomas died in 1993 aged 80.

> *from their bacterial predecessors. The event probably occurred about 1 billion years ago.*

Most researchers in the life sciences now agree that organic evolution does not entirely – or even primarily – depend on chance mutations, sexual recombination (meiosis) and other mechanisms proposed by neo-Darwinists. But strangely enough this fact is ignored in textbooks of Biology most commonly used by high school and even college students. It seems to me that the publishers of textbooks, along with the general public, are obsessed by the absurd evolution/special creation controversy, rather than emphasizing that evolution did, and does, take place; only certain *mechanisms* of evolution are still debated.

Acquisition of new genomes by the coming together of diverse organisms plays an important role in the genesis of new strains and species. In Margulis' words

> *Symbiosis has affected the course of evolution as profoundly as biparental sex has. Both entail the formation of new individuals that carry genes from more than a single parent.*

Amoebas, like many one-celled organisms, do not reproduce sexually, they simply split in two. Hence the acquisition of new symbionts may well be one of the mechanisms by which they create diversity. Lewis Thomas feels that we humans who, wrongly, think of nature as "red in tooth and claw", a jungle where only the strongest survive, could learn from this aspect of evolution:

> *I take the view that the successful and persistent existence of symbiosis, quite aside from the question as to whether it is relatively uncommon or relatively all-over-the-place, suggests the underlying existence of a general tendency toward cooperative behavior in nature. It is simply not true that nice guys finish last, rather, nice guys last longer.*

The field of symbiology has expanded enormously since I first got interested in the phenomenon of organisms living cooperatively. Many such associations have of course been known for a long time, for example the fact that herbivores, such as cows, depend on symbiotic bacteria in their gut to digest cellulose and the same is true of the termites that destroy and digest our wooden houses. We humans, too, harbor billions of microorganisms in our intestines, our mouths, on the skin and in other areas. Indeed the bacterial cells in our body outnumber those of our own cells. Each of the hundreds of species of resident bacteria has its own DNA and it has been said that each of us has really three sets of genes: the ones we got from our parents and those of the "guest workers" living inside us, which also differ in each person. Until modern techniques such as DNA sequencing became available, it was virtually impossible to identify this intestinal flora, since endosymbionts are notoriously difficult to culture (as we found out!). But in the last ten years some progress has been made in sorting out the menagerie inside us.

As I hinted previously, work on the xD strain of amoeba is continuing. Kwang Jeon maintained all our amoeba cultures in his laboratory at UTK from 1970 until his retirement in 2005. Meanwhile, Tae Ahn is continuing research on the X bacteria at Seoul National University. In a 2004 publication in *Environmental Microbiology* Ahn and his colleagues provide evidence that X bacteria resemble *Legionella*, the causative organism of Legionnaire's Disease, a human respiratory tract infection that emerged in 1976 in Philadelphia.

Legionella bacteria are frequently found as endosymbionts of certain species of tiny amoebas, called *Acanthamoeba*, which flourish in soil and water. But, *unlike* X bacteria, *Legionella* can infect humans and can be grown *in vitro*. In spite of these differences Ahn's group propose the name *Candidatus Legionella jeonii, sp.nov.* for the X bacteria.

"Candidatus" indicates that the name is provisional: a lot of criteria must be fulfilled in order to establish a new species name. I am not qualified to judge whether the allocation of X bacteria to the genus *Legionella* is justified. But I would be happy for the X bacteria to have a name at long last, and for Kwang Jeon to be immortalized by having his name attached to our famous bacteria! I await further developments and hope that *somebody* will continue nurturing the amoebas when Tae Ahn retires in 2012.

Non-scientists have often asked me of what possible use research with amoebas could be. Questions such as, "Are you trying to find a cure for cancer?" and "Are amoebas really like human cells?", come my way, not to mention "Why should my tax money support your tinkering in the lab?"

The answer to all such "noise" is that that there is no way to foresee where medical advances or "breakthroughs", as the press likes to call them, might come from. Chance discoveries only happen to those who tinker in the lab, and the "prepared mind" will take advantage of them. Basic research is essential to the progress of science and "playing" with amoebas is part of that vast network.

I began this section by quoting Louis Pasteur's famous dictum: "Chance favors the prepared mind." I would like to end with a remark made by another famous nineteenth century French scientist, Claude Bernard. He said:

> *"The true worth of a researcher lies in pursuing what he did not seek in his experiment, as well as what he sought."*

"Life Begins in Buffalo"

On November 13, 1970 the above and other strange headlines suddenly appeared in newspapers all over the country – indeed all over the world. And they referred to *our* little lab at the Center for Theoretical Biology (CTB)! How did this come about? I will endeavor to reconstruct the sequence of events that led to this media frenzy, which might be looked at as a comedy of errors, though it ultimately had tragic consequences.

Jim Danielli was very interested in the new discipline of *exobiology,* a field that combines research on the origins of life with the search for life on other planets. Some of the research at the CTB concerned the possibility of synthesizing new life forms, especially in connection with NASA's Mars exploration program. Danielli was always full of novel ideas, so I was not particularly surprised when in 1966 he suggested that we attempt to construct an amoeba from its constituent parts. Jim had recently participated in a NASA-sponsored symposium at Pennsylvania State University, entitled *Synthesis of Life,* from which he returned full of enthusiasm. Moreover, a physicist called C.C. Price, had just published a paper in which he suggested that the synthesis of new life forms should be made an American National Goal – rather like putting a man on the moon. There had never been a mega-project comparable to space exploration, in biology. It actually took another 25 years for the first "Big Science" venture in biology to be funded and it was not cell synthesis but the Human Genome Project. However, Jim believed an artificially constructed amoeba would be a good model for life synthesis and he had obtained approval and funding from NASA[6] for his idea.

Joan using a"microforge" to make tiny glass instruments. Center for Theoretical Biology, Buffalo, NY. 1970.

So, together with Kwang Jeon we devised a plan to take amoebas apart and put them together again. If you think this sounds easy, let me assure you that there are numerous technical difficulties. Still, we knew that, in theory, it should be possible. After all, I had successfully transplanted nuclei in amoebas since the 1940s[7], and had injected cytoplasm from one amoeba into another, so this was just an extension of well-established techniques. Kwang and I did

6 The Center for Theoretical Biology had a NASA grant for $100,000 annually.

7 Lorch, I.J. and Danielli, J.F. (1950) Nature 166,329. *Transplantation of Nuclei from Cell to Cell.*

the actual lab work, while Jim Danielli provided inspiration – and funding.

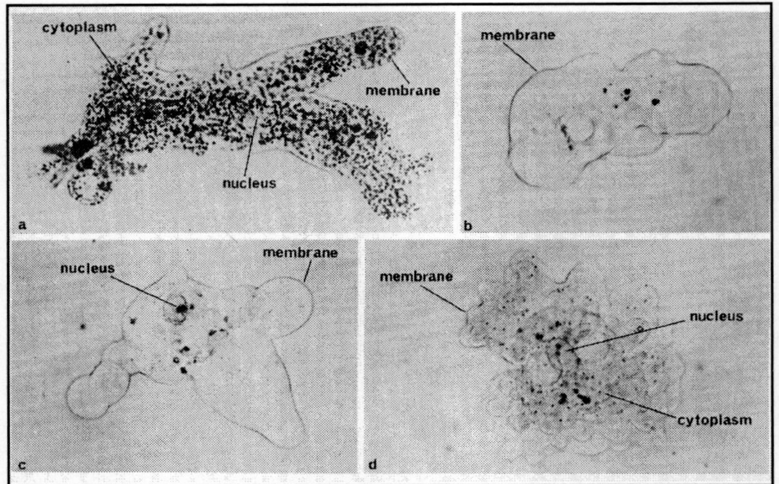

Photomicrographs of stages in the assembly of a viable amoeba. a. Normal amoeba. b. Dissociated membrane obtained by high-speed centrifugation. c. Dissociated membrane into which a nucleus has been inserted. d. Cytoplasm from a third amoeba has been injected into the dissociated membrane containing the implanted nucleus, thus completing the assembly. (Based on experiments described in Jeon et al 1970.)

Here is what we did in order to isolate three different constituents of amoebas (outer surface, cytoplasm and nucleus):

First we centrifuged a lot of amoebas at high speeds. This procedure literally blew them apart, leaving balloon-like little sacs (outer membranes) and debris of nuclei and cytoplasm. We picked out the membrane sacs, discarding the debris. The sacs could not survive of course, having neither adequate cytoplasm nor a nucleus. Then we "renucleated" the empty sacs, pushing in nuclei taken out of living amoebas; still no survivors. Next we took renucleated membrane sacs and injected them with cytoplasm. Most of these cells survived and multiplied. Success! So, we really had been able to assemble viable amoebas from dissociated (non-viable) parts. Based on 258 assembly attempts, the success rate was about 75%, not bad, considering the trauma to which the cells were subjected. The accompanying photomicrograph should make the process easier to understand.

I must stress that all the amoeba parts used came from the same strain of *Amoeba proteus*. When we tried to combine parts of different strains the resulting cells did not survive for long.

Over 2 years later we felt we had enough data to publish a preliminary report. Jim went ahead and drafted a paper for publication in *Science*, entitled *Artificial Synthesis of Living Cells*. In the draft, he pointed out that neither nucleus, cytoplasm nor membranes could live by themselves, but putting them all together had resulted in living reproducing cells. He concluded that we now had the means to synthesize *any* cell from non-viable components.

Kwang and I disagreed with these sweeping claims. We were hesitant to extrapolate from amoebas to "any cells". We also disliked the term "Artificial Synthesis" which implies that our reassembled amoebas were "man-made". After much animated discussion, Jim agreed to modify the language and the final title became:

Reassembly of Living Cells from Dissociated Components

We submitted the manuscript in December 1969. Two months went by before it was rejected. The editors felt the paper was too specialized for *Science*. They suggested we send it to the *Journal of Cell Biology*. Jim would not hear of it. He told the editors that our work was an extremely important breakthrough, and they had better publish it at once. The paper appeared in March 1970[8]

Jim expected that our publication would arouse a lot of interest, and perhaps an editorial in *Science* or other comments, yet this did not happen. We had ordered lots of reprints though few requests came in. In order to impress NASA, whose grants provided our livelihood, Jim planned to take additional steps: a big dinner and press conference to be held in the fall. I was busy working on the endosymbionts project (described in the last section), and quite unaware of these plans. Kwang Jeon was in the process of moving to Knoxville where he had been offered a faculty position at the University of Tennessee. That left me in charge of the amoeba unit.

The media frenzy, that broke out in November 1970, took

8 Jeon, K.W., Lorch, I.J. and Danielli, J.F. (1970) Science 167, 1626. *Reassembly of Cells from Dissociated Components*. Copy of paper is in appendix.

me completely by surprise. Very early on November 13th my phone rang: it was an irate person from the office of public information at the University.

" Dr. Lorch, have you seen the Courier Express (Buffalo morning paper) or the New York Times?" "Are you listening to the radio and watching TV?"

Of course not, I was barely awake.

"Well *turn on your TV*; we are flooded with calls here and don't know what is going on."

Well, that was the beginning. There were so many calls that I was told the University had to install extra phone lines to cope with the inquiries. I had no idea what precipitated the onslaught. Surely our carefully worded publication in *Science,* which had appeared *six months earlier*, could not have induced newspaper reports that we had "created life in a test tube", "are playing God" and other strange stories.[9] What had happened?

Kwang was in Knoxville and did not want to get involved. Jim was at a Mars Study Group meeting in California, but returned as fast as he could to take charge. He cautioned me not to say a word to any reporter, leaving him to be the spokesperson on nationally broadcast TV and radio programs. Finally, he explained to his stunned colleagues at the CTB what had happened:

As mentioned previously, Jim was planning a big event at the University to publicize our success in assembling living cells. Before leaving on his trip he had given preliminary plans, including letters of invitation to numerous dignitaries *and the media* to Kay, his secretary, to type while he was out of town. The letter was worded somewhat flamboyantly in order to make sure the media would take notice. No release date was mentioned, nor was any of the material labeled "confidential". Somehow these invitations got to the media long before they were meant to and mayhem followed!

Jim did his best to control the situation – but I think he actually made things worse by not stating firmly enough that WE DID NOT CREATE A LIVING CELL FROM *NON-LIVING* COMPONENTS. The nucleus and cytoplasm we put into the empty membranes did, after all, come from other *living* amoebas. However, it takes skill to communicate with the press. Reporters tend to misinterpret

9 A few examples of press coverage are in the Appendix. This is just the tip of the iceberg.

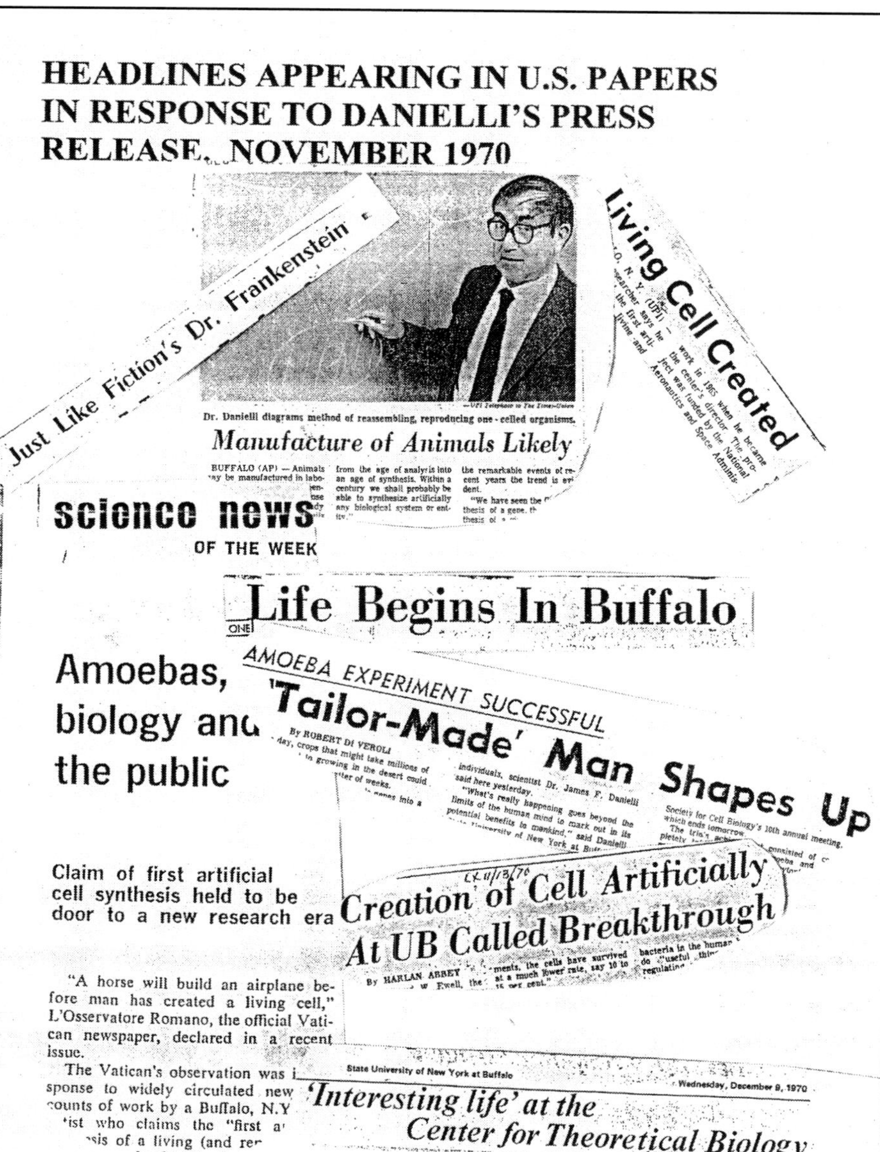
HEADLINES APPEARING IN U.S. PAPERS IN RESPONSE TO DANIELLI'S PRESS RELEASE, NOVEMBER 1970

Just Like Fiction's Dr. Frankenstein

Dr. Danielli diagrams method of reassembling, reproducing one-celled organisms.

Manufacture of Animals Likely

Living Cell Created

science news OF THE WEEK

Life Begins In Buffalo

Amoebas, biology and the public

Claim of first artificial cell synthesis held to be door to a new research era

"A horse will build an airplane before man has created a living cell," L'Osservatore Romano, the official Vatican newspaper, declared in a recent issue.

The Vatican's observation was i... sponse to widely circulated new... counts of work by a Buffalo, N.Y. ...tist who claims the "first a... ...sis of a living (and re...

AMOEBA EXPERIMENT SUCCESSFUL

'Tailor-Made' Man Shapes Up

By ROBERT DI VEROLI

Creation of Cell Artificially At UB Called Breakthrough

By HARLAN ABBEY

State University of New York at Buffalo — Wednesday, December 9, 1970

'Interesting life' at the Center for Theoretical Biology

HEADLINES APPEARING IN U.S. PAPERS IN RESPONSE TO DANIELLI'S PRESS RELEASE. NOVEMBER 1970

The Evening Press
BINGHAMTON, NEW YORK
DEC 8 1970

Synthetic Animal Expected

The Washington Post
WASHINGTON, D. C.
NOV 14 1970

Biologist Predicts Animal Synthesis

BUFFALO, N.Y. (AP)—A biologist says animals may be manufactured in laboratories within ... century.

more types of synthesis will be possible ... 20 years.

plished earlier this year by an eight-member team headed by ... Danielli.

The researchers, Danielli said, ... taken basic parts from different amoebae—one-celled crea-

wall of the cell, the cytoplasm basic substance of the cell ... the nucleus or center of the cell

The press focuses on U/B's international story.

Synthetic Mammals Foreseen

LONDON, Nov. 13—A biologist who has produced living cells — amoebas — from parts of other cells forecast today scientists may be able

Columbus Citizen-Journal
COLUMBUS, OHIO
NOV 13 1970

Cell Synthesis Opens New Scientific Era

NOV 12 1970

Creation of Living Cell in Tube Claimed

BUFFALO, N.Y. (UPI)

Lab Creation of Humans Predicted by Year 2070

By MILDRED SPENCER

Scientist Predicts Hybrid Humans

Shades Of Dr. Frankenstein!

Research Creates Animal Cells

By VICTOR COHN
Gannett News Service
WASHINGTON — Living, ... one-celled ani-

era of synthetic animals begins

Dr. James F. Danielli, set ... create entirely new amoebae ... the basic parts

your statements, either through ignorance or perhaps deliberately. Anything for a "breakthrough" and big headlines!

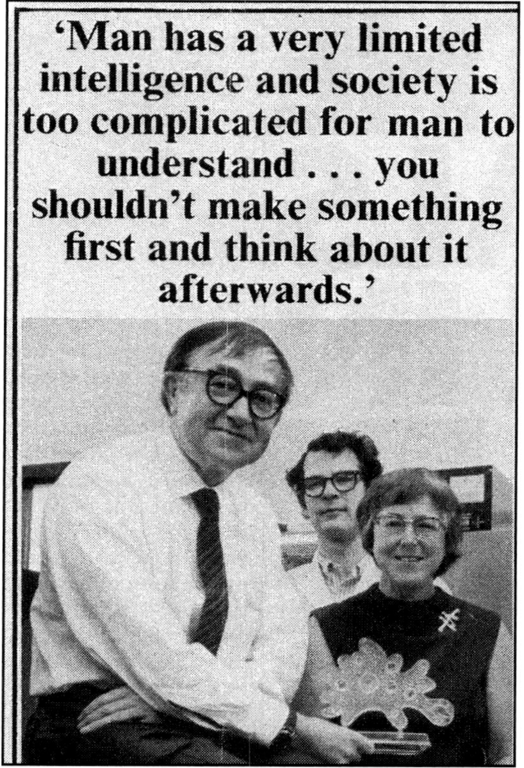

'Man has a very limited intelligence and society is too complicated for man to understand . . . you shouldn't make something first and think about it afterwards.'

Jim Danielli, holding a plastic amoeba model, and Joan, wearing a silver "amoeba" brooch. Our post-doc, Chuck, is in the background. From "Nova" magazine 1972.

There were some notable exceptions, for instance Walter Sullivan, chief science reporter of the New York Times. He insisted on talking to me personally in spite of Jim's attempts to keep me out of this. Mr. Sullivan, a soft-spoken man, and a good listener, understood exactly what we had done. Unlike most of the reporters, he had not only read the controversial paper in *Science*, but our other publications as well. We had a very pleasant conversation, and his article on the front page of in the *New York Times* was a model of what science reporting should be.[10]

On December 7, 1970, almost a month after the "leak", the

---

10 See Appendix

planned dinner and press conference finally took place. Yes, the deans and provosts of the University at Buffalo showed up, as did many members of the media, although the topic was no longer "red hot" for them. Significantly, NASA did *not* send a representative. At the conference, Jim explained the cell assembly project, and encouraged me as well as Kwang, who had flown in from Knoxville, to explain in detail exactly what we had done. We answered all questions from the press as best we could. At no time did we claim to have "created life", but Jim speculated that within the next twenty years it would be technically possible to produce "artificial mammals, even humans", using the methods of cell assembly we had pioneered. He was very concerned about the ethical implications of this type of research and called for guidelines to be put in place *before* man-made organisms were released into the environment.

You might wonder to what extent Danielli's prophecies were fulfilled, so let us pause to review very briefly some of the advances in biology that occurred since that time. Thirty-eight years have passed, so I have the advantage of hindsight when asking questions such as "Has anyone actually synthesized a living, reproducing cell from chemical components?" The answer is NO. But let's rephrase the question: "Have scientists produced artificial organisms, i.e. organisms that do not naturally occur on earth?" Now the answer is a definite YES. How was this done? Here we must backtrack to 1970, the very year our controversial paper was published. That same year H.Gobind Khorana's team at MIT synthesized the first functioning artificial gene, a truly great achievement – but it was still a long way from synthesizing a living cell.

Three years later, two researchers at UCLA, Stanley N. Cohen and Herbert Boyer, reported creating novel bacteria by inserting foreign DNA into their genome. This new technique, called recombinant DNA (rDNA) or gene splicing made it possible to put DNA from one species, e.g. human, into another, such as a bacterium or a pig, and have it function there. That means the bacterium – or the pig – now makes a *human* protein. Indeed it became possible to insert genes from any organism - plant or animal - into any other, thus creating living creatures that had never existed before.

Practical applications soon followed and led to the birth of

Biotechnology. This term now generally refers to gene splicing techniques to produce organisms useful to humans, e.g. genetically modified crops or farm animals, as well as genetically engineered drugs and hormones. The year 1977 is often considered Year One for the biotechnology industry. It saw the production of genetically engineered human *Somatostatin* (a brain hormone) by Herbert Boyer and his team. The following year Genentech, a new biotechnology company founded by Boyer and venture capitalist Robert Swanson, marketed *Humulin* (human insulin) produced by *E.coli* bacteria, followed by Human Growth Hormone (HGH). Thus the biotech industry really took off. Genentech went public in 1980.

According to famous biotech entrepreneur J.Craig Venter, the production of functioning synthetic living organism is imminent, including bacteria that will be the renewable source of cheap, alternate fuels – one of Danielli's early predictions. Venter plans to put the petrochemical industry out of business! Based on his prior record I am inclined to believe him.

Venter started his career at the University at Buffalo in the 1970s and soon made a name for himself as a dynamic personality with a great ego who would go far. I was teaching at Canisius College at the time, and met this bombastic young scientist who presented one of our more memorable seminars.

Since leaving Buffalo, Venter has indeed "gone far".[11] The Institute for Genome Research (TIGR), together with biotech company *Celera*, both founded by Venter, beat the U.S. government-sponsored Human Genome Project in the race to sequence a complete human genome - his own, not surprisingly - in 2001. More recently, his Maryland company, *Synthetic Genomics,* has completed the synthesis of a bacterial chromosome from chemicals. If this chromosome proves to be functional, i.e. can induce the production of novel proteins in a bacterium, then "the creation of life" will indeed have been achieved. What a pity Venter did not stay in Buffalo!

Did these startling accomplishments of biotechnology arouse the wrath of the popular media and cause panic among the public? Indeed they did. Predictions of epidemics caused by artificially created lethal "bugs", deadly "Frankenfoods", horribly deformed animal hybrids and human clone-slaves abounded.

---

11 See his biography *A Life Decoded* (2007)

II 6a

DAILY EXPRESS

Thursday August 26 1976 Weather; Dry, sunny

Life-creating scientists warned:

SUPER BUGS FOR BRITAIN

The reaction of one London newspaper to genetic engineering (recombinant DNA).

Yes, there was reason for concern, although certainly not for panic. Scientists voluntarily called for a moratorium on gene splicing experiments and held a conference (the famous 1973 Asilomar Conference) to consider their safety. This is remarkable! Can you imagine the automobile or the tobacco industry temporarily halting production until the safety of their product was ensured? As a result of the Asilomar conference guidelines were drawn up by the NIH (see the Federal Register of September 9, 1976) and scientists funded by federal agencies had to comply. Over the years the regulations were relaxed, but guidelines are still in place.

Thirty odd years later none of the ghastly predictions have materialized and Biotechnology has benefited humankind enormously. Genetically modified (GM) crops and farm animals are universal in agriculture worldwide. Yes, opposition to the applications of genetic technology still exists, and with some justifications. No technology is without dangers. Consider the enormous toll of deaths and disability due to auto accidents, which far outweighs war casualties, yet the auto industry has never considered safety its first priority. One of the beneficial outcomes of Biotechnology was the development of another new discipline, that of Bioethics, a very active field of study, both theoretical and applied, which is now firmly in place to examine every ethical, moral and legal aspect of new developments in the life sciences

So did Jim Danielli's prophecies come true? Yes and no. He was right in that novel "man-made" organisms were indeed created, but he did not foresee *how* this would be achieved. Recombinant DNA techniques are in no way related to our cell assembly methods. He was also correct to call attention to the many ethical and legal complications that would arise and to urge scientists and the public to pay attention to these potentially serious problems

Did we ever get back to normal after the dust settled on the "cell synthesis event"? Not really. Jim's NASA grant was *not* renewed, and the University announced that the Center for Theoretical Biology would be gradually "phased out". The stress of the previous months had taken a toll of Jim and he seemed less energetic. It came as a great shock to me, however, when he announced that he had been diagnosed with a type of lymphoma and was starting radiotherapy. He resigned from the CTB and, after his successful cancer therapy, accepted an administrative position at Worcester Polytechnic Institute in Massachusetts where he worked until approximately 1980. He died in 1984.

With the demise of the CTB, I now had to decide what to do with the rest of my professional life. I was nearly fifty years old and felt I needed a complete change. Yes, I loved the amoebas; but I hated the constant hassle of writing grant proposals. Research scientists often spend more time "begging" for money than actually doing research! I pondered whether I should try teaching, if indeed I could get a faculty position. I even thought of teaching in a high school, but found out I was not qualified, never having taken any education courses. The sort of job I had in mind was at a college, where I could teach biology to undergraduates, yet still play with the amoebas without the "publish or perish" policy prevalent at major universities. Unlike Kwang, I was not free to leave Buffalo because Peter was a tenured full professor at the School of Dentistry and he had no intention of moving. So I spruced up my resumé, looked up "educational institutions" in the Yellow Pages, and sent out applications to every kind of college within commuting distance. It felt like scattering seeds over rocky ground. Typical replies said something like: "Thank you for your excellent application. We shall keep it on file, in case a vacancy should arise."

Then came a letter from the Chairman of the Biology Department of Canisius College. He indicated that he was searching for two new faculty members with specialties in either cytology or histology. Would I like to visit him to discuss the possibilities? You bet I would!

The "Golden Dome" of Canisius College in Buffalo, NY.

At Fifty: A New Career

Canisius College is a Jesuit liberal arts college in Buffalo with a long tradition of teaching excellence. Since I was educated in England, where education is quite specialized at the high school and undergraduate level, I was not familiar with liberal arts colleges. I was equally ignorant about Jesuits, associating them primarily with Galileo and the inquisition – not exactly reassuring. Yet here I was, applying for a teaching position at *The Jesuit College of Western New York*. What Chutzpah! At this time (1971) Gregory was a student at the University of Rochester, receiving a liberal arts education, and I was aware of the fact that he was studying a great variety of topics, even a little biology, although his major was Political Economy. I also knew that he got report cards at the end of every semester (always excellent!) where both grades and credit hours were listed. This did not happen at British universities: you studied for 3 years without getting much feedback regarding your progress – or lack of it. Then you took the Final Exams, which determined whether you got your degree - or not. Rather brutal, I think, but that's the way it was.

After doing some reading about Jesuits in general and Canisius College in particular, I drove downtown to meet the Chair of the Biology Department, Dr. A. Allan Alexander, whom I liked immediately. He showed me round his department in a venerable building aptly named "Old Main," and emphasized that they would soon be moving to brand-new facilities in a fine Health Sciences Center. The department was full of ancient skeletons, jars of animals in formalin, and apparatus usually seen in history of science museums. I could not imagine how one could teach modern biology in this musty old place. Al was very excited about his plans for the new department, and promised me a state-of-the-art "amoeba lab" designed to my requirements. I met other members of the department, all very pleasant and enthusiastic about their teaching and the impending move. There was only one full-time female professor. Nobody seemed to have an active research program.

Al had arranged for us to have lunch in the faculty dining room with another senior biology professor, Vincent Stouter, as well as Walter Sharrow, Dean of Arts and Sciences, and Executive Vice President, the Reverend Edward Maloney, S.J. They asked questions about my research (Did I *really* synthesize a living cell?) and then the conversation turned to some technicalities about grading. They used terms such as credit hours, GPA and QPA, and I did not have a clue what the argument was about. But of course I endeavored to hide my ignorance of all matters educational, and when asked my opinion, simply said,

"Yes, *very* interesting, I fully agree with Father Maloney (the most senior person present)" or words to that effect.

Dean Sharrow suggested that I give a seminar about my research, as well as a lecture to freshmen. I thought this was a good sign and returned to Al's office to schedule these events.

"Let's see what topic Bio 102 will be covering the day you'd be here – ok, it's the Krebs Cycle. Is that ok with you, Joan?" I vaguely remembered struggling with the Krebs Cycle, an important part of cellular metabolism, when I was a freshman at Birmingham University about thirty years ago, promptly forgetting it after Final Exams, and never giving it another thought.

"*Please*, Al, I would *much* rather give a lecture on how cells move, especially amoeboid movement, now *that's* a fascinating topic, the kids will *love* it, and I can tell them about my *own* experiments."

"OK, I get you," Al laughed, "the Krebs cycle isn't my favorite topic either, we'll call your guest lecture 'How Cells Get Around' and you can talk about anything you like!"

Both the seminar and the lecture went well. There had been one question from a freshman, addressed to their regular teacher:

"Dr. Barker," the young man said, "are we responsible for what she talked about?"

I did not understand the question, but Ken Barker was quick to answer, "Yes, *sir,*" (he was a Southerner!) "There will be a quiz on Monday."

About a week later Dean Sharrow called to offer me a tenure-track position as Assistant Professor. I had always been underpaid, so the entry-level salary he mentioned sounded ok to me. He explained that my "teaching load" would be three 3-credit courses per semester plus labs, including freshman zoology, something called "Biology of Man" for non-science-majors, and an upper-level course in my specialty. I would be expected to continue my research and serve on committees. It sounded overwhelming. I procrastinated, and said I'd think about it. I also made it clear that I could not move until the new Health Sciences Center was completed and my lab was ready to accommodate the amoebas.

Actually, I had grave doubts about my ability to adjust to this strange new world, a world where quizzes, credits and GPAs (whatever they were) appeared to be of greater importance than subject matter, where teaching was regarded as a "load" and labs – surely *the* most important activity for a scientist - were just an afterthought, worth one credit for a three-hour session. The people at Canisius really seemed to want me, which was flattering.

Years later I figured out why they were so keen: President Demske, or possibly the Board of Trustees, had recently decided on a new policy for Canisius: in addition to excellence in teaching, there would be increased emphasis on original research, including undergraduate involvement, and publication in refereed journals. They were also looking for more diversity: The current faculty consisted predominantly of white men, mostly Catholics educated at Canisius and other Jesuit colleges. They were devoted teachers, but - at least in the natural sciences – did little publishable research. So I was a god-sent to them: I was about as different from the typical Canisius faculty as one could be: female, a Unitarian with Jewish roots, educated in Europe, and a full-time researcher with numerous publications. I was also a media personality of sorts!

I decided to have another chat with Al Alexander and Vince Stouter. They understood my hesitation and proposed a compromise: would I like to teach just *one* course for *one* semester, as a sabbatical replacement for Vince? This would enable me to "get my feet wet" (one of Al's favorite expressions). They even offered to schedule the course in the evening, because I was still working at the CTB. And my amoeba lab would be ready for occupation in August 1973, should I decide to accept the Dean's offer of a tenure-track position. How could I refuse? I decided to give it a try.

My teaching adventure began with a course called *BIO 407/513 Cytology*. I learned that the numbers indicated that this course was for seniors as well as graduate students,[12] so I worked hard to prepare an advanced course, which I renamed *Cell Biology*. Looking back on my first attempt at teaching a college course, I must say that I learned a lot. I just hope that my students also learned something, but that is less certain. I had no "mentor", and was totally ignorant of teaching techniques. But the students were very kind. They reminded me that I was expected to give assignments - yes, homework like in high school - schedule quizzes at frequent intervals, as well as a mid-term and a final exam. Peter showed me how to construct multiple-choice questions as used in Dental School,

12 Canisius had a Master's program jointly with Roswell Park Cancer Institute at that time

but they turned out to be much too complicated for my students. Our son, Alan, a student at Amherst Central High School gave me a lot of advice.

"Mother," he said, "first of all you gotta dress smart, these kids have to *look* at you for over an hour! Then you must learn how to write on the board and how to load the film projector."[13]

When Gregory came home for a weekend from Rochester, he organized my grade book and patiently explained the mysteries of grading "on a curve", and how to calculate final grades. I spent many sleepless nights over that process. The average score in my first exam was about 60%. I thought it pretty good, but my students were appalled. I hastily assured them that in *my* courses 40% was pass and 80% an A. Obviously I had set the level far too high, being mislead by the 400-500 course number. True, these students were in their 4th or 5th year of study, but this was their first course in Cell Biology!

It all worked out in the end and nobody failed. I was exhausted. How could anybody teach *three* courses, not to mention do research, advise students, and "give service to the college?" Maybe experience was the answer. So I went ahead and accepted the Assistant Professorship for 1973, starting work two months after my 50th birthday.

My men, Peter, Gregory and Alan, made me a beautiful birthday card depicting a big old turtle (? me) with the inscription "Happy Birthday, Mom, it's time you stopped worrying about the origin of life and started LIVING it!"

"Yes We Can!"

As I am bringing my memoirs to a close during the historic week of President Barack Obama's inauguration, I would like to borrow his campaign slogan to serve as a "signature tune" for this last chapter. Change brings challenge. Sometimes these challenges seem impossible to meet.

As anticipated, I found my new career challenging, but also very rewarding. I liked and respected my students, realizing that many of them were a lot brighter than I and, with some nurturing,

13 Thank goodness for DVDs!

would go far. Inevitably there were things at Canisius I did not find to my liking, and I set about changing them. Change takes time, but since I stayed at the college for many years, I was able to accomplish a fair amount.

The Biology Department did move into their new building. Now, thirty-five years later, plans for another move and upgrade are in the works. Both students and faculty are actively engaged in original research, using excellent equipment. Women, a majority among undergraduates, are also well represented at all levels of faculty and administration. The syllabus has changed beyond recognition, mirroring modern Biology. Laboratory work and field trips now have their rightful place. However, as computers play an increasingly important role, hands-on "wet labs" may in fact be phased out: looking down a microscope at living organisms is being replaced by viewing videos. I regret this particular change. One can learn a lot more from a living frog than from a computer model, and the microcosm in a drop of pond water that you have just collected has never been seen by *anybody*; it's yours alone to discover.

During my long tenure at Canisius, I initiated several new courses, such as *Bio-Moral Problems* (jointly with Dr. Robert Rizzo, an ethicist), *Animal Parasitology* and *The Biology of Women*. The latter is part of the Women's Studies Program, which was probably one of the most ambitious projects I undertook. I have discussed this previously under *Ruminations on Being Female*.

Describing my thirty years as a college professor, including three years as department chair, could easily fill another volume, but I shall not attempt that just now. However, I would like to say that I greatly admire women who hold responsible teaching positions, manage active research programs, and at the same time raise a family – with or without support from a husband. I was perhaps fortunate that I did not start this demanding career until our sons were in their late teens. Most important, I had Peter's support and encouragement: he tolerated being occasionally addressed as Mr. Lorch when joining me at Canisius functions, and cheerfully put up with my frequent absences. He looked after our Siamese cat, Candy (long retired from breeding), while I attended professional meetings in far away cities, including Nairobi. Both of us spent sabbaticals away from home: Peter worked in dental schools in Vancouver, BC as well as in Chicago, while I spent time in Kwang Jeon's lab in Knoxville, TN.

I was forced to retire from my full-time position at age seventy, i.e. on June 13th, 1993. A new law, proscribing compulsory retirement of college faculty on account of age, came into effect only about two weeks later, on July 1st, 1993. However, I was quite happy to teach part-time for another ten years. It allowed me to spend more time skiing and traveling, while earning just enough to support these hobbies. Retirement is a big change and quite a challenge, even if phased in gradually. In fact old age, euphemistically referred to as "The Golden Years", is probably the biggest challenge of all! It is relatively easy to evaluate a period you can look back on, although childhood memories tend to take on an unwarranted rosy glow. In contrast, it is hard to give an unbiased description of one's present condition, since one cannot see it in perspective. Unfortunately, where old age is concerned, you never will! There are no word-processors in heaven.

Acknowledgements

I thank my son, Gregory Staple, as well as my old friend, Heinz Redwood for critical reading of several chapters, as well as Mona Doss for her conscientious proofreading, truly a labor of love. Jack Anchin, as always, encouraged and supported me through some rough passages.

Molly Jarboe scanned the illustrations, assisted with the cover, and exhibited great patience while converting my manuscript into book form. Barbara Greune helped with proofreading and drew my attention to Chekhov's *Ward Six*. I am grateful to Laura Caldwell Anderson of the Birmingham Civil Rights Institute for access to historical data, and to Jeanne Weaver, historian of the Unitarian Universalist Church of Birmingham, Alabama for allowing me to see the draft of her research. Jan Sapp of York University, Toronto made helpful comments on the Endosymbiosis section.

I thank Bill Offhouse for assistance in accessing material in the Archives of the University at Buffalo, and Colleen O'Hara of Canisius College for her help and support. Many friends contributed helpful comments in informal conversations, which is much appreciated. Finally I want to emphasize how much I value the ongoing encouragement of the many readers of *Chance and Choice. My First Thirty Years* who "can't wait" to see what happens next.

Inevitably, errors still lurk on these pages; they are entirely my responsibility. I agree with Lewis Thomas' dictum that *we are built to make mistakes, coded for error.*

The photographs in the book come from my personal albums.

Appendix

Publications by Joan Lorch and Colleagues, 1946-1985

1. Demonstration of Phosphatase in Decalcified Bone, Lorch, Nature, 158, 269 (1946)
2. The Action of Alloxan and Related Compounds on Alkaline Phosphatase, Lorch, and Burgen, Biochem. J., 41, 223 (1947)
3. Note on the Cytological Localization of Alkaline Phosphatase, Lorch, Quart. J. Micr. Sci., 88, 159 (1947)
4. Localization of Alkaline Phosphatase in Mammalian Bones, Lorch, Quart. J. Micr. Sci., 88, 367 (1947)
5. Alkaline Phospatase and the Mechanism of Ossification, Lorch, J. Bone Joint Surg., 31B, 94 (1949)
6. The Distribution of Alkaline Phosphatase in the Skull of the Developing Trout, Lorch, Quart. J. Micr. Sci., 90, 183 (1949)
7. The Distribution of Alkaline Phosphatase in Relation to Calcification in Scyliorhinus Canicula, Lorch, Quart. J. Micr. Sci., 90, 381 (1949)
8. Differentiation of the Sea Urchin Egg Following Reduction of the Interior Cytoplasm in Relation to the Cortex, Horstadius, Lorch and Danielli, Exp. Cell Res., 1, 188 (1949)
9. Transplantation of Nuclei from Cell to Cell, Lorch and Danielli, Nature, 166, 329 (1950)
10. Folding and Unfolding of Protein Molecules in Relation to Cytoplasmic Streaming, Amoeboid Movement and Osmotic Work, Goldacre and Lorch, Nature, 166, 497 (1950)
11. The Amoeba as an Experimental Animal, Lorch, Biology and Human Affairs, 17, 20 (1951)
12. Enucleation of Sea Urchin Blastomeres with or without Removal of Asters, Lorch, Quart. J. Micr. Sci., 93, 475 (1952)
13. The Effect of Enucleation on the Development of Sea

Urchin Eggs, Lorch, Danielli and Horstadius, Exp. Cell Res., 4, 254 (1953)

14. Nuclear Transplantation in amoebae I. Some Species Characters of *A. proteus* and *A. discoides*, Lorch and Danielli, Quart. J. Micr. Sci., 94, 445 (1953)

15. Nuclear Transplantation in Amoebae II. The Immediate Results of Transfer of Nuclei Between *A. proteus* and *A. discoides*., Lorch and Danielli, loc. Cit., 94, 461 (1953)

16. Nucleus and Cytoplasm in Cellular Inheritance, Danielli, Lorch, Ord and Wilson, Nature, 176, 1114 (1955)

17. Cytoplasmic Inheritance in Amoebae: Modification of Response to Antiserum by Micro-injection of Heterologous Cytoplasmic Homogenates, Jeon, Lorch, Moran, Muggleton and Danielli, Exp. Cell Res. 46, 615 (1967)

18. Unusual Intracellular Bacterial Infection in Large Freeliving Amoebae, Jeon and Lorch, Exp. Cell Res. 48, 236 (1967)

19. A New Simple Method of Micrurgy on Living Cells, Jeon and Lorch, Nature 217, 463 (1968)

20. Reversible Effect of Actinomycin D on Amoeba Nucleoli: Nuclear Transplantation Study, Lorch and Jeon, Nature 221, 1073 (1969)

21. Lethal Effect of Heterologous Nuclei in Amoeba, Jeon and Lorch, Exp. Cell Res. 56, 233 (1969)

22. Character Changes Induced by Heterologous Nuclei in Amoeba, Lorch and Jeon, Exp. Cell Res., 57, 223 (1969)

23. The Rate of Attachment of Amoebae to the Substratum: A Study of Nuclear-Cytoplasmic Relationships, Lorch, J. Cell Physiol. 73, 171 (1969)

24. Strain-specific Mitotic Inhibition in Large Monoucleate Amoebae, Jeon and Lorch, J. Cell. Physiol. 75, 193 (1970)

25. Reassembly of Living Cells from Dissociated Components, Jeon, Lorch and Danielli, Science 167, 1626 (1970)

26. Ethics and Trends in Biology, Lorch, Quart. Bull. Center for Theoret. Biol. 4, 143 (1971)
27. Mitotic Inhibition and Nucleic Acid Synthesis in Amoeba Nuclei Jeon and Lorch, Nature New Biology 231, 91 (1971)
28. Some Historical Aspects of Amoeba Studies, Lorch, In: The Biology of Amoeba (K.W. Jeon, ed.) Academic Press, N.Y. 1973 Chapter 1
29. Strain Specificity in Amoeba proteus., Jeon and Lorch In: The Biology of Amoeba (K.W. Jeon, ed.) Academic Press, N.Y. 1973 Chapter 21
30. Compatibility among Cell Components in large free-living Amebas. Jeon and Lorch. Int. Rev .Cytol. Suppl.9 (1979)
31. Resuscitation of Amoebae deprived of essential Symbiotes. Lorch and Jeon. J. Protozool. 27, 423 (1980)
32. Rapid Induction of cellular Strain Specificity by newly acquired cytoplasmic Components in Amebas. Lorch and Jeon. Science 211, 949 (1981)
33. Nuclear Lethal Effect and nucleo-cytoplasmic Incompatibility induced by Endosymbionts in Amoeba Proteus. Lorch and Jeon. J. Protozool. 29, 468 (1982)
34. The formation of vacuole membrane in the Presence and Absence of the Cell Nucleus in amoebae. Jeon and Lorch. Exp. Cell Res. 141, 351 (1982)
35. Differential Effect of Colcemid on mitotic Apparatus in Amoebae as Studied using anti-tubulin monoclonal Antibodies. Lorch and Jeon. Europ. J. Cell Biol. 39, 290 (1985)
36. Symbiont-induced Strain Specific Lethal Effect in amoebae Lorch, Kim and Jeon. J. Protozol. 32, 745 (1985)

Reprinted from
20 March 1970, Volume 167, pp. 1626-1627

SCIENCE

Reassembly of Living Cells from Dissociated Components

K. W. Jeon, I. J. Lorch and J. F. Danielli

Abstract. *Combining the techniques of nuclear transplantation and cytoplasmic transfer, dissociated amoeba nuclei, cytoplasm, and membranes were reassembled to form viable amoebae. The techniques of cell reassembly appear to be sufficiently adequate so that any desired combination of cytoplasm, nucleus, and membrane can be assembled into living cells.*

Interest has developed in the possibility of synthesizing living cells and in reassembling living cells from isolated cell components. In 1965 Price proposed that such syntheses be made an American national goal (*1*). After participating in a symposium on the experimental synthesis of living cells (*2*), we decided that we had the means to carry out the reassembly of *Amoeba proteus* from its major components: namely nucleus, cytoplasm, and cell membrane. We have now shown that new viable amoebae may be produced with the membrane of one cell, cytoplasm from one or more other cells, and nucleus from a third cell. These three components are nonviable individually, and when any of them is missing the reassembled cell cannot live.

The basic procedures of reassembly are (i) removal of the nucleus from an amoeba, (ii) removal of the cytoplasm to the extent that the remaining part cannot survive even when a nucleus has been inserted, (iii) injection of desired cytoplasm to refill the above, and (iv) insertion of a nucleus.

The first two steps can be carried out either by (i) enucleation and removal of cytoplasm by micrurgical methods (*3*) or by (ii) centrifugation of cells at high speed. In a single cycle with the use of micrurgical methods involving removal of cytoplasm and nucleus and refilling the membrane with cytoplasm from another cell, only about 75 percent of the original cytoplasm can be with-

Table 1. Results of reassembly experiments. Letters A, B, and C represent different strains used in an experiment. In actual experiments, five strains (D, P, Q, S, and G) were used, but they were grouped together for simplification. Suffixes n, c, and m denote nucleus, cytoplasm, and cell membrane, respectively. Superscripts indicate the source of a component, for example, in the experiment with $A_n' + A_c'' + A_m'''$ the superscripts indicate that the nucleus, cytoplasm, and membrane came from three separate cells of strain A.

Combination	Cells (No.)		Clone (No.)	Viable (%)
	Studied	Dividing		
$A_n' + A_c'' A_m''$	200	172	170	85
$A_n' + A_c'' + A_m'''$	58	48	43	74
$A_n + B_c' B_m'$	168	72	0	0
$A_n' + A_c'' + B_m$	244	82	2	<1
$A_n + B_c + C_m$	22	4	0	0

drawn. On refilling with cytoplasm, the volume can be brought to about 75 percent of the original. Thus a single cycle results in a cell, the cytoplasm of which still consists of one-third of the original cytoplasm; however, two cycles would reduce this to one-ninth.

For removal of nuclei and cytoplasm by centrifugation, amoebae are layered over 10 percent Ficoll (*4*) and centrifuged first for 5 minutes at 30,000*g* and then for 30 seconds at 40,000*g* at 4°C. The centripetal portions of the cells contain little particulate cytoplasm, except for colored lipid droplets, and are nonviable even after renucleation. The subsequent refilling with cytoplasm and renucleation (the last two steps above) are performed by micrurgical methods in both cases.

Where cytoplasm, membrane, and nucleus are all obtained from cells of the same strain, reassembly is relatively easy and 80 percent of the reassembled cells are normal amoebae, behaving and reproducing so as to be indistinguishable from cells of the original clone (Table 1, experiment 2). However, when one or two of the three components are from different strains, only a small proportion of the reassembled amoebae form viable clones. The great majority are able to maintain normal functions only for a limited period, sometimes dividing not more than four times (Table 1, experiments 3–5). It is likely that the failure of these cells to form clones is partially due to the newly discovered interstrain lethal factors (*5*). However, that we have already obtained two fully viable clones with mixed components suggests that appropriate procedures will probably be found to assemble most combinations of nuclei, cytoplasm, and membranes.

There are many known examples of the partial use of reassembly methods in amoebae. For instance when nuclei from cells lethally damaged by x-ray or nitrogen mustard (*6*) are placed in unirradiated cytoplasm, the nuclei are irreversibly damaged, whereas nuclei from cells lethally damaged by actinomycin D readily recover (*7*). Injection of cytoplasm (*3*) and of cytoplasmic homogenate, either fresh or lyophilized (*3*), can result in a modification of strain-specific characters in the host progeny.

The success of our reassembly experiments means that we now have the technical ability to assemble amoebae which contain any desired combination of components and thus have an excellent test system. This system can be used to test the condition of particular cell components; for example, an organelle from an amoeba which has been prevented from undergoing division for some time can be used in a reassembled cell, the other components of which are from cells undergoing normal, logarithmic growth. Also, the viability of cell components, for example, nuclei or mitochondria isolated by standard procedures (*8*), can be examined. In this way the viability and compatibility of cell organelles from diverse sources can be determined.

K. W. Jeon, I. J. Lorch
J. F. Danielli
Center for Theoretical Biology and School of Pharmacy, State University of New York at Buffalo, Amherst 14226

References and Notes

1. C. C. Price, *Chem. Eng. News* **43** (39), 90 (1965).
2. E. C. Pollard, *Symp. NASA–AIBS, on Synthesis of Life*; preprint copies of the report are available from E. C. Pollard, Pennsylvania State University, University Park.
3. K. W. Jeon and I. J. Lorch, *Nature* **217**, 463 (1968); S. E. Hawkins and R. J. Cole, *Exp. Cell Res.* **37**, 26 (1965); K. W. Jeon, I. J. Lorch, J. F. Moran, A. Muggleton, J. F. Danielli, *ibid.* **46**, 615 (1967); I. J. Lorch, *J. Cell Physiol.* **73**, 171 (1969).
4. Pharmacia Fine Chemicals, Inc., Piscataway, N.J.
5. K. W. Jeon and I. J. Lorch, *Exp. Cell Res.* **56**, 233 (1969); *J. Cell Physiol.*, in press.
6. M. J. Ord, *Quart. J. Microscop. Sci.* **97**, 37 (1956); ——— and J. F. Danielli, *ibid.*, pp. 17 and 29.
7. I. J. Lorch and K. W. Jeon, *Nature* **221**, 1073 (1969).
8. Isolation procedures for organelles are reviewed by several groups of investigators in *Meth. Enzymol.* **12**, section 3, 416 (1967).

9. We thank Mrs. L. Powers for technical assistance. This work was supported by NASA grant NSG 015-16.

8 December 1969

Some Press Cuttings from 1970 and 1973

pg. 235. Scientists Recreate Living Amoebas by Reaasembling Parts of Several.
Victor Cohn
The Washington Post Nov 13, 1970

pg. 236. Buffalo Scientists Report Synthesis of Living Cell
Walter Sullivan
New York Times front page Nov 13,1970

pg. 238. 3 UB Researchers Create Living Cell
Patrick J. Ryan
Buffalo Courier Express Vol. CXXXVI #115
Nov 12, 1970 pg.1 and 5

pg. 239. Scientist Keeps her Two Lives Separate
Buffalo Evening News April 11,1973

pg. 242. Women in Science: Expansion Seen of Female Role
Katherine Smith
Buffalo Courier Express April 29,1973

Scientists Recreate Living Amoebas By Reassembling Parts of Several

By Victor Cohn
Washington Post Staff Writer

Living, reproducing one-celled animals—amoebas—are being recreated from their isolated parts by a laboratory team in Buffalo, N.Y.

In doing so, they are building the first living, reproducing cells from interchangeable components.

The achievement "opens up a new era for artificial life synthesis," in the opinion of Dr James F. Danielli, head of the Center for Theoretical Biology at the State University of New York at Buffalo.

In theory, it could lead to reassembling human cells—to make improved ova (egg) cells to produce better babies.

It could lead to tailor-making human cells in order to treat genetic diseases in which the body's own cells lack some natural component.

It could lead to making new kinds of bacteria to attack human disease.

It might also, Danielli believes, teach man to create organisms that could live in strange environments—such as the planet Mars when man someday colonizes it. Partly for this reason, his center's work has been financed since 1963 in the neighborhood of $100,000 a year by NASA.

All such goals are far off, and will require many more advances. But there may be one early practical application of the Buffalo work: Making special lines of amoeba to test the effects of environmental agents like pesticides or radiation.

See CELL, A7, Col. 1

Scientists Create Amoebas From Key Parts of Others

CELL, From A1

The Buffalo scientists—Danielli, Dr. Joan Lorch and, until recently, Dr. Kwang W. Jeon (now at the University of Tennessee) — separate amoebas into three parts: Their central nuclei, their gel-like cytoplasm or general body matter (which organizes itself into specialized units to meet specific needs like food consumption or digestion) and their cell membranes.

Typlically, they:

- Remove the nuclei from individual amoebas by microprobe, a small microsurgical instrument.
- Suck out most of the cytoplasm through a slim pipette—or remove it by high-speed whirling in an ultracentrifuge.
- Then refill the remaining membrane from one amoeba with cytoplasm from a second and a nucleus from a third.

With amoebas of the same genetic strain, the new hybrid creatures multiply indefinitely, by dividing, to form strong, healthy colonies.

But where amoebas of different genetic strains are combined, permanent colonies have been established in only two cases in 300.

This is an important obstacle to many of the long-range goals of genetic engineering. Such engineering would generally require combining cell components of different strains.

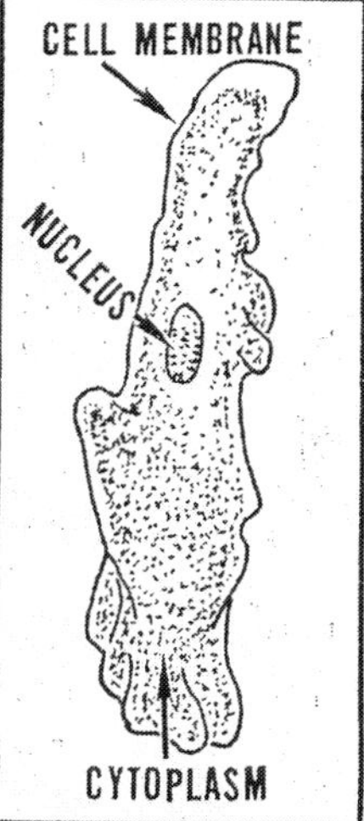

An amoeba with its key parts, now being re-created at the Center for Theoretical Biology, Buffalo.

"We don't know why the parts from different strains aren't compatible," Dr. Lorch said in an interview yesterday.

But the rejection is probably immunological, in the same way the human body rejects organs from other persons.

"We shall probably overcome it by and by," Dr. Lorch added. "It just takes time."

Drs. Jeon, Lorch and Danielli first reported their work in a short technical report in the journal Science last March. Dr. Lorch will give a current report to the American Society for Cell Biology in San Diego next week.

There have been other important recent advances in genetic engineering—making artificial DNA (the genetic chemical), growing hybrid human-animal cells, manufacturing artificial lysosomes (parts of a human cell) from chemicals off the laboratory shelf.

Many scientists now believe these advances tell society it is time to begin thinking about evil as well as beneficial possibilities.

Genetic engineering is inevitable, most scientists feel. "And the way the Buffalo people are doing it," one biologist said yesterday, "may be the way in which it will really be done."

Some political leaders may then want to use genetic engineers to tailor bacteriological weapons or, someday, make servile citizens — simple-minded slaves like the docile workers in Huxley's "Brave New World." Most scientists think it is time to begin to ponder how to prevent this, while using genetic engineering to cure disease and help man.

N.Y. Times 11/13/70

Buffalo Scientists Report Synthesis of Living Cell

By WALTER SULLIVAN

The State University of New York at Buffalo reported yesterday that scientists there had achieved "the first artificial synthesis of a living [and reproducing] cell."

The reference was to experiments at the university's Center for Theoretical Biology in which amoebas were partly dismembered, then put back together, using some components from other amoebas.

The reconstituted amoebas not only survived but also reproduced themselves and were indistinguishable from normal amoebas, it was reported. Amoebas are single-celled animals.

"This work," the report said, "opens up a new era for artificial life synthesis, now being explored."

For example, it continued, it helps clear the way "for the synthesis of new micro-organisms, new egg cells and an organism capable of living on Mars."

The environment of Mars appears so inhospitable that there are serious doubts among biologists that any form of life has evolved there. It has been suggested by some scientists, however, that organisms could be tailor-made to exist on that frigid planet by reconstituting or modifying existing life forms.

The experiment was reported to newsmen in a letter signed by Dr. Raymond Ewell, vice president for research, and Dr. James F. Danielli, the center director who led the team that has done the experiments.

The letter invited newsmen a dinner on Dec. 7 at which further details would be reported. Its contents were made public by several radio stations and news services.

While some researchers in the field were not willing to endorse the somewhat sensational evaluation of the work as described in the sport, specialists at the National Aeronautics and Space Administration, which is supporting the work, described it as "exciting" and "a big step."

They said it went considerably beyond the experiments of Dr. John Gurdon at Oxford Uni-

Continued on Page 16, Column 4

HE NEW YORK TIMES, FRIDAY, NOVEMBER 13, 19

BIOLOGISTS REPORT SYNTHESIS OF CELL

Continued From Page 1, Col. 4

versity, who has implanted the nucleus of a body cell from one frog in the egg cell of another. The result was a frog identical to the one from whom the body cell was taken.

The work of Dr. Danielli and his colleagues, Dr. K. W. Jeon and Dr. I. J. Lorch, was described in preliminary form in the March 20 issue of the journal Science.

They removed the nucleus from an amoeba, as well as about three quarters of its cytoplasm, or "flesh." What remained was the rest of the cytoplasm, plus the cell membrane, or "skin."

All Parts Combined

They then inserted cytoplasm and a nucleus taken from one or more other amoebas. They found that if the inserted material came from amoebas of the same strain, about 80 per cent of the reassembled organisms lived and were able to reproduce by subdivision.

They found that in many cases where the inserted material came from other strains, survival was curtailed and the man-made amoebas divided only three or four times. Apparently material from one strain contained "lethal factors" that acted against another strain.

However, the Buffalo group was apparently able to overcome this effect, at least in some cases, producing amoebas that combined characteristics from strains that were not closely related. To the NASA specialists this was particularly significant.

Experimenters in the past have been able to modify the characteristics of an amoeba gy injecting foreign cytoplasm into it. However, according to the Buffalo group, it should now be possible to remove various parts of the cell — the nucleus, os some other internal component, such as an organolle — and subject them to various tests.

After such tests — with radiation, drugs and the like — the units would be reinserted into cells to see if their function was affected.

As described in the Science report, the Buffalo group has not been able completely to dismember a cell. If more than three-quarters of the cytoplasm is removed, the reassembled cell will not live. Futhermore when reassembly is completed, the resulting cell is only three quarters as large as the original one.

Until now experimentation on the origin of life has focused largely on efforts to reconstruct the process whereby simple substances on the primitive earth interacted with one anothr, spontaneously synthesizing ever more complex compounds. It has thus been possible to reconstruct a plausible pathway for the early stages of such chemical evolution.

CX 11/12/70

3 UB Researchers Create Living Cell

Find Will Open New Era In Artificial Life Synthesis

Dr. James F. Danielli
. . . creates life

By PATRICK J. RYAN

A University of Buffalo researcher announced Wednesday that a research team he heads has created a living and reproducing cell, a biological advance that will have "far reaching implications" in the fields of medicine, biological engineering and genetic engineering.

In a letter to The Courier-Express, Dr. James F. Danielli, director of the university's Center for Theoretical Biology, said the discovery would "open a new era" in the field of artificial life synthesis.

Three Parts

He, and a team consisting of Dr. Kwang W. Jeom and Dr. I. J. Lorch, both of the School of Pharmacy, broke down nature's smallest and simplest animal, the amoeba, into its three basic parts, nucleus, cytoplasm and cell membrane.

The researchers then reconstructed new amoebas from the disassociate, which, although still amoebas, were completely new animals with different gene patterns.

Dr. Danielli's discovery may lead the way for scientists to create new organisms to fit specific needs, opening new doors in the fields of medicine and genetic engineering as well as indicating several industrial possibilities.

Great Advance

Using this process, it may be possible to create new microorganisms, such as bacteria, that could be used to combat harmful, antibiotic-resistant bacteria in the body, researchers said. This would be a great advance in the treatment of patients who do not respond to the present types of treatment.

It also may be possible to create a new organism which could live in nonterrestial conditions, such as Mars, the researcher said. The project has been funded for about five years by the National Aeronautics and Space Administration.

Since the female egg in the reproduction process is a single cell, Dr. Danielli's process could be used to breed offsprings to specifications. The question of gene manipulation, or genetic engineering, in the female egg has often been discussed as a means to end birth defects.

Waste Materials

Dr. Danielli also said that "industrial applications" of his process, including the creation of bacteria designed to break down waste materials, "can be expected to follow."

Dr. Danielli and his associates reported some of their discoveries in last May's Scientific American, a science journal. His letter to The Courier-Express Wednesday announced a dinner Dec. 7 at the Center on the University's Ridge Lea Campus to issue information on his process, and another study conducted on campus.

The other study, conducted by Dr. Richard Gordon, Robert Bender and Dr. Gabor Herman, involves the development of a new method for determination of the three dimensional structure of objects.

Native of England

Danielli, who is vacationing with his wife in California, is a native of England. He came to the University of Buffalo as a professor in the School of Pharmacy in 1962.

Prior to that he had been professor and head of the dept. of zoology in King's College,

LIVING CELL
Continued on Page Five

Living Cell Is Created By UB Team

★ From Page 1

London, when he began his experiments in life synthesis.

He served as the provost of the faculty of natural sciences but resigned that post to assume his present position in 1969.

He holds Ph.D and Doctor of Science degrees from London University and a PhD from Cambridge University.

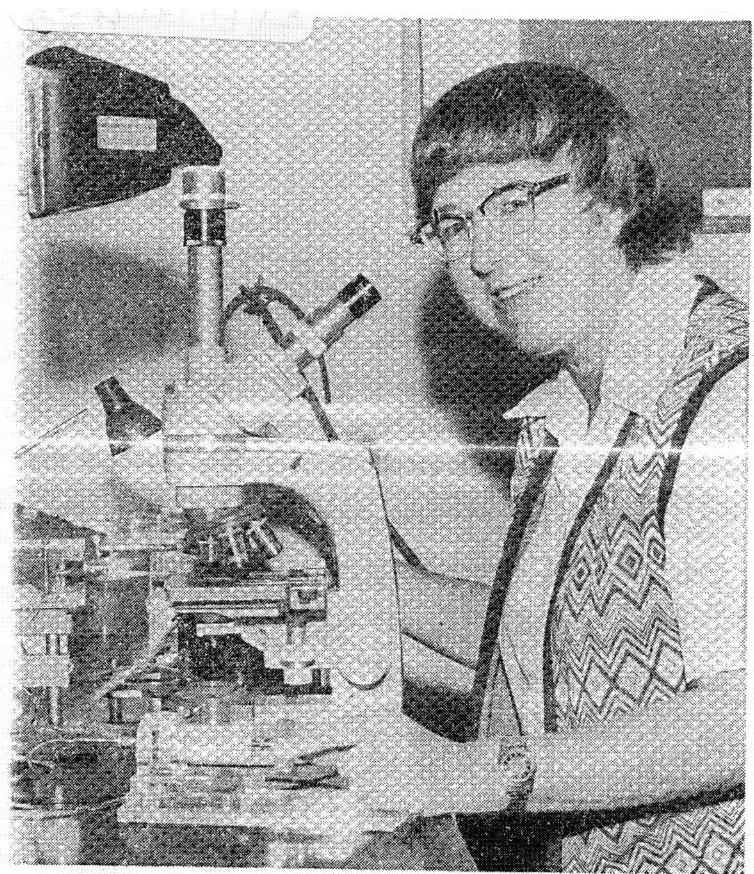

I. JOAN LORCH, an internationally-known biologist and assistant professor of biology at Canisius College, works in her laboratory.

Scientist Keeps

Dr. I. Joan Lorch is an internationally-known biologist who is now assistant professor of biology at Canisius College.

Mrs. Peter Staple is an Amherst resident, mother of two and the wife of a member of the State University of Buffalo Dental School faculty.

If her neighbors, students or her husband's colleagues don't know that Dr. Lorch and Mrs. Staple are one and the same, that's just fine with Joan Lorch.

Had she married at 19 "like too many American women do," she's not sure whether or not she would have chosen to retain her maiden name professionally. But, by the time she married at 29, she had already had work published in scientific publications under the name of Lorch. To change names, she felt, would have been to create confusion.

* * *

FOR EXAMPLE, she cites the publications of a twice-married woman scientist whose work is filed under three different letters. Another colleague who switched to a married name, switched back after "no one knew her."

Part of the three-member team at the State University of Buffalo that received acclaim in 1970 for taking parts from three different single-celled animals and re-forming them into a new, living, reproducing amoeba with a different heredity pattern, Dr. Lorch has a name that's down in the textbooks.

"When my students see the name there and realize it's their teacher, they're really pleased," she says.

* * *

JOAN LORCH was a post doctoral student at Kings College, London when she met her husband, an Air Force veteran who was one of three other graduate students working at the time with Dr. James F. Danielli. The other two, a man and woman, also married after meeting in the laboratory. That woman, too, kept her maiden name professionally.

Joan Lorch left the laboratory shortly after her marriage. She had two sons and moved with her husband to the United States where he taught at the University of Alabama. "Southern ladies don't work," she comments,

Her Two 'Lives' Separate

and for those years she was solely Mrs. Peter Staple, PTA member and church school teacher.

* * *

BEFORE HER husband was offered a job at the State University of Buffalo and, totally unknown to the Staples, Dr. Danielli had come to the university here. He read in a university publication that the Staples were coming and he offered Joan a job.

It was then that she had a chance to re-assess her decision to keep her maiden name. Because she and her husband had published in different fields, she reaffirmed her earlier decision.

"If I go to a convention and wear a name tag as Mrs. Staple, no one would come up to me to discuss work we have in common. They wouldn't know who I was. If I go to a dental convention with my husband, as I once did, then I wear the tag that says Mrs. Staple," she says.

* * *

A DANISH colleague of Dr. Lorch's kept her maiden name and hyphenated it with her husband's. Dr. Lorch thought about this too but decided that Lorch-Staple was "too cumbersome."

Because she and her husband file a joint income-tax, she listed herself at the University of Buffalo with both names. The university directory staff immediately decided she had to go into the directory as Staple. For three years, until she got it changed, she and her husband kept getting each other's mail, some people never could locate her.

"I like to keep my professional life separate from my family life," she says. "Men do that quite automatically. In my case, the different name makes the separation clear."

Expansion Seen Of

By H. KATHERINE SMITH

DR. I. JOAN LORCH, assistant professor of biology at Canisius College, is gratified by the increasing number of American women pursuing careers in the sciences.

She attends regularly conventions of the American Society for Cell Biology. Nine years ago, she recalls, women at those conventions were few indeed. Today, they comprise nearly 50 per cent of those attending. They present papers and hold important offices in the society.

"Today, it is less difficult than at any previous time for women to enter medical schools," she stated. "I can remember when a woman had to be exceptionally brilliant to obtain an opportunity to study medicine. Today, women actually are sought. A woman candidate for the M.D. degree needs only to be as competent as the men trying for the same profession."

DR. LORCH, who obtained her B.S. and Ph.D. degrees in England, cites several differences in English and American education.

At age 16, an English high school student must decide on his field of future study. If he chooses a science, all his courses must be in science.

Dr. Lorch, who spoke German and French at an early age, was not permitted to combine the study of those languages and literature with her work in science.

THE ENGLISH STUDENT does not have the benefit of a faculty adviser as Americans do. He must plan his own curriculum. In an English university, the only test is the final examination at the conclusion of a course.

When Dr. Lorch was preparing for her Ph.D. in London,

Dr. Lorch

no graduate courses were available. She earned her doctorate through pursuing research under the direction of a professor.

IN 1972, when she visited England, she learned that education there had undergone several changes. Some graduate courses were available, and undergraduate students could attend the newly established polytechnic schools which offered courses similar to American liberal arts colleges. She was impressed by the number and variety of university courses offered on British television.

"It is possible to earn a degree through television courses plus written papers and written examinations," she stated.

DR. LORCH IS a member of the Institute of Society, Ethics, and the Life Sciences, also known as the Hastings Institute. This organization studies such problems as artificial insemination; legal rights of the child in a case of artificial insemination; embryo implants, experimentation on human beings, and the ethics of prolonging, by artificial means, the life of

Female's Role

a patient in a coma from which recovery is impossible.

Dr. Lorch, in private life Mrs. Peter Staple, is the wife of a professor in the U.B. School of Dentistry. The couple are parents of two sons, Gregory, a student of political science at the University or Rochester, and Alan, a senior at Amherst Senior High School. At present, Alan is enjoying a three-week visit to an uncle in England.

BORN IN Germany of Jewish parents, Joan Lorch and her father's family were refugees in England during World War II. After graduation from the University of Birmingham, Joan Lorch continued her scientific studies in London and received her Ph.D. from London University.

She and her husband met while both were graduate students. Dr. Staple earned a degree in pharmacology plus his DDS. They were married in England; their sons were born there.

FOURTEEN YEARS ago, they came to the U.S. Dr. Staple accepted a professorship at the University of Birmingham, Ala., and for five years, the family lived in the South.

Dr. Lorch did not work in science until her sons were in school. She resumed her career by taking a part-time research post at U.B. Later, this became a full-time position. In the Center of Theoretical Biology directed by Dr. J. F. Danielli, Dr. Lorch pursued research in protozoology, transplanting nuclei in amebas. In 1972, she taught a course in biology at Canisius. Last September, she left U.B. to become a full-time member of the Canisius faculty.

THE PROFESSOR teaches a course in introductory biology for freshmen and two electives for upperclass students, Cell ~~Building~~ and Protozoology. Dr. Lorch's 30 publications include contributions to the periodicals "Experimental Cell Research," "Celular Physiology;" "Nature," and "Science," also two chapters of the book "Biology of Amoeba" published by Academic Press. She has read papers at several national conventions of the Society for Cell Biology.

In her opinion, it is difficult for a woman to obtain an important professional post because men believe that a woman regards her professional career as an engrossing hobby, and because a wife will leave the city if her husband is transferred.

DURING HER first years as a researcher here, Dr. Lorch discovered with surprise the difference in the meaning of many words when used here and in England. For instance, in England, the word paraffin is used to designate mineral oil, and instead of cotton or cotton batting, the English say cotton wool.

Travel is a hobby shared by the entire Staple family. Dr. Lorch has skied in Switzerland and, during student years, worked two summers in France. She has attended conventions in San Diego, Calif., New Orleans, and other interesting American cities.

DURING HER husband's recent sabbatical year, she and the boys visited him in Vancouver, Canada, where he was engaged in research. The boys have visited the U.S. West Coast. Skiing and tennis are sports enjoyed by the entire Staple family. Among them, the generation gap is unimportant. The boys' long hair is of little concern to Dr. Lorch.

"I am far more interested in what is in their heads than in what grows on the outside," she said, laughing.

8/6/69